A Noble Task

Lewis J. Patsavos

A Noble Task:
Entry into the Clergy in the
First Five Centuries

Translated by Norman Russell

Foreword by Kallistos Ware

Holy Cross Orthodox Press
Brookline, Massachusetts

Original title in Greek: *He eisodos eis ton kleron kata tous penteprotous aionas*
Published in Athens in 1973

© 2007 Holy Cross Orthodox Press
Published by Holy Cross Orthodox Press
50 Goddard Avenue
Brookline, Massachusetts 02445

ISBN-10: 1-885652-97-6
ISBN-13: 978-1-885652-97-3

Library of Congress Cataloging–in–Publication Data

Patsavos, Elias I.
[He eisodos eis ton kleron kata tous pente protous aionas. English]
A noble task: entry into the clergy in the first five centuries / Lewis J. Patsavos; translated by Norman Russell; foreword by Kallistos Ware.
    p. cm.
Includes index.
ISBN 1-885652-97-6 (pbk. : alk. paper)
1. Clergy--Appointment, call, and election--History. 2. Clergy--Office--History. 3. Church history--Primitive and early church, ca. 30-600. I. Title.
BV664.P3713 2007
262'.1411--DC22   2007036779

The saying is sure:
If anyone aspires to the office of bishop,
he desires a noble task.
1 Timothy 3:1

To my students, past and present,
whose calling to ordained ministry or
to service as lay leaders in the Church has led them
to a "noble task."

CONTENTS

PART ONE:
THE FORMING OF CRITERIA FOR
ENTRY INTO THE CLERGY
ACCORDING TO THE TESTIMONY OF THE SOURCES

PART TWO:
THE CANONICAL FORMULATION OF CRITERIA FOR ENTRY INTO THE CLERGY DRAWN UP BY THE COUNCILS

Foreword

I am delighted that the careful and thorough study by Professor Lewis J. Patsavos, *A Noble Task: Entry into the Clergy in the First Five Centuries*, originally published in Greek in 1973, has now been made available in English, in a revised and updated form.

Rereading the work of Dr. Patsavos, with its rich array of key texts from the Fathers and the early synods, I was struck in particular by two things. The first was the remarkably high standard that was expected in the ancient world from members of the clergy and candidates for ordination. We today may well be surprised by the maximalism of Christianity in the first five centuries. Bishops of that period were sharply conscious of their responsibility to prevent the celebration of the Holy Mysteries and the ministry of preaching from being performed by unworthy persons.

The patristic attitude is well summed up in the "Admonition to the Priest," attributed to St. Basil the Great and inserted at the beginning of the Greek *Ieratikon*. "Be zealous, priest," we read, "to present yourself as a worker who is unashamed and rightly proclaims the word of truth. Never attend the church service with hatred against anyone, lest you drive away the Paraclete.... Stand before the Holy Altar with compunction and a pure heart....Never hurry or abbreviate the prayers to please other people, but think only of the King who is before you and the Powers that surround Him."

A second thing that impressed me, as I studied the material that Dr. Patsavos has so helpfully assembled, was the way in which the Fathers and the early synods are flexible in their specific ordinances. There is unanimity in their understanding of what the priestly vocation involves, but there is considerable diversity in their actual practice. Often the canonical regulations vary at different times and from place to place; there is no single, unchanging code of statutes. Bishops and councils left room for adaptation according to the situation of particular individuals and the pastoral needs of local congregations. The Fathers were strict, but they were also compassionate. In their eyes, persons mattered more than rules. They kept in mind the words of St. Paul, "You are not under the law but under grace" (Rom 6:14).

Noting in this work the lofty requirements for candidates to the diaconate, priesthood, and episcopate, we may well exclaim with the Apostle, "Who is sufficient for these things?" (2 Cor 2:16). The answer is given us in the prayer used at ordinations in the Christian East. The words of this prayer, although perhaps later in date than the period covered by Dr. Patsavos, exactly express the Church's standpoint in the first five centuries. With his hand resting on the candidate's head, the bishop says: "The divine grace, which *heals what is weak and supplies what is lacking*, ordains this man....Let us therefore pray for him, that the grace of the All-Holy Spirit may come upon him." None of us can approach for ordination relying on his own strength. Our trust is solely in the mercy of Christ and the power of the Spirit. We approach because we are called by God—called through the voice of the bishop and the local community, as also through the voice of our own conscience. Without this divine call, the priestly ministry becomes impossible.

It is my hope and prayer that bishops, priests, and deacons who read this book will find that it renews their sense of awe and wonder before the service that they are performing in the Church. And may the book, despite the grave warnings that it contains, also encourage and inspire many to offer themselves for ordination: "The harvest is plentiful, but the laborers are few" (Matt 9:37).

When I was pondering ordination, my spiritual father—a Russian priest, Fr. George Cheremeteff—said to me: "I cannot *advise* you to be a priest, for I know how difficult the work of the priesthood can be. But while I do not give you any advice, I will tell you what I *hope*. With all my heart I *hope* you will be ordained." And he added: "As a priest, you will have many sorrows. But you will also experience a joy such as you would never discover in any other way of life."

+ Kallistos [Ware]
Metropolitan of Diokleia

Preface

"Entry into the Clergy in the First Five Centuries" was the original title of a doctoral dissertation written in Greek and submitted in 1973 to the School of Theology at Athens University. As stated in the original preface, the incentive for writing it then was the desire to confront the problems related to priestly formation. More than thirty years later, this incentive still stands, but with even greater urgency. The perilous state of the world places upon the Church the need to provide meaningful leadership of the clergy in the wake of the uncertainty which surrounds us. If, at the time it was written, the goal of this study was to contribute to the spiritual nurture of the clergy, this goal more than anything else has contributed to its translation into English. Its availability to a much larger readership, it is hoped, will thereby be assured. In this regard, a word of praise is due the translator, Norman Russell, who has captured the essence of the original Greek and conveyed it in an intelligible way both for the clergy and for the average layperson. In a certain sense, the virtuous lives portrayed as models of emulation especially for the clergy are also admirable examples for anyone aspiring to live the Christian life.

When one contemplates perceptions of the clergy in the light of reported events in the life of the Church today, one is struck by the daunting task of restoring an image which has been tainted. The Church in the first five centuries was also not without her critics. As a result, she, too, was faced with the task of projecting a favorable image of her clergy. Enemies of the Christian faith portrayed the Church and her clergy in a negative way. Unworthy clergy unfortunately lent credence to these defamatory attacks. References to these facts are to be found in the writings of several of the fathers quoted from this period. At the same time, however, besides the living example of their own lives, these fathers provided a written model of the ideal life of a cleric. It is this life that is the central theme of the present study.

Effort has been given to address modern concerns related to the institution of the priesthood; however, the main focus of the study is approached from a spiritual perspective. As will be apparent to the reader, cleric or layperson, the texts chosen are meant to inspire emulation. Consequently, one should not look exclusively for evidence of text criticism or lengthy historical analysis. On the other hand, in view of the time lapse since the first publication of this study, attention has been given, where necessary, to modern scholarship on the issues addressed. Also, notes and references have been updated, the bibliography expanded, and pertinent sections rewritten. All this has been done to bring the work fully into harmony with contemporary research.

Keeping to the original intent of the work, my primary purpose has been to provide those aspiring to the high office of the priesthood with an account of the virtuous life which should be their goal. To this end, I am ever mindful of the fact that it was the students I have been privileged to teach throughout my career at Holy Cross Greek Orthodox School of Theology for whom this book was envisioned. Whether their calling was to ordained ministry or to service as lay leaders in the Church, this study was to serve as a spiritual resource and guide. This continues to be my hope for the generation of students which follows. It is to my students, therefore, past and present, to whom I dedicate this work.

As in any undertaking of this scope, the support and encouragement of others contributed to its realization. Among them are those who recognized the importance of this task and affirmed it through the generosity of their resources. Of special note here is the exceptional gift of Mrs. Catherine Pappas, ever ready to fund a cause deemed worthwhile, in memory of her late husband Stephen. Also special thanks to Anthony A. Nichols, Ernest Cochanis and Frank Kuchuris for their generous contribution, which helped make this publication possible. Less tangible, but equally important, was the caring and supportive environment conducive to academic pursuits provided by a loving family headed by my recently deceased Uncle Peter, whose concern throughout was like that of a father. I am particularly grateful to Bradley Rice for the invaluable professional services he provided towards the book's overall updating and to my student assistant Seraphim Danckaert for his role in this endeavor. I am honored, finally, that the Most Reverend Metropolitan Kallistos (Ware) of Diokleia graciously consented to write the foreword. To all who in any way contributed to this *noble task*, I express heartfelt sentiments which will accompany me throughout my lifetime.

Lewis J. Patsavos
Brookline, Massachusetts, May 27, 2007
Day of Pentecost

Preface to the Original Edition

This work has a twofold purpose. It is a personal response to a spiritual problem that has exercised the writer and at the same time is the fruit of laborious research and study.

Our age, broadly speaking, is anti-clerical. Hostility to the clergy comes not only from the Church's enemies but also from the body of the faithful itself, some of whose members have rejected the very idea of the clergy, while others would never consider entering its ranks. And that is not all. Even the congregations that constitute the local churches do not agree on the qualities desirable in candidates for the clergy. Some of them wish to have a modern "liberal" clergy, others value "conservative" clerics, yet others dream of a revival of the Church's "golden age," an age in which the ideal requirements of its clergy were first set out.

Furthermore, inspiring figures are rare today among the Church's spiritual leadership. Often unworthy clerics are ordained, who because of their unsuitability for the clerical life not only scandalize the faithful, but put weapons into the hands of the religiously "indifferent" and the Church's enemies which enable them to continue their destructive work.

It is to confront these problems, and also to contribute to the formation of ordinands according to the requirements of Canon Law at the Theological School of Holy Cross in Brookline, Massachusetts, where the future clergy of the Holy Archdiocese of North and South America are trained, that I thought it useful to examine the sources of the Church's first five centuries so as to draw from them elements which would highlight a pastoral ideal that could be spiritually helpful to candidates for the clergy. But since the material I have gathered from a long study of the sources is very extensive, I have restricted myself simply to discussing the prerequisites for entry into the clergy sought for in candidates.

I should like to express my sincere gratitude to those who have made a crucial contribution to my bringing this work to completion. First to my parents, who have supported me at every stage of my life. Their example has guided me since childhood in the study of the Scriptures and the Fathers. Their spiritual and material support has been inestimable. Equally important in the long journey that has led to the completion and publication of this work is the help I have received from my spiritual father, Archbishop Iakovos of North and South America. To my natural parents and my spiritual father I express my profound filial gratitude as a very small part of an unpaid debt. I also extend my warmest thanks to the professors of the Theological Faculty of the University of Athens for their unanimous vote accepting my dissertation, and for their valuable suggestions for its improvement. I should like to thank Professor Constantine Mouratidis especially for his kind supervision of my studies and for his warm interest in the writing of this work, which has a canonical as well as a pastoral character. Finally, I am most grateful to my dear colleagues and friends who have contributed to the linguistic improvement of this work.

Lewis J. Patsavos
Athens, July 20, 1973
Feast of my patron saint, the prophet Elijah

Introduction

The New Testament and later ecclesiastical practice both bear witness to Christ's foundation of a special priestly order in the Church. This priestly order may be understood as a sharing in the priesthood of Christ, who is called priest in the book of Hebrews. This order is called the clergy (from the Greek *kleros*, "that which is chosen by lot") because its members were set aside by lot to be dedicated to the things of God. The foundation of this order coincides with the foundation of the Church itself. The Church was manifested in the person of its divine founder, as he proclaimed the coming of the Kingdom of Heaven on earth and gathered around him his first disciples.[1] These were taught the mysteries of the Kingdom by him, for most people were not yet ready to comprehend their inner meaning. The disciples, as they themselves claimed, were stewards or ministers of the Lord.[2] And the founder and cornerstone of the Church is Christ himself.

Although the foundations of the Church had already been laid through the formation of a hierarchy and the giving of the sacraments, the power was still lacking to give life to this embryonic organism.[3] This came about through the descent of the Holy Spirit at Pentecost, which therefore marks the birth of the Church.[4] Founded in this way, the Church now needed ordering so that it could fulfill its task of bringing salvation to the world. Every organization first addresses the need to create a structure among its constituent members to enable it to achieve its aims. The rights and duties of each member arise in accordance with this structuring. Although the Church cannot, of course, be assimilated to a human organization, insofar as it is divinely created, it is nevertheless like them in its external organization.

Christ therefore founded the Church as "the center and instrument of his redemptive work."[5] But as a visible society and sacred institution, the Church also needs its own administrative system and structure like any human organization. The Church needs this in order to exercise Christ's threefold mission in the world: preaching the Gospel, celebrating the sacraments, and administering the faithful.[6] This enables the Church to fulfill its aim: exercising spiritual authority on earth, teaching the truth, and being the dispenser of divine grace. For the fulfillment of the Church's aim, the Lord chose his disciples to whom he gave the power of the Holy Spirit (cf. Matt 10:1ff.; Mark 6:7ff.; Luke 10:1ff.). The leading position is occupied by the twelve apostles,[7] chosen from Christ's followers and called to exercise an especially important role in Christ's salvific work (Mark 3:13ff.; Luke 6:12ff.).

Sent forth by Christ and possessing supernatural authority, the apostles exercised the function given to them in the name of the risen Lord and granted priestly authority to others. When Christ appeared to his disciples after his resurrection, he said to them: "Peace be with you. As the Father has sent me, even so I send you....Receive the Holy Spirit. If you forgive the sins of any, they are forgiven; if you retain the sins of any, they are retained" (John 20:21-23).

The Old Testament prophecies also clearly proclaim the foundation on earth by the expected Messiah of a kingdom without end, which cannot be compared with any existing kingdom in any way: "It shall come to pass in the latter days that the mountain of the Lord shall be manifest and the house of God shall be established on the highest of the mountains and shall be raised above the hills; and all the nations shall flow to it" (Isa 2:2). "Be joyful, O barren one, who did not bear; break forth and cry aloud, you who have not been in travail! For the children of the desolate one will be more than the children of her that is married" (Isa 54:1). "And in the days of those kings the God of heaven will set up a kingdom which shall never be destroyed, nor shall its sovereignty be left to another people. It shall break in pieces all these kingdoms and bring them to an end, and it shall stand forever" (Dan 2:44). John the Baptist proclaims that "the Kingdom of Heaven is at hand" (Matt 3:2; 4:17; 10:7; Mark 1:15), and Christ himself assures Peter, after his confession of faith, that "the gates of Hades shall not prevail against it" (Matt 16:18), that is, against the Church. Therefore, since the Church is indissoluble and universal forever, it follows that the divine mission entrusted to the apostles also endures forever. This was emphasized by Christ when he sent his disciples out into the world: "Go therefore and make disciples of all nations, baptizing them in the name of the Father and of the Son and of the Holy Spirit, teaching them to observe all that I have commanded you; and lo, I am with you always, to the close of the age" (Matt 28:19-20).

As a consequence of the apostles' exercise of Jesus' salvific work, they manifest their unity.[8] For he prayed to his Father "that they may be one even as we are one, I in them and you in me, that they may become perfectly one, so that the world may know that you have sent me and have loved them even as you have loved me" (John 17:22-23). Thus founded on the foundation of the apostles, with Jesus Christ himself as the cornerstone,[9] the Church teaches divine truth unimpaired, sanctifies believers, and guides them toward eternal life. For it is the ark of salvation, the only channel of grace for all people in all ages. The means and the authority for the Church to fulfill its aim were given to the apostles by Christ, who said: "He who hears you hears me, and he who rejects you rejects me, and he who rejects me rejects him who sent me" (Luke 10:16; cf. Matt 10:40). Thus the apostles are presented as those whose role it is to transmit the revelation of Christ, to proclaim the Gospel, to celebrate the sacraments and administer the Church, a role which is to be performed in the Church for all eternity.[10]

For the perpetuation of Christ's redemptive work on earth, the apostles were charged by the Lord to pass on priestly authority to others, appointing deacons and presbyters in the Holy Spirit and designating successors to their apostolic ministry.[11] In this way, the Church was organized on the basis of two orders, the clergy[12] and the laity,[13] or the hierarchy and the flock.

This distinction in the apostolic Church may easily be observed in the Acts of the Apostles and the Pauline epistles.[14] From this evidence we may conclude that each of the two orders has its own obligations and privileges. The special prerogatives of the clerics charged with the ministry of the divine mysteries are characteristic (cf. James 5:14). The celebration of the mysteries presupposes the existence of the priesthood,[15] and no one could undertake the exercise of this function on his own initiative without a divine calling (cf. Heb 5:4). But apart from the ministry of the sacraments, a fundamental work of the clergy is also the teaching of the divine word to the faithful of the community (cf. 1 Tim 3:2; 4:6; 6:2-3; Titus 1:9; 2:1, 7-8) and their pastoral administration (cf. 1 Tim 3:4-5).[16] Through the exercise of these functions by the clergy, the threefold ministry of Christ is continued eternally in the Church, and God is glorified through the salvation of humankind.[17]

Alongside the clergy, the faithful, or laity, as members of Christ's mystical body (Rom 12:4ff.), also have an active role in the Church, since they constitute with the rest of the faithful a "royal priesthood" (1 Pet 2:9)[18] and participate in a general way in Christ's threefold ministry.[19] Evidence for the activity of the laity goes back to apostolic times. Their active participation may be seen in Matthias's election to succeed Judas (Acts 1:15-26), and also in the election of the seven deacons (Acts 6:2-6), and at the apostolic council of Jerusalem, when by the common decision of the apostles, presbyters, and the whole Church, two men were elected to go to

Antioch with Paul and Barnabas (Acts 15:22).[20] All the faithful participated "according to the measure" (Eph 4:7) of the Paraclete's gifts poured out in the Church (Acts 2:4, 38; 4:29-31), but not all were clerics. All were made participants of the charismatic property promised by the prophets (Joel 2:28ff.; Acts 2:17-22).[21]

The clergy of all three grades of the priesthood—bishops, presbyters, and deacons—constitute the permanent officers of the Church's system of government.[22] In the apostolic Church we also find bearers of charismatic gifts (Rom 12:6; 1 Cor 12:10, 28; 14:1-6, 31).[23] In contrast to the permanent officers, the "charismatics," who appear chiefly in the first two centuries, do not confine their activity to a specific Christian community. Among them are "prophets," "evangelists," and "teachers."[24] It is generally thought that apostles and evangelists concerned themselves chiefly with the foundation of new Christian communities, while prophets and teachers worked to strengthen the faith of existing believers (Acts 15:22, 32-33; 13:1).[25] The precise relationship of prophets and teachers (Acts 13:1; Eph 4:11) to the very early appearance of the three grades of priesthood has been debated.[26] The impression given is that the charismatic ministries of prophet and teacher expressed something beyond the special charisma, analogous to a Church office.[27]

Later, alongside the permanent Church officials, there appeared a new set of permanent ecclesiastical offices, described as the "lower clergy" or "minor orders."[28] Holders of these offices served as assistants to the three higher grades of priesthood. Some of these lower officials, such as reader[29] and exorcist,[30] seem to have been related to gifts of the Holy Spirit and the charismatic office holders.[31] Similar charisms survived not only among the higher clergy but even among the laity.[32]

The divinely instituted hierarchy of the Church therefore includes the three grades of priesthood—namely, deacons,[33] presbyters,[34] and bishops,[35] which were linked together but always distinguished from each other. This hierarchy is distinguished from the laity. The distinction between clergy and laity is fundamental, these terms going back to the third century (to Clement of Alexandria, Tertullian, Origen, and Cyprian). The three priestly grades are clearly documented in the New Testament[36] and in many Church fathers and ecclesiastical authors.[37] It is known, however, that these grades are not found everywhere at the same time from the beginning, nor do the names necessarily imply permanence. The distinction between the three hierarchical grades lies in the authority and particular work of the bishop, presbyter, and deacon. The authority of each is acknowledged in relation to the other two.[38] "The bishop, instituted by other bishops, is the visible head of each local church and its center of spiritual authority. He is the indispensable mark of the Church's existence who appoints the presbyters and deacons. Of these the deacons serve the pastors in their threefold role; and the presbyters, taking their spiritual authority over the flock from the bishop, administer the Church, performing what the bishop does, except for the transmission of priesthood, and the consecration of holy oil, which belong to the bishop."[39] Priestly authority belongs primarily to the bishop and the presbyter, but only the bishop possesses it in its fullness.[40]

That priesthood is a divinely instituted rite and sacrament of the Church, which "through prayer and the imposition of hands by the bishop divine grace descends ordaining the candidate to one of the three priestly grades,"[41] hence the term "ordination,"[42] is also apparent from the New Testament.[43] The charism transmitted by the laying on of hands is a power which sanctifies the person ordained and promotes every virtue in him. The validity of the priesthood cannot be diminished by the bad moral character of the ordainer or the ordained.[44] What is certain is that the divine grace supplied by the ordination to a person worthily is also accompanied by a special strengthening from God to enable that person to perform his priestly functions and to live a virtuous life befitting his priesthood. St. Gregory of Nyssa says of such power:

> This power of the Word also makes the priest sober and honorable, setting him apart from the community as a whole by the newness of the blessing. For yesterday and the day before he was one of the many, one of the public, but suddenly he is proved to be a leader, a president, a teacher of piety, an initiator into secret mysteries. And he does these things not changed in his appearance or in a bodily sense; but remaining outwardly what he was, he is transformed in his invisible soul by an invisible power and grace and improved. (*Bapt.* [PG 46:581Dff.])

Hence it is clear that if someone is to be ordained worthily, it is necessary for him to be endowed with faith, piety, and knowledge. Aware of this vital need, the Church is eager to appoint men to the priesthood who are noted for their faith, piety, morality, and ability, and lays these down as necessary requirements for candidates.

The pursuit of moral perfection is not confined to the clergy and faithful of the Christian community. Something analogous may be observed in the pagans, too.[45] The need for the people to appoint selected persons empowered to represent the people before God in their worship, and especially in the offering of sacrifices, is found in almost all the pre-Christian religions. For worship and the offering of sacrifice to be as acceptable to the gods as possible, strenuous efforts were made by the people to find the most suitable representatives.[46] They therefore drew up lists of the virtues and qualities required in candidates. In this way they hoped that their offering would be well received by the gods.[47]

There was a similar tradition of certain requirements in those who were to offer sacrifices to God or conduct worship in Judaism. The Mosaic law consecrated Aaron and his sons for worship, and the descendants of Levi for "the liturgy of the tent of meeting" (Exod 28:1ff.; Lev 8-10; Num 16-18). Thus the Old Testament priesthood was founded, clearly setting down the requirements demanded in those who were to exercise it. Priests and Levites are threatened and exhorted to live in accordance with the requirements of their office (Lev 10:6-7, 8-11; 22:1-3, 9). Physical defects are also listed which constituted a serious impediment to entry into the priesthood. The basic requirement for Aaron's descendants was their physical integrity.[48] Under no circumstances may such men approach God's altar. There are also strict regulations governing the marriage of priests, especially the high priest, whose wife must be a virgin and of his own people. He is absolutely forbidden to marry a widow, a woman who has been divorced by her husband, or a prostitute.[49] In other words, the moral character of a candidate's wife is a basic consideration of his suitability for the priesthood. Besides physical integrity, the unique privilege of Aaron's descendants as servants of Yahweh also demands bodily purity of them through avoiding any action that might provoke bodily pollution. Lepers, anyone with a discharge, anyone who has touched unclean things, in general anyone polluted in any way, is excluded from priestly service by the prescriptions of the rules of purity.[50] Finally, foreigners are considered profane and are therefore excluded from serving the altar. Transgressors are threatened by severe punishments in the name of God.[51] The purity and perfection of these men was all the more necessary so that the acts of worship and sacrifices offered to God should be pleasing to him. The legal prescriptions adequately served this aim.[52]

The priesthood of the law, that for a time realized the divine plan of salvation, was superseded by the priesthood of the New Testament. The Levitical priesthood was a type of the priesthood of grace (Isa 66:21; Mal 3:3). Moreover, the New Testament preaches that Christ is the supreme high priest, infinitely superior to the high priest of the Jews, and founder of a new priesthood (Heb 5:5-6).[53] Later, many Church fathers and ecclesiastical writers compare the Christian priesthood to the Jewish.[54] Although the Old Testament priesthood had to belong to a particular tribe,[55] in the New Testament there is no such limitation. The clergy of the priesthood of grace could come from any who believed in the Lord. Nevertheless, it is discernible in the Christian tradition that the prescriptions for the Mosaic priesthood have strongly influenced the presuppositions deriving from the New Testament.

In spite of this, there are notable new features in the New Testament and later Christian criteria for the clergy which spring from their authority and work. The model for all the clergy is Christ himself through his teaching and example: "I am the good shepherd. The good shepherd lays down his life for the sheep" (John 10:11). The clergy are the shepherds of Christ's rational sheep. Through asceticism, through being constantly enriched with the virtues, and through ceaseless vigilance, they are distinguished from the unprofitable workers, the false prophets, and the wolves in sheep's clothing who came to pillage the Church. The imitation of Christ, the supreme shepherd, teaches his example to the apostles. Paul proposes as an example his own imitation of Christ, saying: "Be imitators of me, as I am of Christ" (1 Cor 11:1).

Those who through ordination have been invested with one of the grades of priesthood receive the grace of the Holy Spirit, which enables them to fulfill their duties. But not all are worthy of Christ's ministry, which is why Paul says to Timothy: "Do not be hasty in laying on of hands" (1 Tim 5:22). In Paul's pastoral epistles the qualities demanded of the clergy are clearly listed. Addressing his disciples Timothy and Titus, and through them all down the centuries "aspiring" (1 Tim 3:1) to enter the clergy, Paul lays down simply and clearly what kind of man a candidate should be.[56]

This study does not aim to be a general treatise on the priesthood. I examine the presuppositions—the virtues, qualities, and abilities—regarded as indispensable in a candidate for one of the three grades of priesthood and render him worthy of it. I deal only briefly with the priesthood as such, simply to orient the reader for what follows.

One of the two sources for my discussion of entry into the clergy in the first five centuries is revelation both written and unwritten, both Holy Scripture and sacred Tradition, as recorded in the writings of the holy fathers. The other is the works of certain ecclesiastical writers and the decisions of ecumenical and local councils.

The method I have followed is historical and philological. The criteria for entry into the clergy originate in the New Testament. They are developed in the sources of later centuries. Beginning with Paul's pastoral epistles, I examine the sources relevant to my theme until the Fourth Ecumenical Council, which is the period in which the criteria for entry into the clergy are established. The object of this examination is to determine the criteria proposed. I then try to set out the official formulation of these criteria by the councils. Finally, I attempt a systematic exposition of the criteria for entry into the clergy in the first five centuries on the basis of my historical review of hagiographic, patristic, and canonical texts. The study as a whole is concerned only with those criteria which are explicitly mentioned in legislative works. Thus I do not examine the criteria taken for granted by the Church's practice (such as baptism, maleness, etc.).

I recognize that recent scholarship, inspired in part by the increasing popularity of the interdisciplinary study of Late Antiquity, has moved away from the style of this work in several ways. With some notable exceptions, a considerable amount of scholarly work has transcended the disciplinary bounds of theology, patristics, and even biography. With this transformation has come a considerable increase in the methodological complexity of scholarship on early Church history, especially the study of the episcopacy.[57] This topic in particular has presented modern scholars with ample and occasionally controversial material.

By the end of the fourth century, the average Christian bishop was more than a spiritual leader of a local community of faith. He also held an important position of legal authority that placed him near the top of a complicated system of patronage that had been inherited from Roman society. Thus, we find a fusion of legal, political, religious, and moral power in the person of the fourth-century bishop—and, thereby, a fusion of legal, political, religious, and moral identities in the broader Christian church.

These are the topics that captivate many of today's scholars. Today, we find a plethora of monographs concerned with socio-historical, cultural, and literary approaches to the very same texts that are so central to this study. Many of these studies incorporate interdisciplinary techniques and, often, are especially attuned to the centrality of power and ideology in the formation of religious texts and identities.[58]

I offer this study in the conviction that following the historical development of the established canonical requirements for entry into the clergy and presenting a systematic exposition of the Church's teaching in the first five centuries nevertheless fulfills a continuing need to clarify and evaluate the canonical tradition embodied in the canons of the ecumenical and local councils.

Notes

1.   There is a vast bibliography on early ecclesiology. On the origins of the Church within first-century Judaism see, for example, Rowland 2002.

2.   As I. Eutaxias observes: "If the phrase 'stewards of God' (Titus 1:7) is interpreted by 'stewards of the mysteries of God' (1 Cor 4:1)…it clearly suggests the priestly character of the apostles and their successors" (1872, 37).

3.   See Mouratidis 1958, 92.

4.   Ibid.

5.   Androutsos 1907, 264.

6.   Cf. Karmiris 1973, 11ff.; Mitsopoulos 1972a, 93-94; Mitsopoulos 1972b, 24-25.

7.   Cf. Matt 10:5; 26:14, 20, 47; Mark 4:10; 6:7; 9:35; 10:32; 11:11; 14:10, 17, 20, 43; Luke 9:12; 18:31; 22:3, 47; John 20:24.

8.   Cf. Michel 1932, 1200.

9.   Cf. Ps 118:22ff.; Isa 28:16; Matt 21:42; Acts 4:11; 1 Pet 2:6-8.

10. See Schmaus 1958, 494. The uniqueness of apostolic office lies, among other things, in the witness of the resurrection by the eleven, who thus constitute the authenticity of the Church's faith. Cf. Colson 1964, 153-154; Campenhausen 1953, 24-25; Lohse 1953.

11. See Androutsos 1907, 282.

12. "Clergy" and "cleric" derive from the word *klêros*, which

has the primary meaning of "that which is assigned by lot." In the Old Testament, the term is used chiefly to indicate a portion given to somebody by God (Num 18:20). In the New Testament, it manifests the discovery of the divine will, as in the choosing of Matthias (Acts 1:26). It was in this sense of *klêros* that Judas "was numbered among us, and was allotted his share in this ministry" (Acts 1:17). Among the Jews it was of vital importance whether they had a share in Moses (*Assumption of Moses* 2.22). Similarly with Christians in the New Testament, it was important whether one had a share in the word or gift of God (Acts 8:21: "You have neither part nor lot [*klêros*] in this matter"). Elsewhere the term indicates the share in eschatological fulfillment which a person may be given (Acts 26:18: "I send you to open their eyes…that they may receive…a place [*klêron*] among those who are sanctified by faith in me"; Col 1:12: "giving thanks to the Father, who has qualified us to share in the inheritance [*klêrou*] of the saints in light"). The faithful are given a share in the lot of the "saints." The term *klêros* in these passages refers to the divine gift which God grants to each of the faithful called to communion with all the "sanctified" (see Foerster 1965, 3:764). In his letter to Nepotianus, Jerome explains the term "clerics" by the fact that clerics belong to the Lord's portion, or the Lord is for them a special portion: "God's ministers are on that account called clerics [*clerici*], either because they are the Lord's by lot, or because the Lord himself is the lot, that is, the portion of clerics" (*Ep.* 52, *Ad Nepotianum* 5). Cf. esp. Christodoulos 1896, 159; Milasch 1906, 300, n. 7; Karmiris 1973, 14ff.

13. Other expressions used for the laity in the early centuries are: *poimnion* (flock), *plêthos pistôn* (company of believers), *idiôtai* (private persons), and *biôtikoi* (secular persons). See Milasch 1906, 313, n. 8; Eichmann 1967, 23; Karmiris 1973, 9ff.

14. Cf. Acts 15:22; 20:28; Phil 1:1; Eph 4:11-12; 1 Cor 12:28; Rom 12:4ff.; 1 Tim 4:6, 12, 14; 2 Tim 1:6; Phlm 2.

15. On the institution of the priesthood in general, see Fouyas 1971-1972, 5-12, 23-30, 138-160, 174-179.

16. Cf. also Leclerq 1928, 1056.

17. See Anger 1946, 247; Androutsos 1907, 282; Karmiris 1973, 11ff.; Mitsopoulos 1972a, 93-94; 1972b, 24-25.

18. On the "royal priesthood" see Bratsiotis 1955; Trembelas 1957; Kotsonis 1965 (with bibliography); Ryan 1962.

19. On the participation of the faithful in the Lord's three-fold ministry, see Trembelas 1959-1961, 3:288; Karmiris 1970, 21-22; 1973, 11ff.

20. Cf. Trembelas 1931, 20; Leclercq 1928, 1054.

21. See Kalogiros 1965, 661.

22. Cf. Hatch 1881, 17-78; Milasch 1906, 331ff.; Christophilo-poulos 1954, 44; Lemaire 1971; Faivre 1977.

23. Cf. also Harnack 1924, 222ff.; Stephanidis 1959, 42-43; Kotsonis 1952, 7ff.

24. Matt 7:15-20; 23:34; Luke 11:49; Acts 11:27; 21:10; 1 Cor 12:28; 13:2, 8; 14:29, 37; Eph 2:20; 3:5; 4:11; *Didache* 11-15.

25. Cf. also Stephanidis 1959, 42; Fascher 1927; Lietzmann 1932-1944, 1:145; Colson 1956, 354ff.; Daniélou 1958, 406-407.

26. Cf. Acts 13:1-3; 19:6; 1 Tim 4:14; 2 Tim 1:6. See Harnack 1924, 344ff., 365ff.; Preuschen and Krüger 1923, 56; Lietzmann 1932-1944, 1:145-147; Peterson 1949, 577-579; Stephanidis 1959, 42-43; Aune 1983; Stander 1984-1985.

27. Cf. Stephanidis 1959, 42, n. 1; Campenhausen 1953, 195; Daniélou 1958, 406.

28. On the minor orders, the classic study is Wieland 1897; see also Harnack 1886.

29. See the introduction to Harnack 1886 by John Owen in the translation by Wheatley (1895, 79). Owen sets out Harnack's findings, according to which readers were originally charismatic office-holders.

30. Cf. Wieland 1897, 114-132 and 172-174; Stephanidis 1959, 94-95.

31. Cf. 1 Tim 4:13; *Can. eccl.* 17; *Const. ap.* 8.22; 8.26.

32. Cf. Karmiris 1973, 12-13.

33. According to Cyprian the seven were deacons (*Ep.* 3.3; 67.4; cf. Sozomen, *Hist. eccl.* 7.19). Their duties can be guessed from the qualities which Polycarp regards as indispensable

for them in his epistle to the Philippians (*Phil.* 5).

34. In the apostolic age the terms "presbyter" and "bishop" were interchangeable, although the functions of each differed. An ecclesiastical hierarchy (monarchical bishop, presbyter, and deacon) appeared very early in Syria and Asia Minor, and spread from there to other areas where the ancient missionary structure (body of presbyter-bishops originally under an apostle and then under a presbyter-president) had become established. See Michel 1936, 142; Fransen 1962, 1213; Konidaris 1959a, 42ff. and 53ff.; Colson 1964, 163ff.; Jay 1981; Young 1994. From the older literature, see also Lietzmann 1914, 97ff. and 1932-1944, 2:49ff.; Campenhausen 1953, 82ff.; Goguel 1947, 110ff.; Palmer 1937, 768ff.; Schmidt 1937, 314ff. In the primitive Church, those bearing the name of "presbyter" are usually concerned with priestly duties, while those bearing the name of "bishop" are chiefly concerned with administrative and disciplinary duties (Acts 20:28). See Stephanidis 1959, 44. See also below, pp. 24-28.

35. Cf. Geweiss 1958. The term "bishop" (*episkopos*) for an ecclesiastical office appears in the New Testament for the first time in Philippians 1:1. From the pastoral epistles it may be inferred that the bishops exercise the functions that originally belonged to "prophets" and "teachers." The primitive Church adopted a term for an official ministry in the pagan Greek world and gave it a new meaning. See Beyer 1964, 2:608-620; Schnackenburg 1949; Adam 1957; Chadwick et al. 1980; and pp. 24-28 below.

36. Phil 1:1; Acts 14:23; 20:17, 28; Rom 12:8. 1 Cor 16:16; 1 Thess 5:12; 1 Tim 3:1-2, 8, 12; Titus 1:5, 7; Heb 13:7, 17, 24; James 5:14.

37. E.g., Ignatius, *Trall.* 3.1: "So too let everyone respect the deacons like Jesus Christ, and also the bishop, who is the image of the Father; and let them respect the presbyters like the council of God and the band of the apostles" (trans. *Ehrman*, 1:259). See also Theodoret of Cyrus, *Comm. Phil.* 1; *Comm. 1 Tim.* 3.

38. See Eutaxias 1872, 18.

39. Androutsos 1907, 284-285.

40. See Eutaxias 1872, 18ff. On the relationship of the grades of deacon and presbyter to the bishop, see Dix 1947; Luttenberger 1981; Hennesy 1986; Falesiedi 1995.

41. Androutsos 1907, 389.

42. The meaning of the word "ordination" (*cheirotonia*) very early comes to encompass appointment to the ecclesiastical ministries, the sacrament of priesthood, and entry into the clergy. Other terms for this are "consecration" (*kathierôsis*), "sacramental perfection" (*telesiourgia*), "priestly perfection" (*hieratikê teleiôsis*), and, more rarely, "laying on of hands" (*cheirothesia*). Coming originally from popular participation in antiquity in the election of state officials, the word *cheirotonia* originally meant the raising of a hand at the election. This sense of the word, implying the participation of the people and the supervision of their leaders in the election and appointment of ecclesiastical ministers, especially of bishops, endured until Justinian's time. But as the contribution of the laity came to be severely limited, and the main emphasis fell on the sacrament of priesthood, the term remained but its original meaning gave way to that of the sacrament of ordination administered by the laying on of hands. See Feine 1955, 680; Panagiotakos 1951, 30ff.; Christodoulos 1896, 163. There is a detailed discussion of the meaning of the word *cheirotonia* in Siotis 1951. Cf. esp. Behm 1911; Coppens 1925; Lohse 1951; Heubach 1956; Dix 1947, 193-194; Fouyas 1971-1972, 138-140; Gy 1962.

43. To appoint the seven deacons, the apostles prayed and laid their hands on them: "Therefore, brethren, pick out from among you seven men of good repute, full of the Spirit and of wisdom, whom we may appoint to this duty. But we will devote ourselves to prayer and to the ministry of the word. What they said pleased the whole community, and they chose Stephen, a man full of faith and the Holy Spirit, together with Philip, Prochorus, Nicanor, Timon, Parmenas, and Nicolaus, a proselyte of Antioch. These they set before the apostles, and they prayed and *laid their hands upon them*" (Acts 6:3-6). Cf. Acts 13:2-3; 14:23; 1 Tim 4:14; 5:22; 2 Tim 1:6.

44. See John Chrysostom, *Hom. 2 Tim. 3.*

45. This analogy should not be taken too far, however, since most forms of pagan priesthood, with the exception of certain popular cults, such as that of Attis, did not have a professional priesthood. In fact, many of the more important priesthoods were actually civic offices. An extensive analysis of the similarities and differences between pagan priesthood and Christian leadership can be found in Lane Fox 1987.

46. See Marquardt 1881-1885, 3:223; cf. Lane Fox 1987, 76-78. One of the rituals in the appointment of priests by the Romans involved questioning the god's oracle about the worthiness of the man to be appointed.

47. See Marquardt 1881-1885, 3:237ff.

48. Lev 21:17-21: "None of your descendants throughout their generations who has a blemish may approach to offer the bread of his God. For no one who has a blemish shall draw near, a man blind or lame, or one who has a mutilated nose, or cropped ears, or a man who has an injured hand or an injured foot, or a hunchback, or a dwarf, or a man with a defect in his sight or scabs or only one testicle; no man of the descendants of Aaron the priest who has a blemish shall come near to offer the sacrifice to your God; since he has a blemish, he shall not come near to offer the gifts of God." We can observe the influence of these Jewish ordinances very clearly in the Christian ecclesiastical tradition in general. See, e.g., Cyril of Alexandria, *On Worship in Spirit and in Truth* 12.

49. Lev 21:13-14: "And he shall take a wife from his own race in her virginity. A widow, or one divorced, or a woman who has been defiled, or a harlot, these he shall not marry; but he shall take to wife a virgin of his own people." Cf. Lev 21:7 for priests generally. The direct influence of this Jewish precept is observable in Christian tradition concerning the Church. Cf. 1 Tim 3:11; *Didasc. ap.* 2.2.3; Elvira 65; Neocaesarea 8. Cf. also pp. 191-192 below. Since the priestly office was hereditary, it could not be assumed by anyone who did not belong to the priestly class (see 2 Esd 2:61-63; Neh 7:63-65). Similarly, a man born into the priestly class could not be excluded from it. Hence the special regulations for the marriage of priests and the high priest were intended to preserve the purity of

the priestly bloodline. See Philippidis 1958, 437.

50. Lev 22:3-8: "If any one of all your descendants throughout your generations approaches the holy things, which the
sons of Israel dedicate to the Lord, while he has an uncleanness, that soul shall be cut off from my presence: I am the
Lord your God. None of the line of Aaron the priest who is
a leper or suffers a discharge may eat of the holy things until
he is clean. And anyone who touches any uncleanness of soul
or a man who has an emission of semen, or whoever touches
any unclean creeping thing which makes him unclean, or
a man from whom he may take uncleanness, whatever his
uncleanness may be—the soul that touches any such shall
be unclean until the evening and shall not eat of the holy
things unless he has bathed his body in water. When the sun
is down he shall be clean; and then he may eat of the holy
things, because such is his bread. That which dies of itself or
is torn by beasts he shall not eat, defiling himself by them:
I am the Lord." Cf. Lev 10:6-7; 21:1-6, 10-12; Num 19; Ezek
44:25-27, 31. Cf. also Vaux 1961, 347-348.

51. Num 3:10: "And you shall appoint Aaron and his sons
over the tent of witness, and they shall attend to their priesthood and everything pertaining to the altar and within the
hangings; but a *foreigner* who touches them shall be put to
death." Cf. Num 3:1-3; 18:1-7; 1 Chr 23:13. We can observe
a similar influence of the Old Testament on Christianity in
the matter of race, with the difference that in the Christian
tradition a "foreigner" is described as one who is "impious"
and "profane," while a person of the same race is one who
is "pious" and a "lover of God" (Cyril of Alexandria, *Ador.*
12).

52. Cf. Greenberg 1950, 41; Vaux 1961, 536.

53. The teaching on the priesthood of Jesus Christ in the
Epistle to the Hebrews is the first Christian witness to the
theme. It is continued by the earliest Christian writers (Clement of Rome, Ignatius, and Polycarp).

54. See *1 Clement* 40.5; *Didache* 13.3; Tertullian, *Bapt.* 17; Hippolytus, *Haer.* 1 (prooemium); Origen, *Comm. Jo.* 1.3; *Didasc.
ap.* 2.25.7; Cyprian, *Ep.* 1.1.

55. See Num 3:1-3, 10; 18:1, 7; 1 Chr 23:13. The restriction of the service of God to the tribe of Levi is the result of particular historical circumstances. Tested by Yahweh, the Levites remained faithful to him (Exod 32:25-29), which is why their tribe was consecrated to God as the firstborn (Num 3:12-13; 8:18; cf. Exod 22:29).

56. On the description of the ideal cleric, especially of the bishop, in the Cappadocian fathers, see Dentakis 1970; Patsavos 1976.

57. See, for example, Rapp 2005; Sterk 2004; Drake 2000; Brakke 1995.

58. This particular methodological trend has been eloquently championed in Clark 2004.

The Early Sources

The New Testament

Like the Old Testament, the New Testament contains a number of passages describing the qualities required in candidates for the clergy. The Gospels especially reveal Christ's concern for the moral perfection of his disciples. The other books of the New Testament show how the apostles had a similar concern for those appointed by them. The Lord, as the model of the perfect pastor, prepared the apostles through his life and teaching for their saving work,[1] thus sowing the seeds of the criteria for entry into the clergy. The apostles, in turn, exhorted their successors in local communities to maintain the same criteria so as to receive and pass on the sacred apostolic character.

It is especially in Paul's pastoral epistles that we find a shepherd's keen concern to hand on to his spiritual children a list of basic qualities required in those who wish to serve in the Lord's vineyard (1 Tim 3:2-13; Titus 1:6-9). Paul's detailed description of the fundamental virtues of bishops and deacons is caused by a phenomenon which first appears in the apostolic age. As soon as the ideal of messianic poverty began to fade, and with it the moral teaching of Jesus Christ and his apostles, there arose a tendency to list and even codify the qualities sought in those who were to be ordained. The pastoral epistles reflect this tendency. They also show a moral slackening which begins to affect certain representatives of the ecclesiastical hierarchy, and their apostolic concern for protecting the sacred character of the Church, the clergy, and the laity.[2]

When reading Paul's letters to Timothy and Titus, we must bear in mind that the Apostle was addressing men who exercised a hierarchical function in the Church. The words "bishops," "presbyters," and "deacons" have a prominent place in Paul's pastoral epistles. These terms indicate the special offices of each Christian community. Other Pauline letters use different terms, such as "those set over you" (*proistamenoi* [1 Thess 5:12]), "administrators" (*kybernêseis* [1 Cor 12:28]), and "pastors" or "shepherds" (*poimenes* [Eph 4:11]). I should also mention briefly the confusion we find in the apostolic period between the terms "bishop" and "presbyter," and also the problem of the New Testament origin of episcopal office.

The terms "presbyter" and "bishop" are confused in the apostolic period, particularly in the Christian communities founded by Paul (see Acts 20:17, 28; 1 Tim 3:1-12; Titus 1:5-7; Phil 1:1). In these years the terms seem interchangeable (e.g., Titus 1:5, 7). But this confusion does not seem to prevail in all the communities. In Jerusalem, for example, only the presbyters were called by that name.[3] The Church's system of government by the three grades of bishop, presbyter, and deacon was in place there from the beginning. The interchangeability of the terms "bishop" and "presbyter" does not necessarily imply a fusion of the grades. The use of one of the terms in any instance seems rather to refer to the particular duties attached to it. Apart from this, the question of the New Testament origin of the episcopal office has been much debated. A variety of opinions has been expressed by modern scholars.[4] Protestants maintain that in the apostolic Church there were only two ecclesiastical offices, those of presbyter and deacon. In their view the bishop's office arose out of the ambitions of some to preside at religious gatherings,[5] or as a consequence of the later evolution of ecclesiastical ranks.[6] Roman Catholics accept the divine institution of these offices, but, faithful to their monarchical system, maintain that just as among the apostles Peter possessed the plenitude of apostolic authority, so among the bishops instituted by the apostles, Peter's successor, the bishop of Rome, possesses the plenitude of episcopal authority.[7] The Orthodox view is that in the primitive Church the terms "presbyter" and "bishop" indicated particular responsibilities, a "presbyter" having priestly duties, while a "bishop's" responsibilities were administrative, disciplinary, and so on.[8] The three degrees of priesthood were instituted by the apostles. That is to say, their institution was divine; it did not derive from ecclesiastical legislation. In the apostolic period the bishop's office differed from the presbyter's, but at the same time all three offices clearly derive from the apostolic office itself. The immediate successors of the apostles are only the bishops, since they have inherited the apostles' exercise of the highest ecclesiastical authority, with the power to transmit this authority to others and therefore possessing the fullness of the priesthood.[9]

When addressing his representatives, who would soon assume pastoral responsibility for the Church, Paul exhorts them to establish presbyters in each city, laying down precisely which virtues they should possess and the responsibilities of their office. Moreover, he gives instructions for their personal conduct, preaching of the Gospel, ministry toward different kinds of people, and administration of the Church. In a word, he teaches with his full apostolic authority "how one ought to behave in the household of God" (1 Tim 3:15). Writing to Timothy, he gives a detailed description of the qualities he expects in bishops and deacons:

> Now a bishop must be above reproach, the husband of one wife, temperate, sensible, dignified, hospitable, an apt teacher, no drunkard, not violent but gentle, not quarrelsome, and no lover of money. He must manage his own household well, keeping his children submissive and respectful in every way; for if a man does not know how to manage his own household, how can he care for God's church? He must not be a recent convert, or he may be puffed up with conceit and fall into the condemnation of the devil; moreover he must be well thought of by outsiders, or he may fall into reproach and the snare of the devil. Deacons likewise must be serious, not double-tongued, not addicted to much wine, not greedy for gain; they must hold the mystery of the faith with a clear conscience. And let them also be tested first; then if they prove themselves blameless let them serve as deacons....Let deacons be the husband of one wife, and let them manage their children and their households well; for those who serve well as deacons gain a good standing for themselves and also great confidence in the faith which is in Christ Jesus. (1 Tim 3:2-13)

In the letter to Titus he more or less repeats himself:
[I]f any man is blameless, the husband of one wife, and
his children are believers and not open to the charge
of being profligate or insubordinate. For a bishop, as
God's steward, must be blameless; he must not be arrogant or quick-tempered or a drunkard or violent or
greedy for gain, but hospitable, a lover of goodness,
master of himself, upright, holy, and self-controlled; he
must hold firm to the sure word as taught, so that he
may be able to give instruction in sound doctrine and
also to confute those who contradict it. (Titus 1:6-9)

Four qualities appear in both of these lists: the bishop
must not be a drunkard, or greedy for gain, but sensible
and hospitable. Eight virtues are also duplicated, with
the difference that in one list they are required of the
bishop, and in the other of the presbyter.[10] Thus they
are allowed to marry only once. Both the bishop and
the presbyter should be above reproach and blameless
(1 Tim 3:2; Titus 1:7). They should be good heads of
family (1 Tim 3:4-5; Titus 1:6), not greedy for gain or
quick-tempered (1 Tim 3:3; Titus 1:7), but self-controlled
(1 Tim 3:2; Titus 1:8), gentle and hospitable (1 Tim 3:3;
Titus 1:7), and able teachers (1 Tim 3:2; Titus 1:9).

In the first letter to Timothy, Paul emphasizes that the
bishop should not be a "neophyte" or recent convert,
referring to the danger that someone recently catechized
in the faith might lose it through self-congratulation,
and that he might become "puffed up with conceit and
fall into the condemnation of the devil" (1 Tim 3:6). He
also adds that "he should be well thought of by outsiders, or he may fall into reproach and the snare of the
devil" (1 Tim 3:7). His conduct must not give grounds
for criticism by pagans. But we can say that this qual-

ity of enjoying a good reputation among the pagans is emphasized not just as a matter of personal morality but as a factor in the Christian community's effectiveness in proselytizing, and in avoiding provoking pagan hostility.[11] In the letter to Titus, Paul says similarly that a candidate must be a lover of goodness, upright and holy (Titus 1:8).[12]

It is noteworthy that the criteria Paul lays down for bishops and presbyters are repeated almost entirely for deacons. We must therefore conclude that the Apostle regarded these qualities as fundamental. And it is unlikely that these things were enunciated for the first time in the letter to Timothy. But at the end of the second passage from the first list (1 Tim 3:2-13), the ability to teach is mentioned, which is not included among the bishop's main responsibilities, nor has it any relation to the moral criteria applicable to the bishop's office. The importance of this lies in the particular circumstances of the period, and in the needs of the community. Consequently, drunkards, violent men, and lovers of money are categorically excluded from entry into the clergy, which is why in the third passage the attributes of meekness, serenity, and lack of avarice are mentioned as indispensable for the blameless moral behavior of candidate bishops. From the education point of view the exclusion of recent converts (1 Tim 3:6) is surely intended to safeguard the zeal of those who have recently turned to Christ, since it sometimes happens that neophytes lose their enthusiasm for Christ after a while and return to their former inertia and spiritual aridity.[13] Thus by excluding them, the Church acts prudently to avoid creating unnecessary problems.

A bishop should possess three fundamental virtues: the understanding of a leader who knows how to command but also elicits respect and obedience, like the father of a family; justice, whether toward subordinates as a just judge, or whether in renouncing his claims on worldly goods under the guise of magnanimity; and self-control in the broadest sense of the term. The bishop is a person who is satisfied with little, self-restrained, master of his bodily drives and only once married, sober, drinking only a little wine, meek and humble, not falling into the devil's trap of pride. He also exercises the theological virtues of faith, correctly interpreting truth and brotherly love, receiving warmly not only the members of his own Church but also visitors, and being a friend of the good in all its forms. Finally, he is endowed with the gift of teaching to enable him to exhort and strengthen the faithful and refute heretics.[14]

Deacons likewise were no less bound to possess certain virtues, necessary for the exercise of their office. In comparison to the virtues required of bishops and presbyters, they were not assigned any duties to do with doctrine or the offering of hospitality. Although the deacon's office had not yet been fully developed, deacons had to maintain a standing appropriate to the nature of the duties they were called upon to fulfill. The deacon, as the bishop's assistant, served him in his divine ministry and pastoral care of the Church (1 Tim 3:10). The strictest integrity was therefore demanded of him, since he shared in the administration of the worldly goods contributed by Christians, and the distribution of alms to the sick and needy (Acts 6:1ff.; Rom 15:25; 1 Cor 16:15). If he is required to be sincere and not two-faced, this was because he came into immediate contact with the laity. Consequently, he must not be afraid of telling the truth even if it upset people. As the bishop's assistant he participated to some extent in the management of the Church, the conduct of worship, and the administration of the sacraments (Acts 8:5ff.). But we cannot be precise about these duties in the period of the primitive Church.[15] In the list of deacons' attributes, as in that of bishops, we also find the negative expression of certain virtues, the absence of which renders the candidate unfit for this ministry in the Church and is an impediment to his entry into the clergy. Thus the often-repeated accusation concerning the absence of any attribute characteristic of deacons, and the duplication of criteria contained in the list for bishops, lacks weight.[16]

The virtues as they appear in these Pauline lists do not present any particularly Christian characteristic. They are rather virtues which one would expect to find in anybody, whether Christian or not. The similarities between these and the virtues mentioned in the lists of ancient Greek literature have already been noted.[17] According to these, Paul's demands were devised in the same manner as the chief virtues of the Greeks. In demanding virtues with which most Christians were familiar, Paul wanted to emphasize the absolute necessity of their possession by those who wished to enter the ranks of the clergy. A person who cannot give evidence of elementary moral behavior is excluded from them. In spite of the similarity of this pastoral collection to the moral collections of pagan antiquity, the Christian material presents some original features. Even if Paul had the Greek tradition in mind when he was writing to his spiritual children, he omitted some attributes which his predecessors mentioned repeatedly and gives a new christocentric and ecclesiological content to the virtues he lists for candidate clergy. Seeking a basic moral usefulness in holders of ecclesiastical office, he tries to protect them from calumny by "outsiders" and ensure that the authority of evangelical teaching was maintained. Moreover, these basic attributes were indisputable criteria for distinguishing Christ's true servants from false teachers. Finally, Paul gives a new and purely Christian coloring to the traditional meaning of Greek terms, applying to the bishops what Christ taught through his own example and demanded from his apostles.[18]

The Apostolic Fathers

The concern of the bishop, as a shepherd of Christ's Church, for the morally blameless life of aspirants to the clergy has been reiterated so emphatically by all the Church's fathers and teachers that sometimes their statements might be thought exaggerated.[19] The first of these to stress the need for aspiring clergy to possess high moral qualities are the so-called apostolic fathers.[20] Although none of these made a special study of the pastoral ministry, nevertheless they emphasized its meaning and function incidentally, and set our Lord Jesus Christ as a model for the laity as well as the clergy.

The term "apostolic fathers" was unknown to the early Church but is now used of ecclesiastical writers of the first and early second centuries. Because of their early date they reflect the spirit of the teaching of the apostles rather closely, which they received directly from them or from their first disciples. The works of the apostolic fathers are of a pastoral character. With regard to their style and content they resemble the books of the New Testament, particularly the letters of the apostles.[21] They often quote words and phrases from the pastoral epistles verbatim.

The information they give on the institution of the priesthood is surprisingly meager. In none of them do we find details of the qualities required in candidates for the priesthood in this period, or the depth of spirituality which bishops and priests had to have in order to perform the duties of their office. Rarely is a word or phrase used in passing which sheds some light on our subject. But such silence is not surprising when we bear in mind that these fathers were addressing not us but their contemporaries. It was not necessary for them to speak to their contemporaries about things which were part of their daily life. For Christians of the first and second centuries everything was arranged simply, without the need for elaborate documentation.

Clement of Rome

The oldest writing of the apostolic fathers, Clement of Rome's first epistle to the Corinthians, illustrates the truth of this. It describes the creation of the Church's hierarchy and how it was continued as follows:

> The apostles brought us the Gospel from the Lord Jesus Christ. Jesus Christ was sent by God. Christ is therefore from God, and the apostles are from Christ.

Both therefore came in good order from the will of God. Having then received the promises, assured about the resurrection of our Lord Jesus Christ and convinced through the word of God with the assurance of the Holy Spirit, they came out to preach the gospel of the imminence of the Kingdom of God. Preaching in villages and towns, they made the firstfruits of their work, once they had been tested by the Spirit, bishops and deacons of future believers. (*1 Clem.* 42.1-4)

For the writer of this letter, the hierarchy of the New Testament were therefore the bearers of ecclesiastical office transmitted by the apostles. The only way in which legitimate authority could be possessed in the Church was if God provided it. From God, as the source of all authority, it was handed on through Christ to the apostles, who likewise transmitted it to their true successors. This very simple approach to the institution of the clergy in the primitive Church satisfied the needs of the time. But over the years, as the enthusiastic tendencies of the first Christian communities declined, this approach to the question was not considered adequate.

What occasioned this letter was the disruptive behavior of certain members of the Corinthian community who had driven some of their presbyters out of their Church.[22] The news of this scandalous behavior reached Rome, whose bishop intervened to restore peace and harmony. In doing so Clement used the opportunity to emphasize in a striking way the spiritual gifts of the true Christian. His letter is therefore a guide to the Christian life.[23]

To link the new priesthood with the prophecies of the Old Testament and maintain that the priesthood of grace had already been proclaimed in the prophetic age,[24] this apostolic father adapts a passage from the Septuagint: "for many years ago it was written about bishops and deacons. For thus says Scripture: 'I will establish their bishops in righteousness and their deacons in faith'" (*1 Clem.* 42.5).[25] After reminding the Corinthians of the virtuous life they should be following, he goes on to emphasize that God abhors all highhandedness that provokes strife and quarreling in the Church. The apostles, warned by the Lord, knew about the conflict which the episcopal office would provoke (1 Tim 3:1). Suitably informed, they therefore "appointed the people already mentioned,[26] and afterwards laid it down as a rule[27] that when they fall asleep they are to be succeeded by other tested men (1 Tim 3:10) in their office" (*1 Clem.* 44.2).[28] Clement continues in a manner reminiscent of Paul's apostolic exhortations to his spiritual children, Timothy and Titus, and lists the virtues which the ministers of the Most High should possess: "those therefore appointed by them or later by other distinguished men[29] with the consent of the whole Church, and who have ministered blamelessly (1 Thess 2:10) to Christ's flock with humility, peacefully and nobly, well attested for many years by all" (*1 Clem.* 44.3).[30]

Clement's letter is not very revealing about the office of the presbyters. It simply declares that on the death of those appointed by the apostles "to be bishops and deacons of future believers" they should be succeeded by "other tested men." There is no reason for us to doubt that this principle was observed. The succession of ecclesiastical ministers was indispensable for the continuation of the apostolic work in the Church.[31] That is why their successors were chosen by the apostles themselves or "by other distinguished men with the consent of the whole Church."[32] In this way vacancies created by death in the ranks of the presbyters were filled. We can therefore say that for the body of presbyters to be formed their election by the bishops and the consent of the community were indispensable. Clement does not distinguish between bishops and presbyters,[33] nor does he describe the rite or ceremony by which the ministers of God are ordained. We have to be content with his silence.

Ignatius of Antioch

The qualities required for episcopal office are of no particular interest to St. Ignatius. They were already known to his readers and there was no need for him to repeat them. But he does inform us indirectly in his letters of the state of the clergy and especially of the bishops in the various comments he addresses to Christian communities and their pastors.

In his letter to the Church of Magnesia he writes that youthfulness should not be the occasion of excessive familiarity. This suggests that some bishops, such as Damas, bishop of Magnesia, were very young. But as the Magnesians know that the bishop embodies the power of God (*Magn.* 3.1), they should conduct themselves toward him accordingly. The bishop should be the bearer of various virtues, the presence of which is a source of joy to Ignatius when he observes them in his fellow bishops. Thus Onesimus, the bishop of Ephesus,

possesses "inexpressible love" (*Eph.* 1.3). Damas of
Magnesia is "worthy of God" (*Magn.* 2.1). The bishop
of Tralles is "the embodiment of love" (*Trall.* 3.2). His
meekness is such that even the pagans respect him. It is
the virtuous bishop of Philadelphia above all who gives
Ignatius the most spiritual satisfaction:

> [N]ot from himself "nor through men" (Gal 1:1) does he
> possess this ministry, which is a service to the Church,
> nor out of vainglory, but in the love of God the Father
> and the Lord Jesus Christ. I am amazed at his gentle-
> ness. He is more eloquent when silent than those who
> are full of empty words. For he is attuned to the com-
> mandments like a lyre to the strings. Therefore my
> soul blesses his mind directed toward God, knowing
> that his steadfast character and freedom from anger
> is virtuous and perfect in all gentleness of the living
> God. (*Phld.* 1.1-2)

Ignatius also describes the bishop's duties in his letter
to Polycarp, together with the virtues that contribute
to their fulfillment. As he is writing to a very young
fellow-bishop, Ignatius expresses himself freely and
without inhibition:

> It does justice to your official position with all diligence
> of both body and spirit…seek even more understanding
> than you possess…be vigilant as an athlete of God…
> become even more diligent than you are. Observe the
> times. Let nothing be done against your will, and do
> nothing yourself without God…stand firm. (*Pol.* 1-4)

These exhortations reveal the spiritual understanding
and sincerity of an experienced bishop eager through his
example and advice to share his own spiritual virtues.
The possession of such understanding does not come of
its own accord but is a divine gift. It must therefore be
sought through ceaseless prayer (*Pol.* 1.3). So he urges

Polycarp to pray that the incomprehensible things of God might be revealed to him and that he might lack nothing if he desires to possess every gift in abundance (*Pol.* 2.2). As the guardian of unity, endowed with many virtues, the bishop controls all things in the Church concerning worship, administration, teaching the correct faith, and the pastoral care of believers. The bishop's apostolate is not confined to celebrating the Eucharist and leading the congregation in worship, but includes teaching the truth.[34] But Ignatius does not insist on this point as much as one would expect.[35] He says nothing about the bishop's obligation to teach believers the right faith and protect them from the dangers of heresy. No doubt he took this obligation for granted. Finally, when he advises Polycarp not to be disturbed by people "who seem worthy of credence but teach a different doctrine," he has no fears for the steadfastness of his young fellow-bishop. It simply suffices for Ignatius to remind him of this duty among many others.

St. Ignatius is keen to emphasize that the Christian life is always lived in relation to the Triadic God. He therefore exhorts believers to imitate the divine character, that is, to acquire a "divine unity" (*homoêtheian theou* [*Pol.* 3.1]). The model for all Christians in the Church, in which the faithful are united (*enkekramenoi*) with the bishop "as the Church is with Jesus Christ" (*Eph.* 5.1), is therefore God himself. Ignatius's exhortation to imitate the divine character thus applies particularly to aspiring clergy, who will be appointed as ecclesiastical leaders, guardians of the apostolic tradition, pastors, and guides of the Christian community. In Ignatius's letters the role of the bishop in the Church's organization stands out.[36]

The Christians of Asia Minor are taught that they should gather around the bishops, because where the bishop is, there is the multitude, just as where Christ is, there is the catholic Church (*Smyrn.* 8.2). It is also worth noting that the presbyters and deacons occupy a prominent and honored position in the Christian community. The presbyterate is bound to the bishop like the strings to a lyre (*Phld.* 1.2). But Ignatius is more explicit on the place of deacons in the Church.

Polycarp of Smyrna

In his letter to the Philippians, St. Polycarp,[37] bishop of Smyrna and contemporary of Ignatius, discusses at some length the qualities required in presbyters and deacons. He is chiefly concerned with their moral authority and the smooth execution of their pastoral duties. His letter is based on the Pauline pastoral epistles. Indeed there are many similarities.

In his discussion of a deacon's attributes and the basic criteria for undertaking this divine ministry, Polycarp says the following:

> Deacons similarly should be blameless before God's righteousness, as ministers of God and Christ, not of men. They should not be slanderers, or double-tongued, or greedy for money, but self-controlled in all things, compassionate, attentive, walking in the truth of the Lord, who became a deacon to all. (*Phil.* 5.2)

With regard to presbyters, Polycarp stresses that candidates for this rank should be

> ...compassionate, merciful to all, bringing back those who have gone astray, visiting all the sick, not neglecting widows, or orphans, or the needy; but "always having regard for the good in the sight of God and

men" (Prov 3:4; 2 Cor 8:21), abstaining from all anger, partiality, unjust judgment, being far from all avarice, not quick to believe accusations against anyone, not hasty in judgment, knowing that we are all debtors in the matter of sin; if therefore we pray to the Lord that he should forgive us, we too should forgive. (*Phil.* 6.1-2)

As in the Pauline pastoral epistles, Polycarp simply emphasizes human virtues. He demands that presbyters and deacons should be kind and generous and show justice and philanthropy. He does not expect those wishing to serve the Lord to pretend to virtues they do not have, but simply asserts that the shepherds of Christ's spiritual sheep must possess the basic virtues described by Paul. He knows of course that not all of Philippi's presbyters are saints. One of them in particular, called Valens, was guilty of avarice and is therefore severely reprimanded (*Phil.* 11.1-4).[38] But the letters of Ignatius and Polycarp suggest that in general the presbyterate as a whole was served by men full of faith and the Holy Spirit. The information given by Ignatius and Polycarp on the order of priesthood and candidates for it in the early second-century Church may seem sketchy, but it is of prime importance. Even if they do not yet speak about how bishops and presbyters were chosen and installed, at least we see them giving particular emphasis to the importance of their work and apostolate as pastors of the Church. In their letters, bishops and presbyters are presented as those who are continuing the work of the apostles, transmitting what they have handed on, teaching believers and guiding them in the Christian life, and presiding over the Church's liturgical practices. This is a precious testimony.

The Didache

The remaining works belonging to "the apostolic fathers" contain only the sparsest information on the qualities desirable in the Church's office-holders. Among these a special place is occupied by the *Didache*, also known as "The Teaching of the Lord through the Apostles to the Gentiles." Its value lies both in its early date (the first half of the second century)[39] and in its use as a source in later works of comparable content. But although it contains much material on relations of Christians with each other and with their ecclesiastical leaders, there is relatively little on the latter's special characteristics.

The *Didache* is more concerned with itinerant preachers, prophets, and teachers, mentioning bishops and deacons in only one passage: "Therefore ordain for yourselves worthy bishops and deacons of the Lord, men who are gentle and unavaricious and truthful and tested, for they too perform the service for you of prophets and teachers. Do not disdain them, for they are the honorable men among you together with prophets and teachers" (*Did*. 15.1-2).[40] The precise significance of the term "ordain" (*cheirotonêsate*) remains unclear. The way in which bishops and deacons were chosen and installed is not described in the *Didache*. But we may safely infer that the procedure was the same for both. The faithful did not have the right to participate in the choice of prophets and teachers, for these received their apostolate directly from the Holy Spirit. They were not called to spend any length of time in the same Church. As travelers, they did not have a permanent place in the daily life of the community. By contrast, the faithful were indeed those who chose the bishops and deacons. Candidates for these offices had to demonstrate a considerable number of qualities, among which emphasis was laid on impartiality. Four qualities were demanded equally of both bishops and deacons. Of these four, two require that candidates should be "truthful" and "tested," qualities also encountered in prophets (*Did.* 11.11; 13.1) and teachers (*Did.* 13.2), which apply generally to all ranks of officials. Thus emphasis falls on the remaining virtues: gentleness and lack of avarice. These reveal the special nature of the ministry of bishops and deacons.[41]

Hermas

The *Shepherd of Hermas* belongs to the apocryphal writings of the second century. Hermas was a spiritual person with an exalted idea of his work. In one passage he speaks clearly of apostles, bishops, teachers, and deacons who had followed holy paths toward God, having fulfilled their ministries in purity and with dignity in the interests of the elect of God. He then adds that some of them have died, while others are still alive, tirelessly working for harmony, peace, and mutual tolerance (Herm. *Vis.* 3.5.1).

Hermas's severe judgments on "the chief officials and presidents of the Church" give us the impression that the ecclesiastical leaders of his time were ambitious men, no different from ordinary sinners, without discipline or zeal to instruct God's elect. Hermas declares:

> Now therefore I say to you chief officials and presidents of the Church: Do not be like poisoners. Poisoners keep their poison in little boxes, but your poison and venom is in your heart. You are hardened and do not wish to

cleanse your hearts and unite your thinking in a pure heart, that you might have mercy from the great King. Therefore take care, children, that these dissensions of yours do not rob you of your life. How do you think you can discipline the elect of the Lord, when you your-selves lack discipline? Therefore discipline each other and be at peace among yourselves, that I too might stand joyfully before the Father and give account to your Lord on your behalf. (Herm. *Vis.* 3.9.7-10)

Without exaggerating we must admit that Hermas, as a strict moralist, is more interested in exposing and censuring the faults of the Church's shepherds than discovering their virtues and gifts. The *Shepherd* refers to worthy and unworthy officials, to able and useless workers in Christ's vineyard, the Church. It discusses deacons who neglect their duties and seize the property of widows and orphans, thus enriching themselves and turning God's ministry into a business concern (Herm. *Sim*. 9.26.2). It also mentions bishops who have shown a sincere warmth of heart and exhibited all the Christian virtues, having taken God's servants under their protec-tion, bishops who have carried out their ministry wor-thily, as servants of God and of the Church's believers in all things (Herm. *Sim*. 9.27.2). We may therefore take it that the work of the deacons was the organization and execution of good works, and also care of the widows and orphans. The bishops also occupied themselves with philanthropic works. But we cannot conclude that this was their chief work. Without doubt they had a special apostolate and the prerogative of presiding over the Liturgy and responsibility for teaching. The teachers and prophets also seem to have occupied an important position.[42]

The *Shepherd of Hermas* is the last work of the era of the apostolic fathers who, as we have seen, in spite of the sparseness of their information, teach us a good deal about the Christian priesthood. This period of the primitive Church is very important for our study, because during it the spheres of responsibility and duties of bishops, presbyters, and deacons were fixed in a fairly definitive way, as were the criteria and virtues regarded as indispensable for the exercise of their office. I have described the information gleaned from the works of the apostolic fathers as very sparse, since one would have expected rather more from writers considered disciples of the apostles. But as they lived close to the apostolic period, they did not feel the need to describe institutions whose operation was still fresh to them in the example of the apostles and their most prominent disciples.

Other Sources

In this section I shall draw on three distinguished ecclesiastical writers: Clement of Alexandria, Origen, and Eusebius of Caesarea, especially the second and third-century fragments preserved by them.

Clement of Alexandria

Clement, the first of the great theologians of the Alexandrian school, has an eminent place in the history of ecclesiastical literature. Four important works survive.[43] Of these the *Stromateis* is of particular interest to us. When Clement describes the characteristics of the true gnostic, that is, the perfect Christian, in the sixth book of the *Stromateis*, he gives the apostles as an example and discusses their calling (*Strom.* 6.13). They became apostles not because of any exceptional gift belonging to them by nature—Judas too was chosen along with them—"but they were fit to become apostles since they had chosen with a view to the end foreseen" (*Strom.* 6.13). Thus a genuine presbyter of the Church and a true minister of the will of God is a person who acts and teaches in accordance with what has been handed down to us by Christ (*Strom.* 6.13). Like their ordination, their calling is not a human work, but a work of God, who enrolls them "in the presbyterium" on account of their righteousness, and for whom he reserves the highest place in heaven (*Strom.* 6.13). These are "the more elect of the elect" because of their perfect gnosis, "the picked flowers of the Church itself," and "those honored by the most magnificent glory," "judges and administrators" in the Lord's vineyard (*Strom.* 6.13). Hence the Church's hierarchy of bishops, presbyters, and deacons is dedicated to the imitation of the angelic order. "They are imitations of angelic glory and of that dispensation" (*Strom.* 7.1). This is an entirely new element which will later be developed much more extensively in the Areopagitic writings. Clement gives a beautiful description of the functions of presbyters and deacons in the seventh book of the *Stromateis*, where he says that "the presbyters preserve the image of improvement, the deacons of service" in the Church (*Strom.* 7.1). God's minister and servant of his divine mysteries is a true gnostic, "who displays an improving contemplation," is "respectful" towards those who do not respect God, and "serves God blamelessly with regard to human matters." That is to say, he is full of virtues and wise earnestness, far from the passions and the multitude of heresies (*Strom.* 7.1). In the third book of the *Stromateis*, Clement mentions incidentally in the course of his discussion of marriage that those appointed bishops should be men who had shown themselves able heads "of their own household" (1 Tim 3:4) so that they should be able to extend their apostolate successfully in the Church (*Strom.* 3.12).

Origen

Origen's theology is truly the climax of Christian thought in the first centuries. Origen was one of the most prolific authors of antiquity and his contribution to theological thought remains undiminished in spite of the unsatisfactory aspects of his early attempt to present Christian teaching in a systematic form.[44] Of the many testimonies relevant to our theme which could be drawn from his works, I shall confine myself to those which seem to me the most important.

In his apologetic work *Against Celsus*, Origen attempts a systematic refutation of the arguments against Christianity put forward by the second-century philosopher Celsus in his work *The True Doctrine*. In his response, "because no educated or wise or sensible man is converted by words" (*Cels.* 3.48), he says the following: "Not many wise men after the flesh, not many mighty, not many noble are called; but God chose the foolish things of the world, that he might put to shame those who are wise; and God chose the base things, and the things that are despised, and the things that are not, that he might bring to nought the things that are" (1 Cor

1:26-28), and he stresses that this was said not because there was nobody wise after the flesh in Christianity, but because "not many are wise after the flesh" (*Cels.* 3.48; cf. 1 Cor 1:26). Basing his argument on the characteristics of a bishop laid down by Paul in his pastoral epistles, he declares that the bishop must be a "teacher" able to refute his adversaries "by his wisdom" (*Cels.* 3.48). He then goes on to refer in passing to the single marriage, the blameless character of life, the sobriety, prudence, and orderliness that must be considered basic qualities in a man aspiring to episcopal office (*Cels.* 3.48). And he repeats that a candidate bishop should above all be a teacher capable through his wisdom of refuting his adversaries (*Cels.* 3.48). Nor does he fail to remind his readers with regard to such adversaries as Celsus that "the word promises to heal even such people if they come, and makes all men worthy of God" (*Cels.* 3.48). Later in the same work in defense of the Church—"God's country" to those who believe devoutly in God—he speaks of the organization of that country "created by the Logos of God," and briefly recounts the characteristic qualities of its rulers "in accordance with the commands of God" (*Cels.* 8.75). The rulers of the Church are those who are "mighty in word," who have the gift of teaching and disciplining others in true knowledge and wisdom and at the same time refuting adversaries. Accordingly, those "who are sound in doctrine and life" are called upon "to rule over the churches" (*Cels.* 8.75). These are men whose life is blameless and pure in imitation of the Lord and his disciples. They are exhorted to be examples themselves for those under them to follow.

Men who love power are not acceptable for episcopal office. It is not those who aspire simply to the glory and honor of ruling, but "those who on account of their great humility are reluctant hastily to take upon themselves the common responsibility of the Church of God" (*Cels.* 8.75) who are acceptable. These are the true rulers of the Church, "who are called patrons," "instructing as many as possible to live according to God's will in all things" (*Cels.* 8.75).

In his commentary on Matthew, "in a digression" as he himself says, he refers to Paul's "one who aspires to the office of a bishop" (1 Tim 3:1) and emphasizes that one should not seek episcopal authority on the pretext of piety "for the sake of winning glory, or being flattered, or gaining an income from the revenues" (*Comm. Matt.* 11). Because if the aspiring bishop is lured by any of these, "he does not desire a good work (1 Tim 3:1)," nor can he be irreproachable, sober, and moderate, but is drunk with glory, "insatiably seeking satisfaction from it" (*Comm. Matt.* 11). The same is true, says Origen, for presbyters and deacons (*Comm. Matt.* 11). What he stresses and draws particular attention to is wicked thoughts, which are the source of all the sins (*Comm. Matt.* 11). Elsewhere in the same commentary he gives an exegesis of the text: "You are Peter, and on this rock I will build my church, and the gates of Hades shall not prevail against it. I will give you the keys of the kingdom of heaven, and whatever you bind on earth shall be bound in heaven, and whatever you loose on earth shall be loosed in heaven" (Matt 16:18-19). "Those who exercise episcopal office act like Peter" (*Comm. Matt.*

11), he says, and comments that this text only applies to bishops if they make their work that for which Christ addressed Peter with the words "You are Peter," and if their faith is so strong that "this would refer reasonably to those on whom the Church is built by Christ, and the gates of Hades are not obliged to prevail against him who wishes to bind and to loose" (*Comm. Matt.* 11). In his homily on Leviticus, Origen comments on the text: "and the congregation was assembled...and Moses said to the congregation, 'This is the thing which the Lord has commanded to be done'" (Lev 8:4-5). In the life of the Church, too, says Origen, there are often occasions when the presence of the people is needed. It is needed for the election of clerics, so that all may know and be sure that the candidate is better than the others, a good teacher, holy and endowed with all the virtues (*Hom. Lev.* 6.3).

Eusebius of Caesarea

Eusebius of Caesarea's ten-volume *Ecclesiastical History*, although belonging to the fourth century, preserves many fragments of lost works from an earlier period. From these we can easily draw material relevant to our theme. In a letter from a council held in Antioch addressed to Dionysius of Rome and Maximus of Alexandria and their churches, in which the writers warn the recipients of the heretical teaching of Paul of Samosata, we find considerable information on what were considered the necessary qualities of a bishop at that time (*Hist. eccl.* 7.30). The letter's reference to being "adorned with all the good things fitting to a bishop" (*Hist. eccl.* 7.30) reveals, in my opinion, that Paul's list of characteristic virtues had become established in the Church, and consequently those who "aspired to episcopal office" (1 Tim 3:1) had to possess a certain number of qualities. A bishop must not regard piety as a means of income and source of wealth, committing lawless acts, sacrilege, injustices, and every kind of deceit with a view to gain (*Hist. eccl.* 7.30). To "cherish proud thoughts" and arrogantly suppose that "one has assumed secular office and think one should be called a ducenarius rather than a bishop" (*Hist. eccl.* 7.30) does not befit a bishop, who the Apostle emphasizes must not be proud but "above reproach," "temperate," and "dignified" (*Hist. eccl.* 7.30). Boastful talk is a characteristic of sophists and sorcerers, not bishops (*Hist. eccl.* 7.30), who should be humble and the servants of all, after the pattern of Christ the shepherd. Because a man is appointed bishop of the Church "by divine providence" (*Hist. eccl.* 7.30), his manner of life must be "outstandingly eminent" (*Hist. eccl.* 7.30). And as a genuine "disciple of Christ" (*Hist. eccl.* 7.30) he should prove, with his clergy, to be an example through all his good works for his flock to imitate (*Hist. eccl.* 7.30). The bishop should not give occasion through his unseemly behavior for "the faith to be despised and hated" (*Hist. eccl.* 7.30). Even more, not the slightest suspicion should be allowed to arise in the hearts of the faithful on his account which could be a stumbling block to them. In every way he should always be a living example for them to imitate (*Hist. eccl.* 7.30). He should be a teacher of orthodoxy, not of impiety, like Paul of Samosata (*Hist. eccl.* 7.30). The bishop should not cover up sins committed by the clerics under him, but when he discovers them should discipline the wrongdoers for their correction and salvation (*Hist. eccl.* 7.30).

Elsewhere in his *Ecclesiastical History*, in discussing "the Church's presidents who with their blood have demonstrated the genuineness of the piety which they represented," Eusebius emphasizes indirectly the basic virtues expected of clerics (*Hist. eccl.* 8.13). He speaks of bishops and presbyters, who as spiritual leaders and true shepherds "of Christ's spiritual flock" proved themselves "outstanding and beloved of God in all things" and became examples to imitate (*Hist. eccl.* 8.13). These men, "having proclaimed Christ's heavenly kingdom first in word by their defense in court and then in deeds," glorified "the word of God through their endurance unto death" (*Hist. eccl.* 8.13). Their "piety in Christ" was the rich source of their other virtues and brave deeds, through which they proved to be "illustrious, perfect witnesses of Christ" (*Hist. eccl.* 8.13).

Eusebius also tells us that Origen had many students, some of whom became famous, such as Theodore, known as Gregory of Neocaesarea, a "celebrated bishop," and his brother Athenodorus (*Hist. eccl.* 6.30). Eusebius bears witness that these received a secular education: "They were extremely keen to acquire both Greek and Roman learning" (*Hist. eccl.* 6.30). They stayed with Origen for five years, "gaining such improvement in divine matters that while they were still young they were both appointed to episcopal sees in the churches of Pontus" (*Hist. eccl.* 6.30).

Eusebius also mentions some circumstances in his

Ecclesiastical History in which God himself chooses his officials in a very strange manner (*Hist. eccl.* 6.11; 6.29). Those chosen in this way are presented as people adorned with all the virtues in a superlative degree. Finally, Eusebius's references to the Christian life and the Church's administration and struggles against its opponents are full of examples of worthy shepherds endowed with virtues—real models for anyone aspiring to ecclesiastical office to imitate.

Notes

1. The events in the earthly life of the Lord which were to prepare the apostles for their pastoral work are: "the temptation in the wilderness (Matt 4:1-11; Mark 1:12-13; Luke 4:1-13), which vividly represented the shepherd's struggle against temptations; the Sermon on the Mount (Matt 5:13-16); the Mission of the Twelve (Matt 10:1-42; Mark 6:7-11; Luke 10:1-21); the parable of the Good Shepherd (Matt 18:12-14; Luke 15:1-8; John 10:1-16); the parable of the laborers in the vineyard (Matt 19:27-30; 20:1-16), in which the Lord reproves those who labor for the kingdom of heaven only for the sake of a reward; the homily about the Pharisees (Matt 23), in which the Lord censures the false shepherds; the high priestly prayer (John 17), with which the Lord filled out the picture of the ideal spiritual shepherd and sealed it with his sacrifice on the cross" (Papadopoulos 1912, 4).
2. See Schmitt 1962, 74.
3. See Stephanidis 1959, 45.
4. See the discussion of their theories in Konidaris 1959b, 263ff.; Ferguson 1968. Cf. also Hatch 1881, 17-50, 79-111.
5. See Stephanidis 1959, 45-46.
6. See Vapheidis 1884, 460-467.
7. See Vapheidis 1884, 46.

8. See Stephanidis 1959, 45. For detailed studies of the organization of the primitive Church, see Konidaris 1959a and 1959b. Cf. Gy 1962; Jay 1981; Young 1994.

9. See Eutaxias 1872, 21-22. Because of the similarity between the bishop's office and that of the "Guardian" of the Essene community at Qumran, some scholars have speculated that the "Guardian" might have been a forerunner of the bishop. See Hastoupis 1958, 145, n. 12. On the Dead Sea Scrolls generally, see Flint and VanderKam 1998-1999.

10. As mentioned above (pp. 24-25), in the primitive Church the words "presbyter" and "bishop" denoted duties rather than ranks. As ranks, they are not found everywhere simultaneously in the earliest period. It took some time for them to develop. See Stephanidis 1959, 42; Spicq 1947, 84-97; Faivre 1977; Jay 1981; Ysebaert 1994.

11. Cf. Richert 1901, 52-54.

12. Cf. Spicq 1947, 234.

13. See Weiss 1902, 139.

14. See Spicq 1947, 237.

15. See Spicq 1947, 98; Stephanidis 1959, 44.

16. See Weiss 1902, 147.

17. See Weidinger 1928; Campenhausen 1953, 116; Schroeder 1959; Vögtle 1936.

18. See Spicq 1946.

19. See Zimmermann 1933, 123.

20. See Bardy 1937c.

21. Cf. Altaner 1958, 78.

22. See Campenhausen 1953, 93ff.

23. See Altaner 1958, 80.

24. See Fischer 1981, 79, n. 248. Just as the Law of the Old Testament was a training for Christ, so its priesthood was a type and image of the new priesthood of the New Testament. See Tixeront 1925, 9. Prophecies which proclaim the abolition of the Jewish priesthood thanks to the priesthood of grace are found in Isa 66:21; Mal 1:11; 3:3. Cf. Michel 1932, 1203. Some ecclesiastical writers had the impression that the Christian priesthood was a continuation of the Jewish one. For examples, see p. 20, n. 54 above. Cf. Böhmer 1916, 16;

Feine 1955, 45; Grant 1964-, 1:163; Campenhausen 1953, 166; Fouyas 1971-1972, 174-179.

25. Clement gives a free rendering of the Septuagint version of Isa 60:17: "And I will appoint your princes (*archontas*) in peace and your overseers (*episkopous*) in righteousness." The word *diakonos* ("deacon") is not found in the Septuagint version. See Konidaris 1959a, 31.

26. That is, the bishops and deacons mentioned in 42.4. Clement prefers to use the verb *kathistanein* ("to appoint") because he is emphasizing the appointment of ministers by divine law, in contrast to the verb *cheirotonein* ("to ordain"), which is used for the participation of the people in the appointment. Since the Corinthians wrongly believed that they had the right to dismiss ministers on their own initiative, Clement emphasizes the "appointing" (*kathistanein*) to counter their mistaken idea. See Konidaris 1959a, 31.

27. On the use of this word for "rule" (*epinomê*), see Javierre 1964, 195-196.

28. The antiquity of *1 Clement* makes it especially important for the topic of apostolic succession, particularly since this is the first time it is mentioned in patristic literature. Among those who accept that *1 Clement*'s use of *diadechontai* conveys the sense of apostolic succession are Dix (1947, 256ff.) and Javierre (1964, 192ff.; see 193, n. 26 for the relevant bibliography). See also Javierre 1957a. Because of the indeterminacy of Clement's expression, Javierre concludes that here it refers at least to a succession in the work of the apostles (1964, 194). Others, such as Colson, consider it more likely that the term refers only to episcopal succession (1964, 161). Cf. esp. Fouyas 1971-1972, 166-171.

29. That is, ministers appointed by the apostles. See n. 32 below.

30. On the testimony to this "consent of the Church," see Trembelas 1955, 8. Note how Cyprian sees the "consent of the Church" (*Ep.* 67.4.1-2): "Moreover, we can see that divine authority is also the source for the practice whereby bishops are chosen in the presence of the laity and before the eyes of all, and they are judged as being suitable and worthy after

public scrutiny and testimony...so that in the presence of the laity the iniquities of the wicked can be revealed and the merits of the good proclaimed" (trans. Clarke, 23); cf. Granfield 1976. Origen likewise: "Although the Lord had given them commands about appointing the high priest and had made his choice, the congregation was still called together. For in ordaining a priest, the presence of the people is also required that all may know and be certain that from all the people one is chosen for the priesthood who is more excellent, who is more wise, who is more holy, who is more eminent in every virtue, lest afterwards, when he stands before the people, any hesitation or any doubt should remain. This is also what the Apostle taught when he spoke about the ordination of a priest. 'It is necessary to have a good witness from those who are outside'" (*Hom. Lev.* 6.3; trans. Barkley 1990, 120-21). On the contribution of the laity to the appointment of ministers in St. Cyprian's age, see p. 204 below.

31. Cf. esp. Campenhausen 1953, 171-172.

32. There is no doubt that the ministers were appointed by the apostles while they were still living. In the period between the apostolic age and that of Clement, presbyter-bishops were appointed to continue the work of the apostles. See Colson 1964, 161. Thus the "distinguished men" are the genuine successors of the apostles. They were figures in the Church empowered to appoint the ministers, a work which in the past had been performed by the apostles above. See Javierre 1964, 194ff; 1957b, 429. Campenhausen (1953, 171, n. 6) compares the "distinguished men" to the presbyters, as do Müller (1929) and Lietzmann (1932-1944, 1:204).

33. Cf. Konidaris 1959a, 31-32.

34. The teaching that the bishop receives a personal "charism of truth" safeguarding him from heretical influence goes back to Irenaeus (*Haer.* 4.26) as an anti-gnostic measure. Cf. Stephanidis 1959, 73; Alivizatos 1910. Zizioulas (1965, 110ff.) offers yet another explanation for the emphasis on the teaching concerning the "charism of truth": "The death of the living and immediate bearers of this memory (of apostolic teaching) automatically highlighted the need to emphasize

the authenticity of the bishops as teachers" (112). Cf. Fouyas (1971-1972, 179-184, 190-193), who stresses the apostolic succession as a presupposition and guarantee of true teaching.

35. Cf. Bonis 1958, 40; Campenhausen 1953, 10; Chadwick 1950.

36. On the form of Church government in Ignatius, see Campenhausen 1953, 105; Bauer 1923. Cf. Maier 1991.

37. See Campenhausen 1953, 129-130.

38. We are not well informed about the case of Valens, whose wife was equally guilty. The Philippians are called upon to restore the frail and erring member of the body of their own church to his earlier love for God.

39. See Altaner 1958, 44.

40. On this passage, see Campenhausen 1953, 79, n. 6; Jefford 1989.

41. See Harnack 1884, 57.

42. The *Shepherd of Hermas* reproves false prophets at some length, and counsels care and vigilance in distinguishing true prophets from false ones (Herm. *Mand.* 11.7-9): "You must discern the person with the divine spirit by his way of life. First, the one who has the spirit that comes from above is meek, gentle, and humble; he abstains from all evil and the vain desire of this age; he makes himself more lowly than all others; and he never gives an answer to anyone when asked, nor does he speak in private. The Holy Spirit does not speak when the person wants to speak, but when God wants him to speak. When, then, the person who has the divine spirit comes into a gathering of upright men who have the faith of the divine spirit, and a petition comes to God from the upright men who are gathered together, then the angel of the prophetic spirit lying upon that person fills him; and once he is filled, that one speaks in the holy spirit to the congregation, just as the Lord desires" (trans. Ehrman 2003, 2:287-89).

43. See Quasten 1950-1986, 2:6-16.

44. See Quasten 1950-1986, 2:43-75.

Anonymous Canonical Works

In this chapter I shall examine the anonymous canonical works of the early centuries which codify the apostolic tradition and the customs that developed in the Church's life. Some of these works from the first three centuries were mentioned in the previous chapter. Here they will be discussed in more detail, together with other similar works which form a distinct corpus. Their titles usually indicate their indirect apostolic derivation.[1]

Works Dependent on the Didache

The Didascalia Apostolorum[2]

The *Didache* interests us as a work on which others of the same type were based. The oldest of these is the *Didascalia Apostolorum* ("Teaching of the Apostles"), or *Apostolic Constitutions*, as Epiphanius called it, going back to the first half of the third century.[3] While the *Didache* gives valuable information on the organization of the primitive Church, and outlines the qualities required in ecclesiastical leaders, taking their moral integrity for granted, the *Didascalia* is the first pre-Constantinian work which deals at length with the presuppositions for entry into the clergy. It refers first to the person, virtues, and duties of the bishop, as judge and conciliator, and then to those of the presbyter and deacon.[4] Apart from the qualities required for entry into the clergy, the *Didascalia* also examines in some detail the impediments which preclude service at the altar.[5]

The first obligation of the bishop is to preserve those "entrusted" to him from spiritual death. This he is to achieve by his teaching, which he is exhorted to carry out diligently. He is reminded that the responsibility rests with him if the uninstructed sinner dies without repentance. On the other hand, he will be cleared of the charge for the loss of the unrepentant sinner if he has taught him to avoid sin. Since the sinfulness of the ignorant is laid at his door, he is exhorted to teach and reprimand them. Moreover, he is enjoined not to be embarrassed about repeating the same things frequently, in the hope that the sinner will perhaps become conscious of his guilt and repent (*Didasc. ap.* 2.6.12-16). Through his teaching the bishop should, on the one hand, combat sin and spiritual death, and on the other hand, guide his hearers toward good works. He should also extol God's promised reward in the life to come and warn of future judgment (*Didasc. ap.* 2.17.6). The *Didascalia's* author repeats this point, emphasizing that the bishop must reprimand and punish those needing reprimand and punishment, so as to bring them back to the Christian life and save them from perdition. He is called to guide the sinner toward repentance and strengthen the sinner's moral life. He must also exercise care over the person who remains firm in the faith, and lead the people as a whole in peace. Finally he must strengthen the weak by his teaching and heal the sick in faith (*Didasc. ap.* 2.20.2-3). When the bishop teaches the truth, he ensures the divine life in the hearts of the faithful, sustaining them in peace. Through his exalted position as teacher he is also the guardian of the Church's unity in true faith and love.[6]

Using a typological exegesis of a text from 1 Kingdoms (i.e., 1 Samuel), the *Didascalia* makes the prerogatives of a bishop coincide with those of the ancient kings of Israel.[7] The same things apply to the bishop, says the author. But the passage must be interpreted according to its spiritual meaning. The bishop, he says, taking from the people those he considers worthy, appoints them as his presbyters, advisers, and assistants. He does the same with deacons and subdeacons for the service of the house of God.[8] This is the first time that the bishop is presented recruiting and appointing candidates for the priesthood, since he possesses its plenitude. The remaining clergy work with the bishop, performing their tasks under his supervision. Thus the bishop is revealed as the center of unity of the Christian priesthood.[9]

The *Didascalia* also examines the virtues which the bishop should possess as head of the ecclesiastical hierarchy. These are examined in relation to his position once he has become bishop. The bishop should be a model for the people to follow, like Christ. He should be "blameless" (Titus 1:7), "above reproach" (1 Tim 3:2), "untouched by any injustice," and "not less than fifty years old," so that he should be far from "the disorderly behavior of the young," "temptations from outside," and "the blasphemies of certain false brethren." If possible, he should be an educated man. If not, he should at least be "experienced in the word." If in a small community a man "advanced in years," "reputable and wise" cannot be found for the episcopal office, but only a young man "reputed to be worthy by those who have to do with him" and proved to be mature by his seemly behavior confirmed by everyone, such a man may be appointed with tranquility (*Didasc. ap.* 2.1.1-3; *Const. ap.* 2.1.1-3).[10]

The author of the *Didascalia*, referring to the examples of Solomon (3 Kgdms 2:12 [1 Kgs 2:12]), Josiah (4 Kgdms 22:1 [2 Kgs 22:1]), and Jehoash (4 Kgdms 12:1 [2 Kgs 12:1]), all of whom became kings of Israel in their youth, does not regard age as a basic criterion on a par with the others. It is sufficient that the aspirant to episcopal office be "gentle, unassuming, and quiet," free from "any evil and wickedness and injustice" (*Didasc. ap.* 2.1.4-8; *Const. ap.* 2.1.4-8). He should be "temperate, sensible, dignified, stable, undisturbed, no drunkard, not violent but gentle, no lover of money, not a recent convert, that he should become puffed up with conceit and fall into the condemnation of the devil." He should be "the husband of one wife," and "a good manager of his own household" (*Didasc. ap.* 2.2.1-2; *Const. ap.* 2.2.1-2).[11] He should be tested to see if he is "blameless with regard to the necessities of daily life," for it is written: "Examine him who is to be appointed to the priesthood for blemishes" (Lev 21:17). He should be "free from anger," "compassionate," "philanthropic," "loving," "generous, kind to widows, hospitable, helpful, ready to serve, active, having no cause for shame" (*Didasc. ap.* 2.3.2-2.4.1; *Const. ap.* 2.3.2-2.4.1). He should "not be a respecter of persons, or have regard for wealth, or be susceptible to flattery, or neglect the poor, or play the tyrant." He should be "economical and frugal in food and drink," "not given to consumption, or luxury or easy living or feeding on delicacies." He should also be "forbearing, long-suffering in his admonitions, learned, a diligent student of the Lord's books, a keen reader, that he may interpret the Scriptures with care." He should study the word, so that "by his great learning he should richly nourish the people" (*Didasc. ap.* 2.5.1-3.5; *Const. ap.* 2.5.1.3-4.7). A bishop must not be "greedy for gain, especially toward the pagans, for it harms him rather than them…nor should he be a slanderer, or bear false witness, or be prone to anger or contentious… nor double-minded, nor double-tongued, nor giving a ready ear to censure or slander, not a hypocrite, not a person who enjoys participating in the pagan festivals, who uses empty deceits, who is full of desire, a lover of money." He should be "wise, humble, able to admonish according to the Lord's discipline, noble-minded, a man who has renounced all wicked pursuits in his life… who is well able to command, quick to recognize the vicious and protect himself from them, but a friend to all, righteous in judgment, and whatever is or exists that is noble among men, the bishop has made that quality his own" (*Didasc. ap.* 2.6.1.3-4; *Const. ap.* 2.6.1.3-4). And so, far from all evil, the bishop can incite his spiritual children to imitate his good works in accordance with the prophet's injunction (Hos 4:9): "And the priest shall be as the people" (*Didasc. ap.* 2.6.5).[12]

Thus the *Didascalia* describes the ideal bishop. It demands an exemplary life from him, that he may be a model for all the faithful to follow. And the author of the *Didascalia* reminds him again that he should be "pure in his works, knowing his place," because he has been set as a "type" of Almighty God (*Didasc. ap.* 2.11.1; *Const. ap.* 2.11.1).[13] He is truly "a watchman for the house of Israel"[14] that he may protect the flock from the machinations of the evil one, bearing responsibility for its salvation. The zeal of the faithful is dependent on his conduct and example. For if the bishop is bribed by some lawless person and allows him to remain in the Church, he pollutes the flock, leads many others to perdition, and becomes responsible before God and men. It is natural that if the faithful see impiety prevailing amongst them, though they might hesitate for a little, they will follow their impious shepherd, be seized by the same evil, and be destroyed with him. By contrast, when the sinner sees the bishop and deacons delivered of all lawlessness, and the flock without spiritual and moral faults, he will not be so bold as to attend their gatherings. If by any chance he finds himself at one, he will leave quickly with great shame, weeping in his heart, because he has not been able to find any stain in the priesthood and the faithful. In this way the flock will remain pure (*Didasc. ap.* 2.9-10).

Although the bishop must be pure, above any suspicion, and far from any compromise, he must nevertheless not be harsh but gentle and full of compassion and understanding toward sinners. He must not be domineering, severe, rough, "abrupt…unmerciful; he should not mock the people under him, or keep hidden from them…the words of repentance, or be ready to excommunicate them and expel them" (*Didasc. ap.* 2.21.1; *Const. ap.* 2.21.1). The bishop's severity toward sinners means an increase of evil and scattering of the flock. Through such behavior the bishop becomes the cause of his flock's being devoured by wild beasts, that is, wicked men, pagans and heretics, who lie in wait to pounce upon anyone expelled from the Church. A person who is unjustly excommunicated will seek refuge either with the pagans or the heretics and will be entirely alienated from the Church and his hope in God. The bishop is guilty of his loss if he expelled him and did not receive him back when he was repentant (*Didasc. ap.* 2.21.2-3). He will be subject to God's judgment because anyone who mercilessly drives someone out of the Church in effect kills him. God will cast into eternal fire anyone who has driven a sinner out of the Church without regard for the richness of God's mercy and his long-suffering toward those who repent, or for the example given by Christ (*Didasc. ap.* 2.21.8). Just as Christ ate with publicans and sinners, so the bishop should stay in contact with those excommunicated by him, "calling on them, exhorting them, and supporting them," willing to receive them back if any of them sincerely repent (*Didasc. ap.* 2.40.1-2; 2.41.1; *Const. ap.* 2.40.2; 2.41.1). To emphasize to the bishop how compassionate he ought to be, the *Didascalia* describes the Lord's compassionate behavior toward the woman taken in adultery. When the elders asked him if he would condemn her and he gave a negative reply, he said to her: "Go then, neither do I condemn you" (John 8:11). Consequently, the bishops are called to take an example from this act of the Lord, conforming themselves to him, and becoming "'gentle and quiet' (1 Pet 3:4), compassionate, merciful, peaceful, free from anger, 'apt teachers' (1 Tim 3:2), able to reprove, welcoming, consolatory, 'not arrogant or quick-tempered' (Titus 1:7), not abusive, not boastful, not overbearing" (*Didasc. ap.* 2.24.3-4; *Const. ap.* 2.24.6-7).

Elsewhere it is said again about bishops that they must not be hard or tyrannical, quick-tempered, harsh toward the people of God who are entrusted to their care. They must not destroy God's house and scatter his people, but bring back everyone as helpers of God. They should also gather the faithful together with great humility, patience, and gentleness, without anger, for teaching and prayer, as ministers of the eternal kingdom (*Didasc. ap.* 2.57.1). The bishop, judging the faithful of his flock without regard for persons, after the example of the unbribable Judge, the Lord himself, must unswervingly observe his commandments and his will (*Didasc. ap.* 2.22.1). The bishop should not be an implacable judge, because he would then bring the sinner to despair.[15] On the contrary, he must seek him out, exhort him, and bring him back, remembering that God in his mercy promised on oath to forgive sinners their sins through their repentance and return (*Didasc. ap.* 2.20.6). Through his teaching the bishop must bring back those who have strayed and restore them to the Church, not allowing them to remain outside the flock, dismissed on account of their sins. In the same way, he must seek out the lost, not letting those in despair be abandoned to perdition because of the multitude of their sins (*Didasc. ap.* 2.20.5-6).

The author of the *Didascalia* continues his extended description of the good shepherd with images drawn from the Gospels of Matthew and Luke (Matt 18:12-13; Luke 15:4-6). Referring to the authority to forgive sins, he concludes with the following compassionate exhortation. The bishop, as a loving shepherd who lays down his life for his flock, is obliged to go in search of the lost sheep, according to the example of the supreme Shepherd, who leaves the ninety-nine sheep on the mountain and goes in search of the one that has strayed. When he finds it, he takes it up on his shoulders and brings it back to the flock, rejoicing at finding it. The bishop should do the same, "seeking out the lost, guiding those who have strayed, and bringing back those who have separated themselves" (Ezek 34:16), for he has the authority to forgive the sins of those who have fallen since he has put on the person of Christ (*Didasc. ap.* 2.20.8-9).

Christ, then, "as an experienced and compassionate physician" heals "all who have been wounded by sin." Similarly, the bishop, "who is therefore the Church's physician...should prescribe a suitable therapy for each sick person, in various ways treating, healing, and restoring them to health in the Church" (*Didasc. ap.* 2.20.10-11; *Const. ap.* 2.20.10-11). But for such peace to prevail in the Church, the bishop must rule it gently and benignly, and be approachable to all, especially the humble. If a poor person comes, especially one advanced in age, and there is no room for him, the bishop must readily prepare a place for him, even if he himself has to sit on the ground, "that there should not be partiality toward persons, but a pleasing service toward God" (*Didasc. ap.* 2.58.6; *Const. ap.* 2.58.6).

The supreme holiness and perfection which is demanded of the bishop springs from his essential function. The bishops are "to their people levitical priests,
who minister in the sacred tabernacle, the holy catholic
church, and stand near...the Lord our God....Among
their people they are prophets, rulers, leaders, and kings,
mediators between God and his faithful believers, the
recipients of the word and messengers of it, those who
know the written and spoken utterances of God and are
witnesses of his will, who bear the sins of all and speak
in defense of all." The bishops, then, are warned that
they put themselves in peril if they do not announce
the will of God to the people under them. On the other
hand, "a true reward and untold fame" from God awaits
those who have ministered well in the Church (*Didasc.
ap*. 2.25.7; *Const. ap*. 2.25.7). The bishop is the faithful
servant, who does his best for all, and as an "imitator
of Christ" bears the sins of all for whom he has pastoral
responsibility, as a result of which he will be honored by
God. "Since 'he himself bore our sins' (1 Pet 2:24)...so
they [the bishops] must assume the sins of the people"
(*Didasc. ap*. 2.25.9; *Const. ap*. 2.25.9). Consequently, the
author of the *Didascalia* draws from the Old Testament's
vivid image of the suffering servant (Isaiah 53), who
prefigures the redeeming Messiah, and applies this to
the bishop. Like the suffering servant, the bishop is "a
man in suffering and acquainted with bearing sickness...
he was wounded for our sins and was bruised for our
transgressions...and by his stripes we were healed" (Isa
53:3-5). The sinless Lord, who is the bishop's model, bore
the sins of all. So the bishop must bear the sins of all the

faithful under him (*Didasc. ap.* 2.25.10 and 12).

In conclusion the author of the *Didascalia* reminds the bishop that his episcopal office is not "an easy or light burden" (*Didasc. ap.* 2.25.12; *Const. ap.* 2.15.12). It constitutes the highest possible imitation of Jesus Christ, since the bishop has put on his person (*Didasc. ap.* 2.20.9). Clothed in the person of Christ, he transmits, like another Christ, the most perfect possible expression of love. As a source of holiness, thanks to the authority granted to him, the bishop must be a source of the sanctification of the faithful, as he must also be through the radiance of his personal holiness.

The Ecclesiastical Canons of the Holy Apostles

The *Ecclesiastical Canons of the Holy Apostles*,[16] also known as the *Apostolic Church Order*, which draws on the *Didache's* teaching on "the two ways," was most probably compiled at the end of the third or beginning of the fourth century in Syria or, according to some, in Egypt. This work, consisting of thirty chapters, begins by giving precepts on conforming to the Christian ethos, and then deals with the Church's organization, the qualities required in the clergy, and the role of widows.[17] The work has been handed down chiefly in the monophysite Churches of Egypt and Syria and was translated early into Coptic, Arabic, Ethiopic, Syriac, and Latin.

The apostles are presented successively in discussion with each other. They refer to a series of canons bearing their names, and give instructions for the organization of the Church and the qualities required in the clergy. The first canon, which is the one that interests us here, is attributed to Peter. It deals with how bishops are elected, referring to those qualities that ensure the candidate's suitability.

> Peter said: If the community is small, and the number eligible to vote for a bishop is less than twelve men, let them write to the neighboring churches, where they happen to be well established, that three chosen men might come to them and test whether there is a worthy candidate, if someone has a good reputation among the pagans, if he is sinless, if he is a lover of the poor, if he is temperate, not a drunkard, not a fornicator, not rapacious, or abusive, or a respecter of persons, and the like. It is good if he is without a wife, but if not, the husband of one wife (1 Tim 3:2), a man who has had some education and is able to interpret the Scriptures; if he is uneducated, let him be gentle and overflowing in love for all, never censured by anybody, let him become a bishop from the common people. (*Can. eccl.* 16)

As this source reports, the right to elect a bishop belongs to the community. If it lacks the quorum of twelve valid electors, it can make it up from neighboring communities.

Adolf von Harnack[18] compares the tradition of the presence of "three chosen men" with the custom prevailing in Rome in around the mid-third century.[19] According to this tradition, the participation of three bishops was considered necessary for the valid ordination of a bishop. "No doubt," says Harnack, "this established custom is linked with the order in our source, having developed from it."[20] On the basis of this custom canons were drawn up at the councils of Arles (314) and Nicaea (325), laying down that a bishop was to be ordained by at least three other bishops.[21] The participation of three bishops should not be taken as a collective procedure for the transmission of the required grace, for his grace is communicated through their hands by Christ himself. Nevertheless, the participation of three bishops in the ordination was regarded as indispensable, without this precluding the participation of additional bishops.[22]

The qualities required in bishops do not shed much light on their suitability for office. Four of these are worth noting: (i) the bishop should have a good reputation among the pagans; (ii) no age requirement is set; (iii) marriage is not forbidden, even if celibacy is regarded as preferable; (iv) an education is not an absolute requirement, but is nevertheless desirable so that the bishop can interpret the Scriptures.[23] The first requirement is important only when the bishop, in his pastoral role, has contact with pagans (cf. 1 Tim 3:7). From this, and from the absence of any indication of similar activity among presbyters and deacons, we may conclude that only the bishop had the right to represent the community to those outside it. The significance of the second and third requirements lies in their difference from what is specified for presbyters. While the bishop is not required to be unmarried, or of a certain age, both these are emphasized for the presbyter. As in 1 Timothy 3, the qualities sought in bishops are closer to those of deacons than of presbyters. Finally, with regard to the fourth requirement, it is clear that a lack of education is not a bar to episcopal office. However desirable our author considers education, so that the bishop can strengthen the faith of his flock by drawing teachings from the Scriptures, he does not consider it an indispensable criterion.

To return to the general qualities demanded in a
bishop, "if he is free from sin, if he is a lover of the
poor, if he is temperate, not a drunkard, not a fornica-
tor, not arrogant or abusive or a respecter of persons
and the like (*Can. eccl.* 16), we may note that only one
of these, "lover of the poor," is positive; the rest are included in the requirement that he should be "free from
sin." This specific requirement, that the bishop should
be a "lover of the poor," indicates an important duty,
namely, the bishop's care for the poor and destitute.[24]
Thus the expression "lover of the poor" (*philoptôchos*) is
rather like a technical term referring specifically to the
bishop's pastoral role. The bishop, as a pastor caring for
the spiritual well-being of his flock, is the visible head
of the community. He represents it in its relations with
the outside world and is at the same time the president
of its liturgical assemblies. All the members of the community, together with the presbyters and deacons, are
subject to the bishop's spiritual authority.[25]

The next apostle to speak is John:

Once the bishop has been appointed, since he knows
the attentiveness and devotion to God of those with
him, let him appoint them presbyters, provided he has
tested them....They should have spent some time in the
world, avoid meeting women in some way, be generous
to the community, not show partiality, be confidants
and supporters of the bishop, assemble the multitude
and encourage the shepherd. (*Can. eccl.* 17)

Although the community participates generally in
the appointment of the bishop, the appointment of
presbyters is considered a purely episcopal prerogative.

The qualities required in presbyters mark them out as a body of respected persons who stand by the bishop as his "confidants and supporters." No precise age requirement is laid down for presbyters. The author contents himself with the general remark that they "should have spent some time in the world." The following phrase is worth noting: "avoid meeting women in some way," when compared to what is required of bishops and deacons. This phrase implies that presbyters, unlike bishops and deacons, must abstain from marital relations. By "not show partiality" one important duty of the presbyters is revealed concerning their relations with the community. They form a body which watches vigilantly over the life of the community at the side of the bishop, assisting him in calling its assemblies.[26]

The next to speak about deacons is Matthew:

Let deacons be appointed. For it is written: "Every word of the Lord will depend on three people" (cf. Deut 19:15). Let them be tested in every ministry, with a good reputation among the multitude, the husbands of one wife, men who have brought up children, temperate, gentle, peaceful, not grumblers, not double-tongued, not prone to anger, for anger destroys a sensible man. They should not show partiality to the rich, or be oppressive of the poor. Nor should they be fond of drinking a lot of wine. They should be active, proficient at encouraging good works done in secret, compelling those of the brethren who have means to stretch out their hands, generous themselves, willing to share, respected by the multitude with all honor, reverence and fear, diligently paying attention to those living idly (cf. 2 Thess 3:11), exhorting some, entreating others, and reprimanding yet others, and finally excommunicating the contemptuous, knowing that the contentious and scornful and abusive have ranged themselves against Christ. (*Can. eccl.* 20)

The deacons are presented as helpers, servants, and supporters of the community in its daily life. In the execution of their duties they are allowed a certain independent authority. This source first calls for the appointment of at least three deacons, so that in accordance with Scripture they can bear valid witness whenever differences arise between members of the community. It is then specified that they must not only be tested in a general way, as with the other ranks of the clergy, but also be tested "in every ministry." They are responsible for many matters of practical importance to the community, which they should be familiar with.[27] In contrast to the bishops, the deacons are not expected to be held in repute "by those outside," but only "by the multitude," with whom in any case they come into contact. After these general presuppositions there follows a series of specific requirements which clearly delineate the deacons' duties. This series begins with only being married once, which echoes Paul's advice to Timothy (1 Tim 3:12). As we have already seen, the presbyters are obliged to abstain from marital relations, and although the bishop is allowed to have contracted a single marriage, it is preferred that he should be celibate. Only in the case of deacons is it emphasized without reservation that they may enter into marriage once. When a deacon embraces the married life, he must bring up his children in an ideal way, giving all the members of the community an example to follow (1 Tim 3:12). Moreover, the remaining characteristics—temperance, gentleness, peacefulness, not grumbling, not being double-tongued or prone to anger—reflect the close relationship that the deacons should have with the members of the community, "exhorting some, entreating others, and reprimanding yet others." It is especially necessary for deacons always to conduct themselves in a seemly manner with regard to the distinction between rich and poor members of the community. In no way should partiality be shown to the rich or the poor be disparaged. One of the deacon's principal duties is to urge the rich to give generously from their surplus to the community's poor and to incite them to good works, which should be done in secret. The embodiment of all these qualities requires an able and gifted man. As only a generous man can exhort others to generosity, the deacons themselves should be compassionate and generous.[28]

The Apostolic Constitutions

Another work, the first six books of which are based on the *Didascalia Apostolorum*, the seventh on the *Didache*, and the eighth on Hippolytus's *Apostolic Tradition*, is the so-called *Constitutions of the Holy Apostles*, also known as the *Apostolic Constitutions*. This was compiled in the late fourth or early fifth century. Although branded by the second canon of the Quinisext Ecumenical Council as of heretical provenance, and therefore not forming part of the Church's canon law,[29] it has nevertheless been included in this survey because it presents an abundance of material relevant to our theme.

The first six books deal with the duties of laypeople and clerics, and in spite of minor changes, follows the same order as the *Didascalia*, on which it is based. Of the remaining books, the eighth is of particular interest to us because it deals with gifts (chapters 1-2), ordinations (chapters 3-28), and various matters pertaining to worship and ecclesiastical order (chapters 29-46). It concludes (ch. 47) by appending the 85 Apostolic Canons. Because of the close relationship of the first six books of the *Apostolic Constitutions* to the *Didascalia*, to list the qualities required in the clergy would only repeat what has already been said in relation to the *Didascalia*. The eighth book of the *Apostolic Constitutions* and the 85 Apostolic Canons will be discussed below.

Works Dependent on the Apostolic Tradition *of Hippolytus*

The Apostolic Tradition *of Hippolytus*

The *Apostolic Tradition* of Hippolytus[30] has been described as "a fundamental canonical book which cites firm canons and forms for the ordination of officials, the celebration of the holy Eucharist and the administration of baptism."[31] With the exception of the *Didache*, discussed above, it is the oldest and most important of the ancient canonical books. The title of the work, *Apostolic Tradition*, has been found inscribed on the statue of Hippolytus discovered in Rome in 1551. The work was written in Rome after 217. From the critical study and comparison of the *Apostolic Tradition* with other canonical books of similar content, a mutual dependence has been demonstrated,[32] namely, between Book VIII of the *Apostolic Constitutions*, an *Epitome* of this work,[33] the *Testament of Our Lord Jesus Christ*, and the *Canons of Hippolytus*. As we shall see below, these works derive from a common source. I shall therefore set out the contents of the *Apostolic Tradition* in detail insofar as they relate to our theme. Where the original Greek text is no longer extant, I shall refer to the versions.[34]

Before listing the qualities desirable in aspirants to ecclesiastical office, the *Apostolic Tradition* emphasizes the necessity of a divine calling. No one could undertake an ecclesiastical function, or request ordination from the bishop, unless he had been called by God. When this divine calling had been tested, it was recognized and confirmed by official ecclesiastical election, and then the candidate was ordained by the bishop. The divine calling is manifested in most of the ordination prayers by the phrase: "this your servant, whom you have chosen."[35] This expression could have been taken as an indirect call by God, realized through the election of the candidate by the Church, if there had not been other expressions clearly indicating that it implies without any doubt a direct call of God preceding election by the Church. The particular gifts of the clergy are listed after the gift which is common to all believers, namely, the gift of Christian faith. The particular gifts are given only to those called by God. These gifts are correlated to the grades of hierarchy:

> These things then we say, that those who have received these gifts and graces of this kind should not exalt themselves over those who have not received them: we are speaking of the gifts of God which are (accompanied) by signs, since there is no man who believed God through his holy Son, who did not receive a spiritual grace (*charis*) or gift (*charisma*) from him: for the freedom from the ungodliness (*asebeia*) of the service of many gods, and the entrance into the faith of the Father

and the Son and the Holy Spirit, is a gift of God....So (*de*) he who believed this, believed not thus as a matter of course (*haplōs*), nor irrationally either, but rather by a calling and a persuasion, having received the gift from God the Father.[36]

Once he has been called by God, the aspiring cleric must also be chosen by the Church. In this choice the Church is guided by the divine election, confirming the divine calling in persons judged to be worthy of it who are endowed with the canonical gifts required for each grade. So once base and unworthy human motives have been excluded, if the Church chooses those whom it regards as worthy of office, this choice coincides with the divine choice, because it has chosen those already chosen by God and prepared by his grace for priestly office.[37] Hence, too, the importance of the canonical qualities, the presence of which guarantees that his choice by the Church truly reflects the will of God. The Church's choice is exercised by the bishop and people together, as almost all the canonical works witness.[38] Thus the *Apostolic Tradition* lays down that the deacon, chosen according to the criteria just mentioned, is ordained only by the bishop (*Trad. ap.* 72).[39] Then at the election of the bishop, in which all the people participate, the text goes on to say:

Let the bishop be ordained when he has been chosen by all the people, when he has been named and is acceptable to all. Let him come together on a Sunday with the people and the presbyterate, the bishops being present. With the agreement of all, let the bishops lay their hands on him, the presbyterate standing by without saying anything. Let all be silent and pray in their hearts for the descent of the Holy Spirit. Let one of the assembled bishops, at the request of all, lay his hand on him who is to be ordained bishop (*Trad. ap.* 68).

There is therefore no doubt that the people participated in the choice of a bishop,[40] especially since the witness of the *Apostolic Tradition* is also included in other canonical works, as we shall see below. The choice of deacons was made in the same way, as we are informed by the sources being considered here, since the people participated in their election,[41] although we are unable to say precisely how far they participated.[42] The particular contribution of the people lay in their confirmation or denial of the existence of the required canonical attributes in the candidate.[43] If the people consented, this was examined together with the candidate's way of life as a whole before he was ordained a cleric by the neighboring bishops who were present. But if the candidate was found to hold unorthodox beliefs, the participating bishops would refuse to ordain him, even if the people supported him.[44]

The worthiness of the candidate was judged by the intellectual and moral qualities which were indispensable for the performance of his duties. As in the works we have examined so far, the *Apostolic Tradition* tends to take the intellectual qualities for granted, while stressing the moral qualities. The importance of the intellectual and moral qualities may be observed in a passage from the Ethiopic version of the *Apostolic Tradition* which speaks of the qualities of a bishop. Although all the canonical works stress the need that the bishop know the Scriptures and be able to interpret them, only the Ethiopic version of the *Apostolic Tradition* seems willing to overlook this demand so long as the bishop knows the Church's true teaching, which he conveys by his example:

> And he should be one who shares in good doctrine, and who can expound the Scriptures; and if he should be one who cannot expound the Scriptures, he should be humble and abound in love to all men. That the bishop may be condemned in nothing whatever, nor be reproved in anything.[45]

Although it is regarded as obvious that the bishop should teach the flock as much by word as by example, his teaching by example is nevertheless particularly emphasized, since it is regarded as more important. Moral integrity was thus absolutely necessary in the bishop. For the same reason moral integrity was also regarded as indispensable in the deacon. By his example the deacon was meant to teach the virtues which Christ too had taught in his earthly life. The list of qualities expected in the deacon is extensive.[46] The similarity between these and the deacon's qualities listed in 1 Timothy 3:8-12 is striking:

> Deacons shall be ordained, as it is written: by the testimony of two and three every word shall be established. And they shall be tried concerning all the service, having the testimony of all the people, that they live with one wife, and have reared their children in purity, and such as are merciful and humble, and such as are not murmurers, and such as are not double-tongued, nor wrathful, because wrath depraves a wise man.[47]

After mentioning the qualities required in deacons, the text emphasizes the virtue of justice as of equal importance for their apostolate:

> And they shall not respect the person of the rich, nor act unjustly to the poor; nor drink much wine; and they shall work hard for the hidden Mystery and the

beauty of the consolation. And they shall bid those of the brethren who have something to give to him who has nothing, and thus they shall also be sharers in giving. And they shall honor all with all honor and modesty and fear, and they shall keep themselves in all purity. And some of them they shall teach, and some of them they shall question, and some of them they shall reprove and some they shall console. As for the rejected, they shall also expel them at once, and they shall know that those who oppose, the revilers, the rejected, are those who are your adversaries.[48]

The exhortation that the deacons should possess the virtue of justice and avoid partiality was important, especially because deacons were the link between the bishop and the people.

The *Apostolic Tradition* continues its description of the conduct required in clerics when it discusses the *refrigerium*,[49] or memorial supper for the departed:

And if ye are invited on a day, eat orderly and in the fear of God. It may be that ye shall pray for those who have been removed from this world. O presbyters and deacons of Christ, it is proper that ye should be watchful at all times, ye yourselves and others (also), that ye may be able to do according to the saying of the Scripture: the strong, the angry, shall not drink wine, lest they should drink and forget wisdom, and not be able to judge in uprightness (Prov 31:4-5). Because after God the almighty and his only Son, the presbyters and deacons are the authorities of the church. We say this, (but) we do not forbid them to drink (wine), because we cannot despise what God created for the joy of men, but that they should not drink to be drunken. The Scriptures say not that he shall not drink wine, but what is said is that he shall not drink wine to be drunken (Sir 27:37; Hag 1:6), and also that thorns spring up in the hand of the drunkard (Prov 26:9). This is not said only to the clergy, but to all the lay Christian people, those who follow the name of our Master Jesus Christ. These are they concerning whom they say: The woe, but also trouble and contentions and sorrows who hath; and whose eyes are darkened; or wars and wounds shall be to whom? Is it not they who are assiduous in drinking wine, who ask where is the place of drink?[50]

Book VIII of the Apostolic Constitutions[51]

As already mentioned,[52] the eighth book of the *Apostolic Constitutions* is the most important from the point of view of its content. Furthermore, this part of the work is clearly dependent on the *Apostolic Tradition* of Hippolytus. Consequently only this book will be examined here.

Regarding the divine calling of an aspiring cleric, Book VIII of the *Apostolic Constitutions* contrasts the gift of faith with the particular *charismata* and shows clearly that God does not grant these particular *charismata* to all who have received the gift of faith. A person who has been called to faith is not thereby made a recipient of the particular *charismata*. These are given by God, the giver of graces, as he wills: "seeing that the bishop and the presbyters are priests and the laity are laypeople, to be a Christian belongs to us, but to be an apostle, or bishop, or some other thing does not belong to us; it belongs only to God the giver of graces. Let this be said so far for those deemed worthy of *charismata* or office" (*Const. ap.* 8.1.21-22).[53] The divine call to faith does not necessarily imply the gift of the particular *charismata*. Another call was needed by God for the reception of these. Therefore for someone to become a bishop or presbyter or deacon, he has to be called by God and given a particular *charisma* beyond the gift of faith.

Book VIII of the *Apostolic Constitutions* is silent on the election of deacons.[54] It speaks only of the election of bishops, exhorting, like the *Apostolic Tradition*, that they should be elected by the people:

> [T]he bishop to be ordained…irreproachable in all things, elected by all the people. When he has been named and approved, the people assemble together on the Lord's day with the presbyterate and the bishops who are present. The most senior of them should ask the presbyterate and the people if this is the man whom they want as their ruler…and when silence has descended, one of the leading bishops together with two others, standing near the altar, with the rest of the bishops and presbyters praying in silence, and the deacons holding the divine Gospels open over the head of the one being ordained. (*Const. ap.* 8.4.2-3 and 6)[55]

A similar list of qualities required in deacons is lacking in the *Apostolic Constitutions*, even though a considerable number are included in the 85 *Apostolic Canons*,[56] given in Chapter 47 of the *Constitutions*. The same section goes on to outline a bishop's moral qualities:

> And when they (the presbyterate and the people) have indicated their consent, let it be asked further if everyone agrees that he is worthy of this great and illustrious office, if his conduct with regard to God has been pious, if his dealings with men have been just, if his management of his household has been seemly, if the way he has led his life has been irreproachable. (*Const. ap.* 8.4.4)

There follows a discussion of his marital state. A man who has married twice is disqualified: "A man who has

contracted marriage twice after baptism, or has acquired
a concubine, cannot be a bishop, or presbyter, or deacon,
or occupy any priestly office whatsoever" (*Const. ap.*
8.47.17).[57] Clearly the *Apostolic Constitutions* do not prevent the once-married man from entering the clergy, for
in another passage it is forbidden to divorce a wife on the
ground of excessive religious zeal: "A bishop, or presbyter, or deacon may not dismiss his wife on the grounds
of piety. If he dismisses her let him be excommunicated;
and if he persists, let him be deposed" (*Const. ap.* 8.47.5).
Married men who enter the clergy are therefore obliged
to live with their wives, since the bond of marriage has
been instituted by God, and is therefore "very good."
Clerics who have abstained from marriage and regard
it as an evil are also threatened with deposition: "If any
bishop, or presbyter, or deacon, or anyone in the list of
clergy abstains from marriage, or meat, or wine, not out
of asceticism but because he regards them as abhorrent,
willfully forgetting that they are all 'very good' and that
God created humanity male and female (Gen 1:27-31),
he blasphemously misrepresents creation. Let him either
amend his views or be deposed and expelled from the
Church. Likewise with a layman" (*Const. ap.* 8.47.51).
Since marriage, as we shall see below, is prohibited only
after ordination, this constitution applies to those who
have entered the clergy in the married state. The question of the marriage of clerics after ordination occupied
the author of Book VIII of the *Apostolic Constitutions*, who
clearly states which clerics may enter into marriage after
ordination: "Of those who have entered the clergy unmarried, we lay down that only lectors and cantors may

marry" (*Const. ap.* 8.47.26).[58] The *Apostolic Constitutions* also contain other indications of the esteem in which the purity and sanctity of marriage is held. Fornication after baptism and before ordination was in itself an impediment to ordination, while fornication after or-dination was a cause for deposition: "If any accusation of fornication or adultery or any other forbidden act is made against a believer, and is proved to be true, he may not be promoted to the clergy" (*Const. ap.* 8.47.61). "If a bishop, or a presbyter, or a deacon is convicted of fornication, or perjury, or theft, let him be deposed but not excommunicated. For Scripture says: 'You shall not punish the same thing twice' (Nah 1:4). Likewise with the rest of the clergy" (*Const. ap.* 8.47.25). Although both these ordinances refer to public acts which become oc-casions of scandal, they nevertheless reveal an esteem for the purity of marriage. But it is not enough for the marriage to be celebrated according to the Church's rites. It is laid down precisely whom aspirants to the clergy may not marry. The list of such persons includes widows, divorcees, prostitutes, slaves, and actresses. Marriage to any of these is an impediment to ordination: "A man who marries a widow, or a repudiated wife, or a prostitute, or a household slave, or a woman of the stage cannot be a bishop, or a presbyter, or a deacon, or occupy any of the ranks of the clergy whatsoever" (*Const. ap.* 8.47.18). Kinship could also constitute an impediment. Thus the *Apostolic Constitutions* lay down that marrying a sister-in-law in spite of the kinship by marriage, and marrying a niece in spite of the kinship by blood, disqualified a man from entering the clergy: "He who marries two sisters or a niece cannot be a cleric" (*Const. ap.* 8.47.19).[59]

On matters regarding self-control, the *Apostolic Constitutions* do not forbid the use of wine, although drunkenness is condemned (*Const. ap.* 8.47.51). Elsewhere, like the *Apostolic Tradition*, the same source regulates the conduct of clergy at *refrigeria*. The two passages are parallels:

> When you are invited to their memorials, behave at table in an orderly way and in the fear of God, to be able to intercede for the participants. For since you are presbyters and deacons of Christ, you must always be vigilant both with yourselves and with others, that you may be able to admonish the disorderly. For Scripture says: "Princes are prone to anger; let them then not drink wine, lest they drink and forget wisdom, and not be able to judge rightly" (Prov 31:4-5). Therefore, both presbyters and deacons, after almighty God and his beloved Son, are princes of the Church. We say this not to prevent them from drinking, for this would insult what has been made by God to give gladness, but so that they should not get drunk. For Scripture did not say do not drink wine, but what does it say? "Do not drink wine until you are drunk" (Hag 1:6). And again: "Thorns grow in the hand of a drunkard" (Prov 26:9). We say this not only with regard to the clergy but with regard to every Christian layperson, since they bear the name of our Lord Jesus Christ. For to them it is said: "Who has woe? Who has trouble? Who has vexations and disputes? Whose eyes are red? Who has bruises without cause? Is it not those who tarry long over wine, who haunt the places where banquets are held?" (Prov 23:29-30). (*Const. ap.* 8.44.1-4)[60]

On drinking wine both extremes are censured, both its abuse and its total renunciation. For those who held wine in contempt and regarded it as evil, there is the penalty of deposition and excommunication already mentioned.[61] There is another penalty of similar content in the same source: "If any bishop, or presbyter, or deacon does not partake of meat and wine on feast days, let him be deposed as 'one whose conscience is seared' (1 Tim 4:2) and who has become a cause of scandal to many" (*Const. ap.* 8.47.53). The same penalty is applied to the cleric who abuses wine: "A bishop, or presbyter, or deacon who frequents the gaming-tables or carousels must either cease to do so or be deposed" (*Const. ap.* 8.47.42).[62]

Apart from the impediments already mentioned, the *Apostolic Constitutions* also mention several others. Possession by evil spirits and slavery are two removable impediments to entry into the priesthood. It was not permitted for slaves to be ordained without the consent of their masters. If the master consented and the slave was worthy, he had first to be manumitted and released from his master's household. According to the *Apostolic Constitutions*, "If someone has a demon, he may not become a cleric; nor may he pray together with the faithful. But when he has been cleansed, let him be accepted, and if he is worthy, let him become a cleric" (*Const. ap.* 8.47.79).

> We do not permit household slaves to be appointed to the clergy without the consent of their masters, because of damage to the masters who own them, for such an act subverts the household. If at any time a slave appears to be worthy of ordination, as our own Onesimus appeared to be, and the masters give their consent and free him and allow him to depart from the household,

he may be ordained. (*Const. ap.* 8.47.82)[63]

Although there was no moral guilt attached to these impediments, it was nevertheless considered to be in the community's interest to prevent such persons from entering the priesthood. For the same reason deaf and blind people were not allowed to become bishops: "If a man is deaf or blind, he may not become a bishop, not because he is defiled but so that ecclesiastical administration may not be impeded" (*Const. ap.* 8.47.78).[64] As in this case the episcopal office is mentioned explicitly, it is possible that blind and deaf people were admitted, but only to the lower ranks of the clergy. But we do not have any positive information on this. It is more likely that poor eyesight or lameness did not prevent promotion to these ranks because, according to the *Apostolic Constitutions*, they were not an impediment to episcopal office: "If any disabled person is afflicted in the eye or the leg, and he is worthy to become a bishop, let him become one. For it is not the maiming of the body that defiles him, but only the pollution of the soul" (*Const. ap.* 8.47.77). Being a eunuch was also an impediment only when it was accompanied by moral culpability. In such cases the man who had castrated himself was excluded from ordination. But if he was a eunuch because of a malicious act done by others, or because it was a punishment inflicted on him in time of persecution, or because it was congenital, he could, if worthy, be admitted to any of the grades of the clergy.[65] "A man who has mutilated himself may not become a cleric, for he is a self-murderer of himself and an enemy of God's creation" (*Const. ap.* 8.47.22). "If anyone has been made a eunuch as a result of assault by others, or has been castrated in a persecution, or is such by nature, and is worthy, he may become a bishop" (*Const. ap.* 8.47.21).[66]

The Testament of Our Lord Jesus Christ

The ancient canonical collections deal for the most part with the same matters, yet each work contains something of particular interest to the student. Noting how much of the material found in the *Canons of Hippolytus* and the so-called *Egyptian Church Order* is embodied in the *Testament of Our Lord*, R. H. Connolly says "[T]he 'Testament' is something more than a mere redaction, or adaptation, of either of those other texts, or of their possible source. It is strongly marked by the individuality of its compiler, who used, indeed, matter which is found in the other two documents, but made it his own in such a way as to produce a distinct and rather more extensive treatise."[67] Although other ecclesiastical canonical works claim descent from the apostles, the *Testament of Our Lord Jesus Christ* is presented as the last will and testament which Christ gave to the apostles in the forty days after his resurrection. It was written probably in Syria in the second half of the fifth century, originally in Greek. It survives today only in Syriac, Coptic, Ethiopic, and Arabic versions.[68]

Like the related works, once the *Testament* has dealt with the divine call of the bishop, followed by his election by the people as a whole, it goes on to list the qualities with which the aspirant to episcopal office must be endowed.[69] Presbyters and deacons are ordained in the same way, that is, by the participation of the bishop and the people in their election.[70] It is notable that the qualities required for a bishop are missing from the other related works, with the exception of the *Apostolic Constitutions* (2.2 and 8.4). As in the latter work, the list of qualities in the *Testament* is based on Paul's pastoral epistles. The whole series of qualities is summed up in a phrase which emphasizes the bishop's moral integrity in all things, for by his example he is to become the teacher of the flock.[71] Similar requirements are made with regard to the presbyter, who must possess piety and mildness so as to be worthy of God's revelation of what is useful and necessary.[72] The deacon is presented as the Church's eye and an example of piety to the people.[73] He must also possess fear of God, purity and modesty, and always act with zeal.[74]

It is on the marriage of the clergy that the *Testament* is particularly informative. With regard to the bishop it declares that it is good that he should be without a wife, without this implying that he should never have been married. The least expected of him is that he should have married only once. In this way, as the husband of one wife, he can be sympathetic toward the weakness of widows.[75] Nothing is said about the marriage of presbyters.[76] But on the marriage of deacons, as with bishops, the author of the *Testament* clearly aligns himself with Paul, especially as regards the requirement that a man who enters the clergy should be the husband of one wife (1 Tim 3:2, 12; Titus 1:6). A deacon must also lead a virtuous and pure life. If he has not remained in a state of virginity, he should at least, like a bishop, have only entered into a single marriage. The faithful are also asked to testify that he is not involved in secular affairs, does not exercise a profession,[77] and has neither wealth nor offspring. But if he is married and has offspring, they should be pious and pure as befitting the Church's ministry.[78] Even if he does not emphasize absolutely that deacons must be unmarried, the *Testament*'s author nevertheless indicates his preference for the unmarried state.[79] In any case, it is accepted that the deacon must be "the husband of one wife." This expression gives the impression that the *Testament*'s author misunderstands Paul, thinking that he wanted widowers as bishops and deacons, although Church practice, at least in the East, rejected this interpretation, especially for deacons.[80]

The Canons of Hippolytus

According to R. H. Connolly, these canons are a clumsy adaptation of the *Apostolic Tradition*.[81] They were probably composed in Syria around the year 500. Their original language was Greek, like the other collections of ecclesiastical canons. But as not even a fragment of the original text survives, we have to rely on the Arabic and Ethiopic versions.

The *Canons of Hippolytus* also emphasize first the need for a divine call in those aspiring to become clerics. Accordingly, the clergy and the laity are directed to pray for the man just chosen to become bishop in the words: "O God, strengthen him whom you have prepared for us" (*Can. Hippol.* 2). Election to all three ranks of the priesthood is carried out in this way with the assistance of the laity.[82] The *Canons of Hippolytus* do not introduce anything new so far as the qualities required in bishops are concerned. They simply refer to the precepts laid down by Paul.[83] H. Achelis sees in this brief reference to episcopal attributes an allusion to spiritual *charismata*, which were closely associated with the office in the region in which the *Canons of Hippolytus* were composed.[84] Among the spiritual *charismata* mentioned are the expulsion of demons and the healing of illnesses. As the leader of the community, charged with such authority, the bishop is the model of moral conduct in his community, precisely because of the functions of his office. "He is, of course, the instrument of administration and representative of the community; but more importantly he is the exerciser of his *charisma* and representative of his community before God."[85]

Nor is a list of qualities given for the deacon. Only from the ordination prayer, which asks for the necessary qualities, that the deacon might fulfill the demands of his office in a fitting manner, may we infer the qualities required in a candidate: "that you may grant him the strength to overcome all power of the evil one by the sign of your cross, by which he himself is signed; and that you may grant him moral conduct without sin in the presence of all men, and teaching for many, by which he might lead those desiring it to salvation in the holy Church without any scandal" (*Can. Hippol.* 5). Elsewhere it is said about the deacon that he is responsible for catechesis in the Church.[86] No doubt for the deacon to be able to fulfill the requirements for this apostolate, he had to be a man of deep spirituality, so that he could draw from it the strength to subdue the power of Satan by the sign of the cross, as the ordination prayer says.[87]

According to the principle laid down in Canon 4, the presbyter stands on an equal footing with the bishop, except for occupation of the *cathedra* and the power to ordain.[88] Therefore, like the bishop, the presbyter is endowed with authority which allows him to exercise his office in a worthy manner. Assuredly, his high status in the community presupposed moral irreproachability.

Notes

1. See Christophilopoulos 1954, 20.
2. See Colson 1951.
3. See Altaner 1958, 48; Connolly 1924.
4. The term "deaconess" (*diakonissa*) is mentioned for the first time in the *Didascalia* (2.26.6). Deaconesses constituted a specific order in the Church. The beginnings of this are already discernible in the apostolic age in the work of Christian women on the basis of Christian love and an active participation in the Church's missionary work. Later we find an organized women's diaconate, which lasts almost to the end of the Byzantine period. Deaconesses were thus engaged in the work of Christian love from the earliest days. They were appointed by the Church to their office by a special "ordination" (*cheirotonia*) and "laying on of hands" (*cheirothesia*). See Theodorou 1954, 15-19; Davies 1963, 1-6; Ysebaert 1991.
5. Cf. Campenhausen 1953, 264-265.
6. Cf. Zizioulas 1965, 112ff.
7. "This will be the right of the king who will reign over you. He will take your sons and appoint them to his chariots and to be his cavalry, and to run before his chariots; and he will appoint them for himself to be commanders of hundreds and commanders of thousands, and to reap his harvest and to gather his grapes, and to make his implements of war and the equipment of his chariots; and he will take your daughters to be perfumers and cooks and bakers" (1 Kgdms 8:11-13 [1 Sam 8:11-13]).

8. "[S]o now does the bishop also take for himself from the people those whom he accounts and knows that they deserve him and his office, and establishes unto himself presbyters as counselors and assessors, and deacons and subdeacons, all as it is required for him in relation to the service of the house" (*Didasc. ap.* 2.34.3; trans. Vööbus, 106-107).

9. See Bartlett 1943, 75ff.; Chadwick et al. 1980.

10. Where not otherwise specified, the words and phrases in quotation marks are from the *Apostolic Constitutions*. See pp. 73-74 above.

11. The influence of Paul's pastoral epistles is clear. The author of the *Didascalia* has borrowed not only words but also entire phrases from them. Cf. 1 Tim 3:2-6.

12. Cf. Achelis and Flemming 1904, 270-272.

13. Cf. Perler 1962.

14. *Didasc. ap.* 2.16.13. Cf. Ezek 33:7.

15. On the bishop's role and activities in the forgiveness of sins in the *Didascalia*, see Rahner 1950; also Poschmann 1940, 112ff.; Schwartz 1911, 16-20; Galtier 1932, 191ff.; Bartlett 1943, 75ff.; Beaucamp 1949.

16. See Altaner 1958, 49; Quasten 1950-1986, 2:119-120.

17. In the *Ecclesiastical Canons of the Holy Apostles* it is said that "it is useful for a diaconate to be established for women." Such widows were elected and appointed "that they might support women in need." These canons mention the widow-deaconesses as a parallel institution to the order of "widows," who did not exercise any diaconal function. By contrast, the widow-deaconess had to spend her time "attending to women afflicted by infirmities," and be "willing to serve, be sober, be ready to report what was needed to the presbyters, not be given to sordid gain, and not be addicted to too much wine, that she might be able to remain alert during the night services." See Theodorou 1954, 32-33.

18. See Harnack 1886, 40.

19. See Eusebius, *Hist. eccl.* 6.43.

20. See Harnack 1886, 40.

21. Arles, Canon 20; Nicaea, Canon 4. Cf. Laodicea, Canon 12; Antioch, Canon 19; *Const. ap.* 8.4.

22. See Pheidas 1969, 45. The coming together of several bishops for an episcopal ordination is the model for the convening of local synods in the second century (44ff.).

23. The compiler of the work wants the bishop, of course, to be able to interpret Holy Scripture, but emphasizes that this obligation belongs mainly to the reader, who, according to Canon 19, must be "able to interpret, and be knowledgeable, because he occupies the place of the evangelist. For he who fills the ears of the ignorant will be considered learned by God."

24. On the duties of the bishop, see Stephanidis 1959, 46; Chadwick et al. 1980. For a historical and sociological analysis of the bishop's care for the poor, see Brown 2002.

25. See Zizioulas 1965, 153ff.

26. See Zizioulas 1965, 153ff.

27. On the duties of a deacon, see Stephanidis 1959, 43-44; Colson 1960; Hardy 1968; Echlin 1971; Barnett 1981.

28. On the institution of deacons generally in the early Church, see Leder 1905; Hennesy 1986; Falesiedi 1995.

29. Cf. Altaner 1958, 49-50; Christophilopoulos 1954, 25.

30. See Otterbein 1945.

31. Connolly 1929, xxvii.

32. For a synoptic review of the theories that have been expressed on the authenticity of the *Apostolic Tradition* by Hippolytus, together with the order of priority of the other works dependent on it, see Connolly 1916b, 8; Wordsworth 1901, 18ff.; Achelis 1891, 3-4, 27, 242-243, 271; Funk 1905, xiii.

33. The *Epitome* is also known as the *Constitutions of Hippolytus*.

34. Because of the loss of the original Greek of the *Apostolic Tradition,* we have to rely on later translations. These include the Latin and Sahidic versions in Hauler 1900 and de Lagarde 1883, respectively. There is a German translation from the Sahidic in Achelis 1891. The Ethiopic, Arabic, and Sahidic versions, together with English translations, are in Horner 1904.

35. *Trad. ap.* 72 (Hauler 1900, 110; Ethiopic version in Horner

1904, 145); *Const. ap.* 8.18.1ff. (Funk 1905, 522); *Test. Dom.* 1.38.
Cf. Turner 1915; Bartlett 1916; Nairne 1916; Connolly 1916a;
Simonin 1939.

36. English translation taken from G. Horner's rendering
of the Sahidic version (Horner 1904, 334-335). Cyprian of
Carthage agrees with the teaching of the *Apostolic Tradition*
and its dependent works on the divine origin of the aspiring
cleric's call. Writing in the first half of the third century, he
says that anyone who rises up against the bishops and priests
of the Church of Christ and opposes God's ordinances is
punished by the divine justice for his presumption (Cyprian,
De catholicae ecclesiae unitate 17: "[W]hoever opposes God's
institution is punished for his reckless insolence by divine
retribution" [trans. Bévenot, 87]).

37. See Achelis 1912, 2:9. Referring to the belief that God
himself chooses the ministers of his Church, Achelis mentions the following anecdote from Eusebius's *Ecclesiastical
History* (6.11): While on a visit to Jerusalem, a Cappadocian
bishop called Alexander was persuaded by the people there
to become their bishop. The occasion was a revelation during a night service, at which the more devout heard a voice
commanding them to go outside the gates and welcome the
man called by God to be their bishop. Alexander obeyed the
voice, and leaving his own community without a shepherd,
became bishop of Jerusalem while his predecessor, Narcissus,
was still alive.

38. Only one work, the *Didascalia*, which we have already
examined, speaks of bishops appointing deacons: "Therefore,
O bishop, appoint for yourself workers of righteousness,
helpers who cooperate with you unto life. Those that please
you out of all the people, you shall choose and appoint as
deacons...." (*Didasc. ap.* 3.12.1; trans. Vööbus, 156). Cf. *Didasc.
ap.* 2.34.3. For a historical examination of the laity's participation in the election of bishops, see Poulitsas 1946, 274-326. See
also Trembelas 1955; Karmiris 1973, 74ff.

39. The Sahidic version reads: "Further (*de*), when the
bishop will ordain (*kathista*) a deacon, who has been chosen
according as we said before, the bishop shall lay his hands

upon him" (trans. Horner 1904, 307).

40. Cf. Feine 1955, 39.

41. Cf. Tixeront 1925, 118; Michel 1936, 160.

42. See Achelis 1912, 2:416; Kirsch 1930, 238, 469; Bréhier 1937, 538.

43. The evidence for this is furnished by Cyprian in a letter to his flock. In this letter (*Ep.* 38), he explains why he did not consult the laity before ordaining the confessor Aurelius, although he was accustomed to consulting them in order to establish the candidate's good character. In Aurelius's case his integrity was obvious, Cyprian says, for it was clearly confirmed by his courageous confession of the faith on re-peated occasions during the persecutions (Cyprian, *Ep.* 38; cf. *Ep.* 67.5 and *Ep.* 59.5).

44. See Pheidas 1969, 45.

45. From Horner's translation of the Ethiopic version (Horner 1904, 133-134).

46. Curiously, the *Apostolic Tradition* lacks an analogous list for bishops.

47. Translation of the Ethiopic in Horner 1904, 135.

48. Ibid.

49. See Quasten 1940.

50. Taken from Horner's translation of the Arabic version (Horner 1904, 287-288). Cf. Prov 23:29-30.

51. *Epitome*, the title of another work related to Book VIII of the *Apostolic Constitutions*, is misleading. This work is not, as the title wrongly suggests, a summary of Book VIII of the *Apostolic Constitutions*, but is an extensive excerpt from it. This may be deduced from the verbal similarities in the two works. See Funk 1905, xi-xix, where the text of the *Epitome* is also given (72-96).

52. See pp. 73-74 above.

53. The following passages, too, clearly reveal the teaching of the *Apostolic Constitutions* on the existence of a divine call addressed to those whom God chooses to serve him: "For not every one that will is ordained, as the case was in that spurious and counterfeit priesthood of the calves under Je-roboam; but he only who is called of God" (*Const. ap.* 8.46.9;

trans. *ANF* 7:499); "For we have affirmed only that no one snatches the sacerdotal dignity to himself, but either receives it from God, as Melchisedek and Job, or from the high priest, as Aaron from Moses. Wherefore Philip and Ananias did not constitute themselves, but were appointed by Christ, the High Priest of that God to whom no being is to be compared" (*Const. ap.* 8.46.17; trans. *ANF* 7:500).

54. Particularly in Book VIII of the *Apostolic Constitutions*, there is a long discussion of the "ordination" and duties of deaconesses, and their appointed place in the hierarchy of the clergy. The ordinal of the *Apostolic Constitutions* gives a "constitution" and "epiclesis for the ordination of a deaconess." It was the understanding of the Church, then, that deaconesses were "ordained" like the other clergy "by a divine command," their "ordination" being set out in the ordinal after the ordination of deacons and before the ordination of subdeacons, giving it a prestigious status among the clergy and in the whole Church. See Theodorou 1954, 33, 51ff., 70-71.

55. Cf. Trembelas 1955, 16-17; Poulitsas 1946, 279.

56. These 85 Canons, bearing the name "Apostolic" pseudepigraphically, but nevertheless imbued with the apostolic spirit, had great influence on the Church in general and on the prerequisites for entry into the clergy in particular. They were convalidated by the Quinisext Ecumenical Council, the Council in Trullo, and thus constitute a valid source of Orthodox canon law. Cf. Milasch 1906, 110ff.; Bardy 1937b.

57. The same precepts are laid down by the following passages from other books of the *Apostolic Constitutions*: "We have already said that a bishop, a presbyter, and a deacon, when they are constituted, must be but once married, whether their wives be alive or whether they be dead; and that it is not lawful for them, if they are unmarried when they are ordained, to be married afterwards; or if they be then married, to marry a second time, but to be content with that wife which they had when they came to ordination" (*Const. ap.* 6.17.1; trans. *ANF* 7:457); "Such a one a bishop ought to be, who has been the 'husband of one wife,' who also has herself

had no other husband, 'ruling well his own house'" (*Const. ap.* 2.2.2; trans. *ANF* 7:396).

58. Canon 10 of the Council of Ancyra of 314 also allowed deacons to enter into marriage after their ordination, provided that they had declared their intention to marry beforehand. See Hefele 1907-1952, 1:230. The entire subject of the marriage of clerics is discussed at length below.

59. A man who married his wife's sister was excluded from the clergy on account of having contracted a second marriage. But this ruling excluded him even from the ranks of the minor clergy.

60. Cf. Prov 23:29-30.

61. See p. 82. above.

62. Another prohibition of excessive drinking is implied in the penalty laid down for a cleric who frequents taverns: "If any one of the clergy be taken eating in a tavern, let him be suspended, excepting when he is forced to bait at an inn upon the road" (*Can. ap.* 54; trans. *ANF* 7:503).

63. Two reasons are mentioned for the Church's attitude on slaves who wish to join the ranks of the clergy: (i) the desire to maintain the master's property rights; and (ii) the fear that the master will have undue influence over his slave. See Jonkers 1942.

64. Here we have a clear influence of the Old Testament on ecclesiastical tradition. Cf. Lev 21:17-21.

65. The Church moved very slowly towards a clear prohibition of eunuchism. It was in connection with the well-publicized case of Origen, against whom Bishop Demetrius of Alexandria took action on account of his self-castration, that eunuchism was first put forward as an impediment to entry into the clergy (Eusebius, *Hist. eccl.* 6.8).

66. Cf. Achelis 1912, 2:427-428.

67. Connolly 1916b, 6.

68. Altaner 1958, 51.

69. "[L]et the bishop be appointed, being chosen by all the people according to the will of the Holy Ghost, being without fault, chaste, quiet, mild, without anxiety, watchful, not a money-lover, blameless, not quarrelsome, ready

to forgive, a teacher, not given to much speaking, a lover of
good things, a lover of labor, a lover of widows, a lover of
orphans, a lover of the poor, experienced in the mysteries,
not lax and distracted in company with this world, peaceful,
and in all good things perfect, as one to whom the order and
place of God is entrusted" (*Test. Dom.* 1.20; trans. Cooper and
Maclean 1902, 64-65). Cf. Poulitsas 1946, 274-326; Trembelas
1955, 16-17.

70. "Let a presbyter be ordained, being testified to by all
the people, according to what has been said before" (*Test.
Dom.* 1.29; trans. Cooper and Maclean 1902, 90); "The deacon
is appointed, chosen like the things which have before been
spoken of" (*Test. Dom.* 1.33; trans. Cooper and Maclean 1902,
97). It is interesting that the *Testament* refers on the one hand
to ordained widows ("*viduas*" or "*viduas canonicas*") and on
the other to non-ordained deaconesses ("*diaconissas*"). The
former are classed with the clergy, the latter with the laity.
The work of widows is to be doorkeepers in the churches.
The organization of the women's ministries is peculiar to this
source. This peculiarity, however, is only external, not affect-
ing the essential nature of women's ministries. In the *Testament's* ordinal there is also an "*oratio*" for the "ordination"
of widows—deaconesses entitled "*Oratio constituendarum
viduarum.*" See Theodorou 1954, 34-35, 51-52.

71. The bishop should be "in all good things perfect, as one
to whom the order and place of God is entrusted" (*Test. Dom.*
1.20; trans. Cooper and Maclean 1902, 65). On the bishop as
teacher, see p. 78 above.

72. "[I]f in all things he be pious, quiet, so that being [thus]
he may in all respects be worthy to have those things that
are fitting and suitable revealed to him by God" (*Test. Dom.*
1.29; trans. Cooper and Maclean 1902, 90).

73. "Let him be in everything as the eye of the Church,
with fear admonishing, so that he may be an example to the
people of piety" (*Test. Dom.* 1.35; trans. Cooper and Maclean
1902, 99).

74. "Let the deacon be such as this, so that he may appear
with fear and modesty and reverence. With regard to fervor

of spirit, let him have a perfect manner of life" (*Test. Dom.* 1.36; trans. Cooper and Maclean 1902, 102).

75. "It is good indeed that he be without a wife, but at any rate that he have been the husband of one wife only, so that he may sympathise with the weakness of widows" (*Test. Dom.* 1.20; trans. Cooper and Maclean 1902, 65). Cf. Kirsch 1930, 347, 486, 747; Funk 1901, 63.

76. The *Testament* speaks only of the marriage of bishops and deacons perhaps because only bishops and deacons are mentioned in Paul's pastoral epistles. See Cooper and Maclean 1902, 186. Funk (1901, 63) sees in the words *purus et sine macula* ("pure and without blemish"), which refer to the presbyter (*Test. Dom.* 1.29), the same sense as the ordinance for bishops.

77. Although Paul says that those who proclaim the gospel have the right to be maintained by the gospel (1 Cor 9:14), he did not make use of this right "not to put an obstacle in the way of the gospel of Christ" (1 Cor 9:12). Since the deacon is not allowed to pursue a profession, it is assumed that he will be maintained by the Church. On the prohibition of undertaking secular business in general, see pp. 223-227 below.

78. "The deacon is appointed, chosen like the things which have before been spoken of. If he be of good conduct, if he be pure, if he have been chosen for purity and for abstinence from distractions; if not, yet [if he] be the husband of one wife, borne witness to by all the faithful, not entangled in the businesses of the world, not knowing a handicraft, without riches, without children. But if he be married or have children, let his children be taught to work piety and to be pure, so that they may be approved by the Church, according to the rule of the ministry" (*Test. Dom.* 1.33; trans. Cooper and Maclean 1902, 97).

79. See Rahmani 1899, 161.

80. See Cooper and Maclean 1902, 154; Funk 1901, 64.

81. See Connolly 1916b, 132.

82. For the bishop: "Let the bishop be chosen by all the people....The week when he is ordained, all the clergy and the people say, 'We choose him'" (*Can. Hippol.* 2; trans. Bebawi,

11). For the presbyter: "When a presbyter is ordained, one is to do for him everything which one does for the bishop" (*Can. Hippol.* 4; trans. Bebawi, 13). And for the deacon: "When a deacon is ordained, one is to do for him according to the same rules" (*Can. Hippol.* 5; trans. Bebawi, 14). This last canon is referred to in *Can. Hippol.* 2. Cf. Trembelas 1955, 16.

83. "[L]et him be without reproach, as it is written concerning him in the Apostle" (*Can. Hippol.* 2; trans. Bebawi, 11).

84. See Achelis 1891, 159-160.

85. Achelis 1891, 160.

86. *Can. Hippol.* 10: "If he comes with a true faith, he is to be received with joy, questioned about his occupation, and instructed by the deacon. In this manner he is to be instructed in the Scriptures, so that he may renounce Satan and all his service" (trans. Bebawi, 17).

87. Achelis 1891, 169-170.

88. *Can. Hippol.* 4: "The presbyter is equal to the bishop in everything except the seat and ordination, because to him is not given the power to ordain" (trans. Bebawi, 14).

Authors of the Fourth and Fifth Centuries

The sources studied so far reflect the Church's first efforts to present material of a canonical nature. For the most part, these sources are not cast in the form of legal canons, being rather moral exhortations based on the Old and New Testaments.[1] The exhortations had a practical aim which was later to be enshrined in the Church's canons. They are not simply collections of precepts regarded as necessary to the Church's life, but guides for the laity, and especially for the clergy, to help them resolve their moral perplexities and elucidate the Church's customs.

Some of the writings of the fathers and other ecclesiastical authors had the same aim. For various reasons, these authors set down their views on the priesthood and the life of the clergy, either in letters to their spiritual children or in extensive treatises. The authority of the fathers was such that passages from their writings were adopted by Church councils in the form of canons. The fathers wanted to enhance the prestige of the priesthood. They therefore emphasized the high moral standards required in those who aspired to it. This tendency, observable in the earliest years of the Church, reached its climax in the fourth and fifth centuries, not so much in legislative texts as in biblical exegesis and patristic literature in general.[2] Although many fathers refer incidentally to qualities desirable in clerics, relatively few discuss the priesthood and its requirements in detail.[3]

The fathers who have written specific works on the priesthood describe its eminence and strongly emphasize the supreme need for moral integrity in the clergy. In this chapter I discuss the contribution of these fathers. Of the many pastoral works which deal with the functions of the clergy, I have limited myself to a representative sample of those which treat them at some length, taking as my criterion how fully they present a picture of the ideal cleric.[4]

Ephraim the Syrian

In his discourse *On Priesthood*, St. Ephraim the Syrian[5] expresses his amazement that anyone should have the audacity to approach the priesthood without first having received a divine call: "I am astonished, my dear brethren, that some foolish people are accustomed to be so shamelessly bold as to seek the priesthood rashly without having been called by the grace of Christ, not knowing, wretches that they are, that fire and death are heaped up for them. I do not say to you simply that a person may not rashly lay hold of the priesthood, but he may not even touch any other vessel of all-holy worship" (*Priesthood* 5). Filled with holy fear before the mystery of the priesthood, the gift of which "transcends all thought and understanding" (*Priesthood* 2), he describes it with wonder. Because it is a gift of God, "through which the world is saved and creation is illuminated" (*Priesthood* 1), it is "an ineffable power, which has been made to dwell within us by the laying on of hands of holy priests" (*Priesthood* 3). And he adds: "Blessed is he who lives his life in this dignity purely and blamelessly" (*Priesthood* 3).

Aware of the divine origin and purpose of the priesthood, Christians are called upon to show appropriate respect and love to the priests of God, "because they are friends of Goodness himself, and intercede for us and the world" (*Priesthood* 4). They should not pass judgment on any particular priest, whether he is worthy or not, for they should pay heed to Christ's commandment in which "he who receives a prophet with joy in a prophet's name will receive a prophet's reward" (*Priesthood* 4).[6] The unworthiness of an aspiring cleric in no way diminishes the mystery of the priesthood or the sacraments celebrated by him when he has been ordained: "For just as the brightest gold is not harmed when it is smeared with clay, nor is the most shining pearl when it is dropped in filth, so the priesthood is not polluted by anyone, even if the person who has received it is unworthy" (*Priesthood* 4).[7] On the subject of the worthiness or otherwise of members of the clergy, Ephraim goes on to say: "If anyone proves worthy of the priestly office, and conducts himself in a holy and blameless manner, he wins life and an incorruptible crown. But if anyone dares to enter upon it unworthily, he procures for himself the outer darkness and implacable judgment" (*Priesthood* 5). So as not to incur the latter, anyone who seeks priestly office is forewarned "not to assume the grade of priesthood in a presumptuous way unworthily, because God, who is pure, does not approve of those who have been ordained presumptuously" (*Priesthood* 5). Moreover, mention is made of Old Testament figures such as Moses, Aaron, and Eleazar, whom Christian priests too are urged to imitate. Then the various virtues are mentioned which the priest must cultivate throughout his life. It is of the greatest interest that the cultivation of these virtues is mentioned after entry into the grades of the clergy. We must of course accept that these qualities are considered indispensable to the aspirant's career before his ordination. But here, in referring to them in relation to the cleric's life after his ordination, Ephraim emphasizes rather their prior existence and the consistent struggle afterwards to build on them and develop them. Thus he exhorts: "You have been granted, brother, the grade of priesthood. Seek earnestly to please him who has recruited you in purity and righteousness and divine wisdom and radiant virginity. Become a fervent emulator of Joseph's continence, Joshua's purity, Abraham's hospitality, Job's generosity to the poor, David's fatherly affection, and Moses' gentleness. Bring back the wanderer, bandage the lame, raise up the fallen, help the weak, and so on" (*Priesthood* 5).

In conclusion, to set a seal on what he looks for in priests, St. Ephraim urges them to remember "the fearful words of almighty God, spoken through the mouth of the prophet Isaiah: 'On whom shall I rest, but on him who is meek, humble, peaceful, and trembles at my words?' (cf. Isa 66:2). Always keep this saying in mind, and devote yourself to acquiring a treasure, namely, purity of thought" (*Priesthood* 5-6).

Athanasius the Great

Athanasius the Great was one of the leading person-alities of the First Ecumenical Council of Nicaea. The standard-bearer of orthodoxy, he fought strenuously against Arianism, and when he was elected patriarch of Alexandria, became a distinguished pastor of the Ortho-dox Church.[8] Although, unlike St. John Chrysostom and St. Gregory of Nazianzus, he did not write any specifical-ly pastoral works, his role at the council and his handling of the difficult problems facing the Alexandrian Church show that only a leader endowed with the richest moral, religious, and intellectual gifts could have successfully steered the Church's ship through the stormy seas of Arianism. Athanasius was rightly accorded the title of "Great," in view of his greatness in thought and action. His name was regarded as synonymous with virtue. In the eulogy St. Gregory the Theologian delivered on the anniversary of Athanasius's death, he says: "In praising Athanasius I shall praise virtue" (*Athan.* [PG 35:1081ff.]). The struggle against Arianism was his life's work, and he pursued it systematically and with self-denial. He resisted any interference of the civil authorities in the Church's affairs, regarding the ecumenical councils alone as possessing ultimate authority in ecclesiastical matters. He gathered the orthodox bishops around him. He was frequently humiliated and suffered all kinds of ill-treatment, but he never ceased to encourage and exhort, or to mount a vigorous resistance.[9] He thus suc-ceeded in becoming a pillar of orthodoxy.

Contemporary scholarship, nevertheless, raises another image of Athanasius. In fact, the corpus of

Athanasian scholarship has devoted much attention to
the political machinations, strategic decisions, and even
the alleged violence of the great Alexandrian hierarch.
In a certain sense, this is nothing new: others in the past
saw Athanasius as a cunning politician, but modern
scholarship has subjected him to particularly intense
and sophisticated scrutiny.[10] In any event, one cannot
deny that Athanasius played a pivotal role in the rise of
the so-called monarchical episcopacy.

A more nuanced and less acerbic attempt to catalogue
this rise shows how Athanasius was able to redefine
Alexandria's occasionally extreme theological and
ascetic tendencies into a productive tension between
otherworldliness and social cohesion.[11] Viewed from
this perspective, Athanasius's famous *Life of Anthony* attempts to persuade the reader that the Christian ascent
to the divine can only be fully experienced when ascetic
endeavor also includes submission to the authority of
the bishop.[12] From his pastoral activity and his works as
a whole a number of testimonies can be drawn which
together constitute a picture of his clerical ideal.

Pastoral authenticity

Athanasius dwells on the clergy's role especially in
the surviving fragments of his commentary on St. Matthew. He compares the bishop or the presbyter to the
eye of the Church's body. Just as the physical eye is the
body's most precious organ, so the bishop or the presbyter is a unique organ of the Church, like eyes. These
eyes, however, are of value only when they fulfill their
function, when they lead the faithful on the true, life-

giving path of salvation. Otherwise they fail in their purpose and cause harm, and because they are no longer of value, they should be put out (cf. Matt 5:29). Thus the bishop and the presbyter, like eyes full of light, should guide the Church's body safely away from the stumbling blocks of error along the life-giving path of truth. But if these eyes grow weak, they themselves can also be deceived. If they become a scandal to the faithful, they should be cut off from the body. For it is preferable that the faithful gather in the houses of prayer without them (*fr. Matt.* [PG 27:1369C]).

The deacon's service to the Church is similar to the service which the hand offers to the body. With use of the hand, a person accomplishes a host of tasks; one only has to lose it to realize its importance. In spite of this, it is better to cut off one's hand if it becomes a cause of scandal (cf. Matt 5:30). Thus deacons, too, according to Athanasius, should be worthy of the diaconate to which they have been appointed, for if they exercise it unworthily, they should be banished from the altar (*fr. Matt.* [PG 27:1369C]). In his constant battle against Arianism, Athanasius stresses that any false prophet who follows this heresy may have "a dignified outward form" and be "dressed in sheep's clothing," and may be called a presbyter, or a bishop, or a deacon, or even an ascetic, but his authenticity is judged only by his conduct. If he proves to be chaste, hospitable, merciful, loving, persevering in prayer, and patient, he is a true shepherd, or, as Athanasius puts it, "an intelligent shepherd." Conversely, if he makes "his belly a god and his gullet Hades," and is possessed by such a pernicious love of money that he makes a business of the Christian faith, then such a man, exposed by his works, is not a worthy shepherd but a false prophet and a "wolf in sheep's clothing." Just as trees are valued according to their fruit, and good people are distinguished from the bad by their deeds, in the present case "those who make Christ a source of gain" and have only the "reputation of piety" while in reality "their souls belong to the devil" are distinguished from the intelligent shepherds, the true imitators of the Great Shepherd, who is Christ (*fr. Matt.* [PG 27:1380D-1381A]). In describing the true shepherds and distinguishing them from the false prophets, Athanasius thus emphasizes the following qualities: piety, chastity, hospitality, mercy, love for God and neighbor, patience, perseverance in prayer, and basic virtues, with which the shepherds ought to be endowed, so that their works, flowing from these virtues as a whole, should distinguish them from the wolves in sheep's clothing that devastate Christ's Church.

Irreproachable life

In his *History of the Arians*, while speaking of the damage done to the Church by the followers of the "Arian madness," Athanasius emphasizes incidentally the great importance of the bishop's "irreproachability" (*H. Ar.* 1-3). Since the Emperor Constantius was pro-Arian,[13] he frequently drove the orthodox bishops out of their sees and replaced them with heretics. Athanasius describes this as "utterly novel" because the faithful do not have the pastor they themselves want, whose irreproachable life they know intimately, but one the emperor sends them "from afar supported by soldiers and an imperial rescript," whom they do not know at all (*H. Ar.* 2). At issue here is the importance of the irreproachable life of one who intends to assume priestly office, especially a bishop (*H. Ar.* 2). This episcopal quality is repeatedly emphasized by Athanasius in the *History of the Arians*. The heretics are "full of filth" and described as "spies" (*kataskopoi*) rather than "bishops" (*episkopoi*) (*H. Ar.* 2). They are deaf to the Apostle, who urges: "a bishop must be above reproach" (1 Tim 3:2; *H. Ar.* 2).

Unshakeable faith

In Athanasius's view a basic virtue of every believer, and especially of the pastor, is his unshakeable faith in the orthodox teaching handed down by the Lord and his disciples to the Church. If they are inspired by this teaching and are vigilant guardians of it, the clergy, as worthy zealots for the truth, will be able to keep the Church free from stain and safely guide the souls of the flock entrusted to them (*H. Ar.* 4). Athanasius therefore gives special emphasis to the adherence of the clergy and particularly the bishops to orthodox teaching, which they must defend against every danger without fear of exile, expropriation, or violence from whatever quarter, even death itself, but rather regard them as a "ministry of service," or even a living proclamation of the truth against falsehood and deceit (*H. Ar.* 32).

The saints' heavenly calling or imitation of Christ

Athanasius gives special emphasis to the heavenly calling of clerics in his *Letter to Dracontius*. Referring to the example of Jeremiah, who "out of reverence for him who had commissioned him, fulfilled his prophetic mission" (*Ep. Drac.* 5), although previously he had said: "I will not mention the name of the Lord" (Jer 20:9), he explains to Dracontius that his assertion that he is "too young to preach" is invalid. He should rather take account of the fact that God in his omniscience had called him: "but show reverence for him who knew you before you were created" (*Ep. Drac.* 5). In the same letter Athanasius stresses that Dracontius would do better "to imitate Paul and emulate the deeds of the saints" (*Ep. Drac.* 7). He calls those who "pursued the prize of their heavenly calling" "stewards of the mysteries." And he offers as examples some of the leading figures of the Old and New Testaments, Paul, Peter, Elijah, Elisha, and the Savior's disciples (*Ep. Drac.* 8). In this way he assures Dracontius that he should not be persuaded by others who say "that episcopacy is an occasion of sin." One can practice the ascetic life in any place, and "the crown of righteousness" (2 Tim 4:8) depends not simply on offices and functions, but on deeds (*Ep. Drac.* 8ff.). In the same letter, Athanasius also provides evidence that in that period there were many celibate bishops: "and many of the bishops have not married" (*Ep. Drac.* 9).

Finally, in his *Letter to Rufinianus* in which he deals with the problem of clerics who have returned from heresy, he pardons those who have erred through deceit or violence, since they have assured him that they "had not changed to impiety."

From these references we may conclude that in the midst of all the dangers that were threatening the

Church, Athanasius wanted the clergy to be zealous for the truth, above reproach, chaste, hospitable, merciful, loving, persevering in prayer, and patient. He wanted them to be luminous eyes and experienced guides on the unerring and life-giving path of truth. He wanted them to be concerned with knowledge, not rapacious, but guardians of orthodoxy, respectful of their divine calling, imitators of the Lord and of Paul, and zealous emulators of the deeds of the saints and the fathers.

Basil the Great

Basil the Great was the organizer of the monastic life in Cappadocia and the founder of a philanthropic institution. He lays down as the primary mission of the shepherd in a cenobium a concern for the healing of souls and their purification from the moral pollution of sin that defiles them, and their guiding toward spiritual perfection and redemption in Christ.[14] In his ascetic writings, the *Longer Rules* and the *Shorter Rules*, he emphasizes the virtues which the monks should acquire, and in particular the supreme religious, moral, and intellectual qualities which the shepherds of the cenobia should acquire in addition.[15] I refer to these monastic writings of St. Basil, because already from the first half of the fourth century the custom developed of choosing bishops from monks distinguished for their sanctity of life and Christian education, so that many of the qualities required in monks were also regarded as necessary for entry into the clergy, especially for those promoted to episcopal office.

The shepherd represents our Lord Jesus Christ. The

exercise of his office imposes on him the assumption of supreme responsibilities. It requires considerable abilities and virtues for him to succeed in imitating Christ, so that he can be an "example to believers" and a "living gospel" in the cenobium. The Apostle's injunction, "Be an example to believers" (1 Tim 4:12) should always be kept vividly in mind. "The shepherd should make his life a clear example of every commandment of the Lord, and not give those he is teaching any occasion to abandon a commandment as impossible to keep, or to hold it in contempt" (*Reg. fus.* 43). A model life is therefore required from the shepherd for his monks to imitate, since the monks regard the leader of the flock as a more proximate example of the Christian life (*Reg. fus.* 43).

The basic virtues which the shepherd should possess are the following:

Love of God

This is the commandment which the Lord laid down as the first and greatest (Matt 22:37-38). It crowns the virtues (*Reg. fus.* 1).[16] Basil regards the supreme quality of a monastic superior as complete love for God in Christ Jesus (*Reg. fus.* 1). A shepherd filled with this love becomes "immovable," so that he prefers nothing to God himself (*Ascet.* 2). If he devotes himself to this, it will contribute to the successful fulfillment of his apostolate, which consists in carrying out the will of the beloved, who is God.[17] Basil gives the vivid example of the thirsty deer, which runs "to the sources of the waters" (Ps 41:2). He uses this Old Testament image to show that the pastor's soul, and indeed the soul of every believer, should hasten to quench its thirst in love for God (*Reg. br.* 157). Love is the chief characteristic required in serving God, because when love is present, there is nothing that can hinder or deflect the service of God. The profundity of this virtue is expressed in the words of the Apostle, "Who shall separate us from the love of Christ? Shall tribulation, or distress, or persecution, or famine, or nakedness, or peril, or sword?" (Rom 8:35). The shepherd's whole life, as revealed in his deeds and words, should be inspired by love for God with all one's heart and all one's strength and with all one's mind (Matt 22:37-38), so that he should become "a witness to the love of God" (*Ascet.* 2).

Love for the flock

In addressing the shepherds of the cenobitic communities, Basil emphasizes love for the monks under them. This love must consequently be shown by every shepherd toward the members of their flock. Moreover, love for one's neighbor, which is stressed by the Lord himself as similar to love for God (Matt 22:37-39) and completes it and depends on it, constitutes in Basil's view the shepherd's fundamental virtue (*Reg. fus.* 1). This was the chief distinguishing mark of the disciples of the Lord, who loved us and commanded us to love one another (*Reg. fus.* 3.1-2; John 13:34). The shepherd's love for his neighbor includes self-sacrifice for the flock.[18] Characteristic are the Lord's words and example as the Good Shepherd, who leaves the ninety-nine sheep to search for the one lost (Matt 18:12-13; Luke 15:4-7): "The good shepherd lays down his life for the sheep" (John

10:11). In particular, the shepherd's love for his neighbor
is manifested as an affectionate paternal concern for
those in his care (*Moral*. 80).[19] The pastor as a spiritual
physician heals those sick with the maladies of the soul
(*Reg. fus*. 7) and, like the good Samaritan, does this out
of love (*Moral*. 80.15-17).[20] When a member of his flock
is ill, he suffers alongside him (cf. 1 Cor 12:26). Thus,
referring to the shepherds' love for their flocks, Basil
describes them as affectionate fathers, compassionate
physicians, and diligent teachers of souls for the sake
of the life in Christ.

Humility

When a person truly appreciates, on the one hand,
the sublimity of the divine majesty and glory, and on
the other hand, his own smallness, he "boasts in God"
(Rom 2:17) and recognizes his own indigence (*Humil*.
3).[21] Humility in general is the fundamental virtue of
monks and is specifically the indispensable presupposition of every shepherd.[22] This springs from the primary
virtue, which is love for God (*Reg. fus*. 43). The shepherd, the one who undertakes this service, must reject
completely any arrogant thought which can lead to his
being stripped completely of all the virtues: "Do not
aspire to clerical rank, but rather be humble" (*Humil*.
10). A shepherd should bear in mind that "responsibility for the majority is service of the majority" (*Reg. fus*.
30).[23] The shepherd's first duty is therefore to follow the
example of humility, which was given by the Lord himself when he said: "Learn from me, for I am gentle and
lowly in heart" (*Reg. fus*. 43.2; Matt 11:29). Gentleness

and lowliness in heart, then, should be characteristic marks of the shepherd. The example of the Lord, who "did not come to be served but to serve" (Matt 20:28) and who condescended to serve his creation, "taking a towel" (John 13:4) and washing his disciples' feet, demonstrates the true measure of humility for all believers, especially his ministers, the shepherds (*Reg. fus.* 43.1). Before anyone approaches the altar and assumes the burden of priestly office, he must be freed completely of every boastful and arrogant thought and be filled with humility and gentleness, since these are "the imitation of Christ" (*Humil.* 10). Having become an imitator of the Master, he will always be compassionate, merciful, a lover of humankind, "advancing in the virtues," "imitating the cherubim," an able worker "by God's grace" in his vineyard, "rejoicing together with Christ for all eternity" (*Humil.* 10).

Gentleness – Forbearance

Gentleness, to which Basil gives special emphasis as a virtue required in the shepherd, was mentioned in the previous paragraph. The Lord, who blessed "the meek, for they shall inherit the earth" (Matt 5:5) and was himself an example of gentleness, led Basil to stress the need for this virtue especially in shepherds. Gentleness is the presupposition which ensures success in the shepherd's work of service: "imposing therapies in all compassion and moderation, not in a self-willed way, but admonishing and teaching with gentleness" (*Reg. fus.* 44.1).[24] Gentleness and forbearance are a shepherd's basic virtues in the exercise of his office. It is with these that he teaches the obdurate, in expectation of their repentance (*Moral.* 70). These virtues will endow the shepherd with the ability and the patience to bring this difficult work to fruition.

The remaining pastoral virtues

The shepherd, moreover, should possess the virtues of continence, fervent prayer, and a firm and unshakeable faith.[25] Basil wants the shepherd "to be the bearer of virtues, undistracted, no lover of money, free from worldly cares, quiet, God-loving, free from anger and malice, zealous for the edification of his neighbors... preferring nothing to God" (*Ascet.* 2). In his letter to Amphilochius, bishop of Iconium, he emphasizes that it is difficult to find worthy men who are trusted by the multitude to assume an ecclesiastical ministry (*Ep.* 190). Wise judgment is needed in the bishops for the choice of the most suitable candidates and their ordination after careful examination and true testing (*Ep.* 190). Such men should be extremely observant, having fear of God, because their ministry is not an earthly and human office but a heavenly and angelic one, for they are God's laborers, expounding the word of truth in an orthodox way. They are also soldiers of the great king, and since they are not enmeshed "in the ordinary business of life, so that they may please him who has recruited them," they must expend all their energy in the execution of their duties, even if they are called upon to sacrifice their own lives (*Ascet.* 1).

The religious and moral qualifications of shepherds set out above should be supplemented by excellent intellectual abilities for solving various problems, especially those of a psychological nature.[26] The shepherd, as physician of souls, imitating in all things the Lord, who is the true physician of souls, should have a deep sense of the therapeutic rules and procedures laid down by the Lord in the Scriptures and should observe them (*Attend.* 1).[27] As a healer of souls, the shepherd should have a deep understanding of the human soul and rich practical experience, since the healing of the soul is more difficult than that of the body (*Reg. fus.* 40). The principle of individuation[28] is given particular emphasis by St. Basil in the carrying out of pastoral work. It is a principle established by the Lord himself, principally in the parable of the ninety-nine sheep and the one that was lost, which the shepherd, abandoning the many, goes to seek (Matt 18:12-13; Luke 15:4-7). Through this principle the value of human personality is underlined. The same principle was confirmed by the apostles, especially Paul. Referring to the Lord's words, "Which of you, having a hundred sheep, if one of them has gone astray, does not leave the ninety-nine, and go in search of the one lost until he finds it?", he teaches that "you should treat the sick person by every means and, as it were, reset the dislocated limb" (*Reg. br.* 102).[29] Intellectual qualities assist the shepherd's work. Basil emphasizes that the shepherd of a cenobitic community should be "vigilant with regard to the present, proactive with regard to the future, able to share the contest with the strong, support the frailties of the weak, and say and do everything that can strengthen those sharing the common life together" (*Reg. fus.* 43). He should especially be "capable intellectually and seek the righteousness of God with a perfect heart" (*Reg. fus.* 35). Moreover, he should have "the power to speak and listen knowledgeably for the building up of faith" (*Reg. fus.* 32).[30] But the presupposition for all these qualities is the divine call for "the service of the saints" (*Ep.* 161).

Finally, according to St. Basil, the shepherd who is suitable for this apostolate is "a support to his country, an ornament to the Church, a pillar and foundation of truth, a bastion of the Christian faith, a security for his own people, a man indomitable to his adversaries, a guardian of ancestral institutions, an enemy to novel doctrines" (*Ep.* 28).[31]

Gregory of Nazianzus

Gregory of Nazianzus[32] was the first to lay the basis of a description of the indispensable qualities required in clerics and discuss the duties of their pastoral ministry.[33]

On the attitude of candidates to the weighty
responsibilities of the priesthood

In his "Apology for His Flight to Pontus" (*Or.* 2)[34] St. Gregory discusses the reasons for his flight and return after his forced ordination.[35] He stresses the excellence of the priestly office, the dangers and heavy responsibilities attending it, and his own sense of unworthiness.[36]

St. Gregory's exhortations in this work refer principally to the duties of a priest, as may be inferred from the occasion of its composition. But since the episcopal office possesses the fullness of the priesthood, Gregory's words also apply to bishops. Both priestly grades are mentioned, since the Pauline precepts referred to are addressed to both bishops and presbyters. The requirements of the priesthood emerge from this apostolate. As Gregory emphasizes at the outset, the priesthood constitutes the most beautiful and most perfect order when all things have their beginning and end in God (*Or.* 2.1). But to realize this we need divine mercy, and the Holy Spirit, through whom alone is God known and understood (*Or.* 2.39).[37]

But what should happen on the human side? Anyone who wanted to devote himself to the work and apostolate of a pastor, and took stock of his own inadequacy, would have withdrawn in the face of its weight and responsibility. If this had happened generally, the Church would have been stunted. But the priesthood is a divine and indispensable institution in the Church. It cannot be set aside but coexists with the Church, against which "the gates of Hades shall not prevail" (Matt 16:18). To emphasize how necessary the priesthood is to the Church, Gregory puts the question: How and from whom would God have received worship, which vastly exceeds in majesty and value anything we have or know? (*Or.* 2.4; cf. Hos 3:4). Worship, therefore, is an indispensable service in relation both to God and to believers, and it is precisely for this reason that it is an institution of divine providence (*Or.* 2.3). Hence it would have been unreasonable for anyone to wish to avoid the office in all circumstances. But the greatness of the office is matched by the danger that accompanies it. A person should therefore examine himself with great care to see if he is worthy (*Or.* 2.10). There is, in fact, a special reason why Gregory says this. During the persecutions, when the authorities targeted the clergy in particular, many avoided ecclesiastical office.[38] But after the triumph of Christianity, the clergy became a respected and powerful body. The pressure of persecution had hardened their character and kept away undesirable people.

The picture of the clergy which Gregory presents in his time, however, has the following characteristics.[39] Many unworthy people gathered around the altar without the virtues required for the priesthood, for which they could have become models for others. They regarded the priesthood as a livelihood and source of wealth, rather than as a divine office for which they would have to render account. This sinful ambition had become widespread. Everyone wanted to teach, no one wanted to learn, with the result that subordinates were lacking. In these circumstances the need naturally arose for exhortations drawing attention to the danger and warding off the evil. Such a clergy would clearly not fulfill their apostolate properly. And for this reason worthy people were refusing to enter the clergy.

Apart from this situation there was another abuse. Young men without ability or experience were seeking honorable positions in the Church. Gregory therefore emphasizes that before one undertakes to teach others, one must first have been taught oneself, for if one wants to guide others to piety but lacks it oneself, the enterprise is impertinent. One must first learn and then teach. One must be virtuous oneself and then presume to be a teacher of virtue (*Or.* 2.47). The soundness of this approach is proved by the correct method of teaching practiced by the Jews. They did not teach the whole of Scripture to everyone, regardless of age, but reserved the fullness and the more difficult parts solely for the mature (*Or.* 2.48). A second argument is drawn from the nature of the office itself. With regard to any other craft, an apprentice would have expended much precious time and effort. How much greater time and effort is required for mastering the supreme craft and ultimate science, which is the priesthood? (*Or.* 2.16). Rejecting the accusation that his flight from Nazianzus was on account of ambition for higher ecclesiastical office, Gregory proceeds to condemn another abuse prevalent at that time. Clerics were frequently promoted to the higher grades without having first been examined or tested in the lower ones (*Or.* 2.5).[40] Gregory draws examples from seafaring and military life. A good sailor is first a steersman's mate and only then, after gaining the necessary knowledge, does he take over control of the rudder. A brave fighter becomes an officer, and an experienced officer a general. The same principle should be applied to the grades of the clergy.[41] He thus maintains that only those who have been sufficiently tested in the lower grades of the priesthood should be promoted to the higher.

Purity and moral probity of the celebrant and shepherd

The priestly apostolate requires that the cleric should be like pure gold or silver (*Or.* 2.10). This requirement derives from his relations with God, whose servant he is, with the Savior, with whom he exercises the priesthood, and with other human beings, whose shepherd and teacher he is. Moral integrity and exemplary virtue are required in the first place for the exercise of the priestly office in the strict sense. Gregory discusses sacerdotal duties in a letter to Amphilochius, in which he asks him for his pious intercession in the Liturgy, "when you draw down the Word by the word, when you divide the Lord's body and blood by a bloodless incision, the sword having a voice" (*Ep.* 171).[42]

He addresses bishops and presbyters as "offerers of bloodless sacrifices" (*Od.* 10 and 13). Anyone, however, who wishes to offer God this external sacrifice, which is a representation of the great mystery, the sacrifice accomplished on the cross, must first have offered himself as a living and holy sacrifice to God (*Or.* 2.95). This requirement is also derived from the relationship of the priest to the people, whose shepherd and teacher he is. Such a difficult apostolate presupposes intense effort.

On analogy with the shepherd of real sheep, the shepherd of Christ's rational flock must teach morality, presenting himself to the community as an example to follow (*Or.* 2.9). This is difficult both for the teacher and the taught, because it is much easier to pick up vice than virtue. Virtue is learned rarely and with difficulty. Vice, as a polluting disease, spreads everywhere easily and rapidly (*Or.* 2.11). How much internal conflict the priest must go through before he arrives at exemplary moral perfection! It is only just possible after a long personal struggle to liberate his soul from everything base and unworthy. Yet the priest is called up to achieve this not only for himself, but also so that he can contribute to increasing the moral stature of the faithful entrusted to him (*Or.* 2.91).

Persuasion and censure by the shepherd in the community

Alluding to 1 Peter 5:2, Gregory shows that obedience is acquired only through suggestion in love, not by the use of force. Whatever is acquired simply through external pressure is not only unworthy of a human being, but does not last very long. This is brought home by an apt example. Just as a plant, when bent by force by a human hand immediately afterwards returns to its original position, so is the conduct of someone who has been constrained by force. Only that which comes as a result of free will and consent is enduring. Just as gold is purified by fire, so the soul must be tested by moral struggles, so that it should receive the good things of eternity not only as a divine gift, but also as a reward for virtue. St. Gregory rightly sees the proof of this, through God's mercy, in the conviction that only through willing consent, through personal choice, and through our own effort can virtue become the possession of each one of us (*Or.* 2.17). When external pressure alone is applied, God's purpose is always thwarted. One thus understands that the Christian teacher's apostolate is a difficult one. Real success in his apostolate is only achieved through persuasion. But although Gregory puts it in this way, he does not exclude severe censure when circumstances require it. When he proposes Paul as an example for all spiritual workers, he makes it clear that he combined severity with gentleness in such a way that gentleness was never transformed into weakness, or severity into harshness (*Or.* 2.54).

The shepherd as an example to be imitated

In this relationship with the community, the priest's primary task is to acquire Christian virtue and moral perfection. The priest must not be satisfied simply with the avoidance of evil and putting every vice out of his heart. He must also manifest the good in every aspect of his life, and indeed in this matter must surpass the faithful committed to his charge. But even this should not satisfy him. The measure of his moral conduct is not what others do or omit to do, but what God's law commands (*Or*. 2.14). He should always not only surpass others in virtue, but regard it as a sacred obligation continuously to pursue perfection on the path of virtue (*Or*. 2.15). Through his morality the priest should always be growing in perfection, and surpass his flock in the measure of his virtue, not according to the rank of his ecclesiastical office (*Or*. 2.14). His teaching should consist not only of words but of deeds. Gregory rightly requires the spiritual worker to be a model for his flock. But he equally rejects the erroneous conclusion that makes the validity of Christian doctrine depend on the personal condition of the teacher, just as the validity of baptism does not depend on the officiant: "Do not inquire into the credentials of the preacher, or the baptizer. There is another judge of these, another tester of what is more invisible" (*Or*. 40).[43]

The shepherd as teacher

With regard to the cleric's duties as a teacher, Gregory requires an appropriate ability and an elementary formal education (*Or*. 2.35). This is indispensable because a preacher of the divine word is obliged to proclaim Christian teaching and expound it at length, as well as communicate to the people the deepest mysteries of the faith (*Or.* 2.36). In this apostolate above all, it is necessary to eschew hyperbole and extreme statements. The occasion for this statement was given to Gregory by the current trinitarian heresies (*Or.* 2.36-38). Here, as elsewhere, we meet appropriate comparisons. Just as a tree which has been blighted by nature cannot be righted by force, so also heresy is not overcome by falling into the opposite extreme position. The safety of an acrobat who walks a tightrope depends on his ability to keep his balance. And for Christian teaching to be precise and successful, it must follow the golden mean. The preacher of the divine word must seek the grace of a precise understanding of the teaching, and an appropriate way of expounding it, which must answer the various needs of his hearers.

St. Gregory draws attention to people belonging to the following categories (*Or.* 2.40-43): (i) those holding assumptions lacking not good will but only a precise understanding; (ii) those like them who have already been corrupted by earlier heresies—a double effort is needed to restore these, because the heresy must be uprooted first before it can be replaced by the truth; (iii) those dominated by pride, who rebel imprudently against the truth and resist sound teaching; (iv) those who attack the teaching like ferocious beasts and dishonor it with their polluted souls; (v) others who have no understanding and accept any teaching and any teacher indiscriminately, as a result of which they fall into skepticism; (vi) by contrast, others have already attained a high level of understanding. These follow a teaching which corresponds in form and content to their higher understanding. To cope with so many different categories of people a homiletic approach is needed which is simple and straightforward but at the same time intelligent, so that it can win the hearts of all (*Or.* 2.44). But so that a preacher who gives all his attention to the points listed above does not fall into a different error, St. Gregory gives a due warning. The true teacher of the divine word should also be aware of each person's needs, but in addressing them he should treat popularity with contempt. He should speak to people directly and with care (*Or.* 2.46). That is why a formal education is not in itself sufficient. The heart too must be conquered and must be on fire when the Scriptures are proclaimed and expounded. The priest must have a christocentric understanding,[44] dealing with spiritual things in a spiritual way when he approaches the mysterious treasures of God, that he may contemplate devoutly the good things contained within them and thus enrich others (*Or.* 2.96).

From what we have seen so far, we have established that St. Gregory considers a capacity to give guidance and to educate people indispensable in a priest (*Or.* 2.78). He must not only have a perfect grasp of theory, but of practice as well. The priest needs culture and pastoral sensitivity not only for preaching, but also for his personal spiritual work. He must always have the appropriate word at hand for every situation and the right means for dealing with any difficult situation.

Many situations are mentioned, amongst which are different ages, economic and social class, and spiritual development, which must be taken into account (*Or.* 2.28ff.). How much, for example, do men and women differ from each other, young people and the elderly, rulers and the ruled. Moreover, the same person needs to be treated differently, according to his spiritual disposition at different times. Sometimes praise is needed, sometimes censure, and this must be administered sometimes publicly and sometimes in private. Another difficulty arises from the fact that sometimes a person who is rich and powerful, sometimes one who is poor and weak, must be praised or censured. With the passage of time, not only diligence and intelligence but, most of all, experience renders the pastor capable and worthy in his apostolate (*Or.* 2.33).

St. Gregory continues to develop his teaching, drawing freely on passages from the Old Testament (*Or.* 2.56-58). In this way he tries to demonstrate the priest's mission and responsibility, and also show what misfortune unworthy priests bring on themselves and their people. Then, as congruent to his theme, he refers to the qualities which the Apostle Paul sets out in his pastoral epistles as basic presuppositions for bishops and presbyters. These are followed by the Lord's commandments given to his disciples when he sent them out to preach,[45] in which meekness and self-denial are emphasized (*Or.* 2.69).

Finally, Gregory proposes the Apostle Paul as the model for all priests of every age, for he embodied the ideal of the Christian priest (*Or.* 2.52ff.). From this

example the spiritual laborer must maintain an indomitable zeal in the difficult aspects of spiritual work, an
unfailing hope in even the most painful failures and
bitter disappointments, a patient endurance in all misfortune and persecution, a fervent zeal for the glory of
God and the salvation of believers, a sincere solidarity
in every spiritual and bodily need of his fellow human
beings, a ceaseless willingness to sacrifice himself for
the grace of Christ and the Gospel, so that he should be
"all things to all men" (1 Cor 9:22).

John Chrysostom

John Chrysostom speaks with no less awe about the
mystery of the priesthood in his apologia to his friend
Basil justifying his refusal of the office of bishop. The
similarity of this work, *Priesthood*, to the earlier work of
St. Gregory of Nazianzus suggests that John made use
of it when composing his own treatise. The purpose of
the work is to present the greatness of priestly service
and define both the qualities and the duties of candidate
clerics.[46] It is a treatise in which the author expresses
himself with great power and left a lasting impression
on his successors. Written in 375 or 376,[47] it is the first
important pastoral work in ecclesiastical literature.[48] In
view of its importance and length, it is worth examining
in some detail.

In spite of the fact that in this work the discussion is
centered on the role of the bishop, which is natural, since
it was written as an apologia for his refusal of the office,
nevertheless John's exhortations are also directed toward
presbyters. Elsewhere he examines why, after describing

the ideal bishop, the Apostle Paul does not refer to pres-byters but deals immediately with deacons (*Hom. 1 Tim. 2*). He explains that this is because there was no essential difference between the bishop and the presbyter, since presbyters also exercised a teaching role and shared ad-ministrative authority.[49] Thus what is said about bishops also applies to presbyters (*Hom. Phil.* 1).[50]

Comparison of the episcopal office with the monastic state

John Chrysostom was particularly well disposed to-ward monasticism.[51] He nevertheless contrasts the monk with the priest to show that the priestly office is the more important, the broader in scope, and the more difficult. The difference between the two is as great as that be-tween a simple subject and a king. While the monk is concerned only with himself and his own perfection, the holder of ecclesiastical office is responsible for the salva-tion of many. And since he is a model for many others, his morality must be higher and more perfect than that of the monk. The monk is like a steersman whose ship lies in harbor, rendering his capacity or incapacity su-perfluous. By contrast, the priest's mistakes are revealed at once, because he is steering the Church's ship through dangerous waves. Since monks live in the desert and are free from worldly disturbances, they enjoy peace and tranquility. Yet priests too try to make sure in various ways that they keep themselves pure before God. One can therefore imagine how strongly the priest must struggle, on the one hand, to maintain his own purity, and on the other hand, to ensure the purity of the souls under his pastoral care. Living in the world, he is subject to incomparably more pressures than the monk that can pollute his soul if he ceases to be vigilant. Here it may be noted that peace and seclusion contribute to the monk's spiritual progress. In this way the monk can more easily resist temptations. The priest, on the other hand, who is active in the world and must be fully informed of all the conditions of life of different types of people, is exposed through his spiritual concerns to every kind of danger and temptation. He therefore needs to be mentally agile and have great powers of spiritual endurance. The priest lives in the world but not with the world nor in the manner of the world. He must be as detached as possible from every aspect of worldly existence. In spite of his external ties, in his interior life he must be less at home in the world than monks are, who live in isolated places in the mountains. Much is required to bring about his perfection and correspondence to the pattern of the perfect priest as set out by the Apostle Paul (1 Tim 3:2; *Hom. 1 Tim.* 10). The monk's field of action is therefore smaller and more accessible. It is easier for him to attain his goal of perfection, and his responsibilities are not as great. By contrast, the priest's field of action is greater and his apostolate more difficult. Hence his responsibilities before the Lord are greater (*Sac.* 6.2).

Ambition as a stumbling block for the priesthood

With regard to these exhortations and others like them, one must not overlook the following: Chrysostom praises the priestly office in vivid, almost extravagant language. That is to say, he emphasizes the office, not the holder of the office, distinguishing clearly between the office and the priest's worthiness as a person (*Hom. 2 Tim.* 2). His description of the priestly office is for him the basis of his presentation of the great duties and weighty responsibilities which a person vested with it undertakes. One can gain some understanding of the nobility and responsibility of the priesthood if one reflects that the priest is concerned not only about himself but also for the members of the community entrusted to him, for whom he must give an account to the Lord. The priest must therefore regard his office not as a dignity but as a burden. Through ceaseless vigilance and constant self-examination the priest must protect himself and others from all corruption and perdition. The model put forward is the Apostle Paul, who ascended to the third heaven and saw the ineffable mysteries of God. He always strove for others, never for himself, and although he did more than God required of him, he nevertheless always stood before the majesty of the office full of awe and humility (*Sac.* 3.7).[52] On the basis of Chrysostom's information, we gain some idea of the life of the clergy of his age,[53] as we also do from the picture presented by St. Gregory of Nazianzus in the apologia we have already discussed (*Sac.* 3.15).[54] The greatest danger for the clergy and the Church generally came from unbridled ambition. It was the motivation behind unsuitable and entirely unworthy candidates, who struggled successfully to attain ecclesiastical office, while suitable and worthy candidates were overlooked or excluded altogether. To this it may be added that the addresses delivered in the struggle to attain ecclesiastical office are associated with wholly unacceptable motives.[55] Aware of all this, Chrysostom often says that whoever desires to approach the priesthood must of necessity be free from all ambition, even though struggling, without love of gain, to attain ecclesiastical office. In the contrary case, he should abandon it. Ambition is presented as a dangerous impediment to the priest's spiritual tranquility and is the main hindrance to a fruitful spiritual ministry. A thirst for glory stimulates other polluting passions in the soul: sharpness of temper, falsehood, slander, envy, obsequiousness, etc. Such priests, indeed, even succumb to the influence of women with authority over them. But the Apostle Paul forbids women not only to teach but even to speak in Church (*Sac.* 3.9).[56]

The shepherd's love for the Savior

Among the other spiritual criteria, Chrysostom emphasizes above all love for the Savior as an essential element of the priest's soul. The Lord's question to Peter (John 21:15ff.): "Do you love me?" and his response to Peter's reply: "Feed my lambs" clearly demonstrate how concerned the Savior was for those he made his heirs through his own blood and whom he loved more than any other. He therefore wishes to entrust them with a shepherd who loves the Lord and the Church more than anything else (*Sac.* 2.1). Such love should attain the heights we admire in Paul, when he says: "For I could wish that I myself were accursed and cut off from Christ for the sake of my brethren, my kinsmen by race" (Rom 9:3). But how difficult and how rare is such love that does not seek gain! (*Sac.* 3.7).

Relations between the shepherd and the flock

On relations between shepherd and flock, Chrysostom says the following. The priest is truly a recipient of God's commandments and an instrument of Christ, commissioned in the Church to administer it and build it up, thus receiving from him his spiritual authority over the flock and being appointed shepherd of Christ's rational sheep. From this derive the duties of both shepherd and flock. Chrysostom constantly reminds the shepherd of the responsibility given to him, tells him to put away pride and the lust for power, and urges him to exercise true guidance to those entrusted to him. Then, referring frequently to the Epistle to the Hebrews (Heb 13:17), he sets out the shepherd's duties towards the flock. He dwells especially on this theme in his *Second Homily on the Second Epistle to Timothy*. We read in this homily that the cause of every misfortune is the disturbance of harmonious relations between the shepherds and the flock. Respect for them is then lost. As a result, there is no longer any respect for God, since the priests have been sent by God. When there is respect for the shepherd, then God is also honored in his person (*Hom. 2 Tim.* 2). The next point is also very instructive. No one is obliged to obey the shepherd, even if it is the Apostle Paul himself, if he speaks as a private person. But when the shepherds speak as apostles and servants of Christ, all should obey them. As regards the relations of believers with an unworthy shepherd, Chrysostom, relying on Matthew 23:2-3, counsels obedience,[57] which God will not overlook. If the unworthy shepherd teaches the truth, then one should follow not his manner of life but his words (*Hom. 2 Tim.* 2). Only when the shepherd teaches heresy are the faithful not required to follow him, even if he is an angel. In other matters they should realize that the priest performs spiritual operations solely in an external manner, for it is God who accomplishes them. This being the case, neither can the unworthy priest harm the believer, nor can the worthy priest help the unrepentant.[58]

Another topic Chrysostom touches on, not only for clerics but also for the laity, is the study of the Bible. He recommends this to both groups, so that Christ's word may live more richly in them. Only by studying the Bible will they always be in a position to give an account of their faith. One will be able to support the other (*Sac.* 4.8).[59]

Qualities relating to the priest's relationship to God

The priest is presented as a mediator, to whom the whole community has been entrusted, and he fulfills the role of a father to the faithful. As their leader, he intercedes to God for them. That is why he must surpass everyone in all things. Since the priest is required to have certain qualities relevant to his relations with the community, it is understandable that he should have moral qualities in an even greater degree relevant to his relations with God. It is he who invokes the Holy Spirit, who celebrates "the most dread sacrifice," whose tongue pronounces sacred and wonder-working words, whose hands touch the most precious sacrament, while angels from heaven surround him and fill the altar for the honor of the One who lies there as sacrifice, and before whom all fall to the ground in an attitude of worship. What kind of soul, Chrysostom asks, should this be? How much attentiveness, purity, and holiness should adorn the priest's soul, which should shine like the sun, and even more! It must be as pure as if the priest were standing in heaven in the midst of the souls of the saints (*Sac.* 3.4; 6.4).[60]

The detailed examination of the candidate

One of the strict obligations that Chrysostom imposes on the bishop is the detailed and careful examination of the candidate in the course of his ordination and appointment to ecclesiastical office. The bishop should not regard the opinion of the populace as sufficient,[61] or the esteem in which the candidate is held by those outside the Church.[62] The bishop himself is responsible when he promotes an unsuitable candidate to the priesthood and shares in his sin, just as in the opposite case he shares in his virtues. The bishop, then, must be sufficiently strong to resist, if necessary, unreasonable advice and the unjustified demand of the people. In this matter, too, as in every aspect of the exercise of his priesthood, he should have regard only for the Church's best interests (*Sac.* 2.4; 3.15-16).[63]

The qualities needed for preaching

When speaking of the preacher's teaching authority,[64] Chrysostom mentions how dangerous this authority is for him who exercises it without the basic qualities required for it. The chief of these requirements is goodness and diligence. He who does not possess these prerequisites should not come forward (*Sac.* 5.1). Elsewhere, he writes on the same topic that it is very important for the edification of the community that the leaders of the Church be capable preachers, because otherwise the communities can suffer great harm (*Hom. 1 Tim.* 15). It is right that after listing the bishop's other qualities—hospitality, gentleness, and blamelessness—the Apostle Paul should have added the gift of teaching.

But what goal should the preacher have before his eyes and what qualities must he have to attain it? The criterion and goal in this work must be pleasing God. This is what his teaching should aspire to (*Sac.* 5.7). In another of his homilies, Chrysostom expresses himself in similar terms, since the aim of preaching in his view is the salvation of the souls of believers (*Stat.* 2.4). The Church, he says, is not a theater. He goes on to ask: What purpose does loud applause serve? His audience has come to hear him in vain if they do not take away something useful. He reminds them that praise of him is the practical application of his words. It is the preacher's duty always to have something useful before his eyes, not simply the desire to please his audience. He is thus obliged to speak the whole truth without giving thought to the approval or disapproval which he might provoke. This, in brief, is the aim and manner of teaching which the pastor should practice in the Church (cf. *Grat.* 2).

In his first homily on the first Epistle to Titus, Chrysostom invokes the Lord's words: "You did not choose me, but I chose you" (John 15:16), stressing that, like the apostles, the preacher should generally carry out his work not in his own name but according to the Lord's precept. The layman has no obligation at all to do this, while the cleric who does not proclaim to the people their religious duties is punished. Precisely because he has the fulfillment of the Lord's commandment as his work, he must not make the teaching of the Gospel a matter of satisfying his lust for power (*Hom. Tit.* 1.2). The same point is made in the Prologue of the *First Homily on 1 Timothy*, where Chrysostom attributes preaching to the common commandment of the three divine persons of the Holy Trinity (*Hom. 1 Tim.* 1.1). In connection with this commandment and the goal of teaching, there follow two indispensable qualities for the Christian preacher, namely, humility and eloquence, which are of equal benefit for both the preacher and the community. The preacher is regarded as worthy of his apostolate only when he possesses both of these virtues. The possession of one or the other in isolation diminishes the effectiveness of the priest's work as a preacher (*Sac.* 5.2). From an examination of the audience to whom sermons are addressed, the following points emerge: (i) The hearers are presented in various ways. They are not easily taught students but behave as if they were at a secular entertainment for their own enjoyment. Instead of embracing what they have heard and following it, they regard themselves as able to judge. They seek entertainment, not instruction. (ii) They are immediately annoyed with the preacher if he ceases to present something notable in a constantly new form. (iii) The hearers are quick to blame the preacher when he makes use of foreign works and appeals in his homily to the views of others. Even the suspicion is enough to cause annoying difficulties.

(iv) Parties are easily formed, whose members prefer one preacher or the other and hear the sermon with a bias at the outset (*Sac.* 5.1). (v) Because of the great variety in the cultural level of hearers, they are often unable to distinguish the able preacher, and sometimes there is no applause for the homily that deserves it. This happens because the same sermon that gives full satisfaction to the educated leaves the rest, who constitute the majority, unmoved (*Sac.* 5.6). (vi) Another and even bigger difficulty arises from the moral level of the crowd, which is ready with groundless accusations and unjustified slander, privately and publicly, to heap up praise on the inept preacher, so as to damage the reputation of those with ability (*Sac.* 5.6). (vii) Moreover, despite the good that he may have done, the fame and reputation of a powerful speaker may be destroyed by a small fault. The crowd easily overlooks great virtues, while small errors are pounced upon immediately and are not forgotten (*Sac.* 5.5). The audience usually does not know that an orator's physical and psychological state can greatly affect his performance; he cannot always be successful (*Sac.* 5.5).

In view of these and similar considerations, the preacher must have humility and also a resilient spiritual disposition free from vainglory and tested by patience. This is necessary for the good of the community and of himself, because when vainglory remains unsatisfied, it becomes a source of constant thought and deep intellectual despondency (*Sac.* 5.4). The vainglorious search for fame can easily lead to envy of one's more successful colleague. The community does not shrink from treating him with enmity, slandering him maliciously, and finally holding him in contempt, even if this leads to its own destruction (*Sac.* 5.8). Then Chrysostom shows that the preacher must avoid seeking systematically to build up a reputation among the people.[65] The pursuit of a fine reputation easily prompts the preacher to say what is pleasing to the people rather than what is necessary and beneficial to them. Thus instead of becoming the people's guide, the preacher is himself guided by the people (*Sac.* 5.2). On this point the preacher must make his position clear. It is he who is the teacher and they who are the taught, he who is the father and they the children. No one is carried away by the shouts and claps, the applause and flattery of children. Similarly, the people's praises should not make the preacher proud, nor should unjustified censure make him dispirited (*Sac.* 5.4). He should endure hatred and insult with patience and a calm spirit and remain unperturbed when others are preferred unworthily (*Sac.* 5.6). To acquire the ability to do this, he should always bear in mind that most people lack proper awareness. He should forgive them because they act in ignorance. To those that act out of malice he should show compassion as people to be pitied, considering he neither wins nor loses through people's favor or disfavor. He should be content with the thought that he has done his duty as a teacher to please God (*Sac.* 5.6-7).

Chrysostom then goes on to present the other side of the matter. If the preacher should not give too much weight to public opinion, he should nevertheless not ignore the people's judgment completely. It helps to

protect him against laziness, while at the same time
stimulating him to constant effort and self-examination.
He should even try to win the confidence of the people.
This makes it essential that every suspicious thought be
banished at the outset. No one magnifies a reputation,
whether negative or positive, as much as the inarticulate
crowd, which passes on what it has heard without first
ascertaining the truth. Only when he has exhausted
every possible alternative should the preacher condemn
the slanderers (*Sac.* 5.4).

A preacher's necessary qualities also include eloquence. Chrysostom emphasizes the need for this gift in
the delivery of sermons (*Sac.* 5.1). Eloquence is not only
a natural gift; it is also the result of diligent and constant
practice, which should therefore never be omitted (*Sac.*
5.5).[66] Even in the rare case when one happens to be a
perfectly accomplished speaker, the duty of constant
practice should not be neglected. Quite the contrary,
a person gifted with eloquence should make greater
efforts than one with a modest talent. More is always
expected of the more skillful. They should therefore seek
improvement with every new sermon (*Sac.* 5.5). The
only perfect speaker is one who has acquired all these
attributes simultaneously. He can then be sure that he
is useful to the people. If a man is free of vainglory but
inept at public speaking, his words are wasted. Because
of his ineptitude his hearers believe that they conceal indifference and faulty thinking. But if the reverse is true,
it is unavoidable that he will abuse his gift, because he
is only seeking an empty popularity. But someone who
is at the same time humble and eloquent will commu-

nicate to the faithful that which is really indispensable and profitable in the appropriate form (*Sac.* 5.3).

Thoughtfulness, patience, individuation

On the basis of the above, the following qualifications are put forward as indispensable in a cleric: First he must have an enlightened understanding and a thousand eyes, so that he can discern the state of the soul at any moment in all its aspects. A priest, however, expends his effort pointlessly if he does not plumb the depths of the soul with accurate psychological insight so as to identify its faults and apply the appropriate remedy. The remedy requires thoughtfulness, patience, and attention to the individual case.[67] Thoughtfulness because a careful approach is needed if people are going to put themselves under priestly guidance and be grateful for the remedy; patience and perseverance, because an approach which is too swift and abrupt will put the remedy in jeopardy. One must always bear in mind that patience brings about every good in people. Finally, attention to the individual case because the shepherd, as physician of souls, must understand very well that the soul's maladies are various, as are the spiritual state and character of each sufferer. Thus in accordance with the principle of individuation the pastor must adapt his approach to the needs of each case, depending on the nature of the illness and the character of the patient, if he is to have any hope of a successful cure.[68] Some are weak and listless, others are enmeshed in worldly pleasures, others have succumbed to melancholy. Some are proud of their origins, others of their wealth and influence. All these things and more should be taken into account, so that such people might gradually and with sympathy be weaned away from their habit of sin and healed of their maladies.

The shepherd's readiness to deal with quibblers, those who have lost their way, or opponents of the faith

There is another class of people who create severe difficulties in the shepherd's spiritual work. These are the quibblers who love to delve into difficult questions. By spending much time in discussing the faith they are in danger of forgetting how to live it. Here Chrysostom, with his characteristic skill, gives the practical advice that in coping with this difficulty one should do neither more nor less than is necessary. The bishop should not enter into hair-splitting arguments, strictly exercising the rights that flow from his authority. Such an approach would make him vulnerable to accusations of arrogance and ignorance. He should avoid exposing himself to such charges, while trying to draw those entrusted to his care away from such pointless questions. But the means available for this is simply the power of the word (*Sac.* 4.5). The same is true when doubts arise in the community about one or another of the Church's doctrines (*Sac.* 4.9).[69]

Special care is needed in the case of those who have abandoned the path of the true faith. A shepherd has an obedient flock and can easily bring back the lost sheep. But great care and effort are required to restore the members who have separated themselves from the Church. The priest should never lose hope but always think with Paul and say: "God may perhaps grant that they will repent and come to know the truth, and they may escape from the snare of the devil" (2 Tim 2:25-26). Those who have strayed should not be made to return by force. The power of persuasion should be used to restore the lost to the truth which previously they had despised. But in the application of this unique means one must demonstrate firmness and decisiveness. The bishop must be simultaneously serious and friendly, severe and mild, imperative and accommodating, impetuous and gentle (*Sac.* 3.16). In his homilies on the pastoral epistles, Chrysostom also reserves the right to the spiritual worker frankly to impose his authority (*Hom. Tit.* 5.3). His behavior should always be governed by the circumstances and be proportionate to the nature of the fault to be corrected. There are sins which can be banished by friendly counsel and gentle guidance. But there are others which can be corrected only by harsh severity.

A painful duty is imposed on the ecclesiastical superior when he has to exclude a member of the Church's community. But because the purpose of such action is to bring about the sinner's repentance, great care is needed in case he is "overwhelmed by excessive sorrow" (2 Cor 2:7).[70] This measure has been laid down for the spiritual benefit and repentance of the person who has erred. Used without care, it can cause even greater harm. The bishop must beware that he does not by thoughtless action push the sinner, and therefore himself, into eternal perdition (*Sac.* 3.17). House visits to the rich and the poor, and relations with the community in general, also require great care (*Sac.* 3.17). The exercise of teaching authority, as well as the pastoral care of the body of Christ, impose on the cleric the duty of defending Christian teaching and protecting the Christian community against the inroads of heresy. For that is why it was said: "Always be prepared to make a defense to anyone who calls you to account for the hope that is in you" (1 Pet 3:15). And with the priest as intermediary, the faithful also share in this role (*Sac.* 4.3). In this regard, the Church must be like a fortified city. The bishop's readiness and understanding must be like a wall surrounding it, to defend it against enemy attack and guarantee the safety of the inhabitants. In this struggle he has to be ready to confront three different enemies: pagans, Jews and heretics (*Sac.* 4.4).[71]

What qualities does this struggle on so many fronts demand? First is experience, together with a full and precise knowledge of the adversaries and their conduct. For the Church's opponents are many and varied, and so are their modes of attack. In this war each has his own special task and his own role to play. The bishop, however, must be present everywhere simultaneously, because if the enemy manages to make even a small breach in the walls, then all is lost. He must be victorious over every adversary in all points. And he must be able to combat all of them successfully (*Sac.* 4.4). The basic requirements for success are intelligence and moderation. Chrysostom recommends a line of conduct, the neglect of which leads to failure. Just as in the art of war, it is essential to follow the golden middle way. Not only must the bishop overcome what is heretical in his adversary's teaching, but he must also emphasize the corresponding truth in his own. Chrysostom discusses the appropriate line to take in two examples. The gnostics reject the Old Testament, while the Jews value it very highly. If one wishes to depreciate Moses' precepts in the course of polemic against the Mosaic law observed by the Jews, one renders a welcome service to the heretics. The Mosaic law was good. The Jews were right in this, but only in the age of the Old Testament. The gnostics, on the other hand, reject the Mosaic law in its entirety. The truth is that the law of the Old Testament ceased to be obligatory after the arrival of the law of grace. The Jew and the gnostic, each in his own way, exaggerates. For each attributes absolute validity to what is valid only for a limited period. Accordingly, the Church recognizes the Mosaic law, but only for the age of the Old Testament. It abrogates it because in the New Testament it has lost its significance (*Sac.* 4.4). For his second example, Chrysostom refers to the teachings of Sabellius and Arius. The former emphasized the unity of God at the expense of his triadic being, the latter the difference between the three persons, causing a differentiation to be made in their essence. If one wishes to counter both of these positions, then one must emphasize simultaneously the unity of the divine essence and the difference of the divine persons, without falling one-sidedly into one or the other heresy (*Sac.* 4.4). Finally, a precise understanding of Christian doctrine is needed and a dialectic skill in defending and establishing the Church's doctrine. At this point Chrysostom embarks on an eloquent eulogy of the Apostle Paul, whom he proposes as the ideal model to follow (*Sac.* 4.6).

Ambrose of Milan

In the West, Ambrose of Milan addressed a treatise called *De officiis ministrorum* to his clergy. It was composed after 386.[72] In the arrangement of his material Ambrose follows Cicero's *De officiis*, attempting to Christianize the Stoic ethics found in this work. As a result, Ambrose emphasizes five virtues: almsgiving, poverty, self-denial, purity, and humility.[73]

Almsgiving

Nothing is more apt to win the laity's respect and affection than the generosity the priest shows toward those in need (*Off.* 2.7).[74] The first among these are the destitute, who must find the food they need for their survival. Ambrose fittingly focuses his attention on those sometimes called "the ashamed poor," those who because of some reversal of their fortunes, as often happened in the later Roman Empire, had fallen into destitution, having enjoyed sufficient means before, and were ashamed to confess their need. He urges clerics who discover cases of this kind to make them known to the bishop, that they might be supported so far as possible (*Off.* 2.15.69; 1.30.158). Generally speaking, less visible poverty is not always less harsh. And the most importunate are not always the most needy. They should not gain by their clamor more than their due and distract the almsgiver to the disadvantage of those whose voice cannot be heard. One should not only lend an attentive ear to those who come and beg, but should open one's eyes to discover concealed misfortune and even see those who do not see us (*Off.* 2.16.77). Such people are the sick and the imprisoned (*Off.* 2.16.77).[75] Prisoners and, more generally, those afraid of the severity of the law should find in the priest a person who is always ready to defend them. Certainly he should not make this his mission, so as to be a cause of civil disturbances. Otherwise he would give the impression that he is acting out of vainglory rather than compassion. And although he is seeking healing and relief, he would cause instead grievous wounds (*Off.* 2.21.102). If a convicted man finds himself in prison because of debts, it would be good for the priest to pay them off and free him (*Off.* 1.30.148; 1.50.252; 2.15.71). As for prisoners of war who fall into the hands of barbarians, Ambrose tells his readers that the barbarians are avaricious and release their prisoners only when they have been paid a ransom. This moves him to ask: Is there any more admirable form of generosity than saving men from slaughter and women from a violence worse than death, and restoring children to their parents and citizens to their homeland? In Ambrose's time there were plenty of opportunities for showing this kind of compassion (*Off.* 2.16.70-71). In pursuing the work of almsgiving, Ambrose did not hesitate even to sell the Church's sacred vessels. Indeed, he expresses the greatest joy that these sacred vessels have been able to ransom from the hands of their enemies those whom the blood of Christ has ransomed from sin (*Off.* 2.28.136-143). The needy, especially the "ashamed poor," the sick, the imprisoned, the wretched, the debtors, the prisoners of the barbarians—all these should find help and support in the priest's person. There are other difficult situations in life which compel those oppressed by them to have recourse to the priest for aid. The priest should protect elderly people (*Off.* 1.30.158) and children. He should have a very special concern for orphans (*Off.* 2.15.71) and find dowries for young women when their parents are unable to provide for them, so that their purity should not be put in danger (*Off.* 2.15.72). Closely connected with almsgiving is the virtue of hospitality. Following Paul's precept (1 Tim 3:2; Titus 1:8) the cleric should also be hospitable (*Off.* 2.21.103-105, 107; 2.21.111). At that time, when invasions and wars were almost continuous, there were many refugees, such that there were frequent opportunities for the exercise of this virtue. Certainly the first to benefit from the Church's almsgiving should be the faithful (*Off.* 1.30.148), but this should not exclude the excommunicated if they do not have enough to live on (*Off.* 2.16.77). Finally, the priest should not forget the needy members of his own family. But he must be careful not to help them to the extent of making them wealthy. One does not dedicate oneself to God to enrich one's own family, but to become worthy of eternal life through good works (*Off.* 1.30.150).

St. Ambrose therefore wants to see in the clergy an inexhaustible willingness to give alms. But this must not lack measure or discretion. Generosity must not be confused with prodigality. One must also regulate one's generosity so that one does not exhaust one's means all at once, but has something to give to all. A concern for vainglory should never be allowed to usurp the virtue of justice. It is then easy for one to be put upon. Many pretend to be poor. They come and seek alms when they are not in distress. They are professional beggars who roam the streets. They dress in rags and conceal their real age so as to receive more. They maintain that they are in debt or have been stripped by robbers. All these claims must be carefully investigated, that the money of the poor might not be distributed to the fraudulent. In a word, the priest's generosity must steer a middle course between thoughtless prodigality and miserly avarice (*Off.* 2.16.78).

Poverty – Self-denial

The bishop, as the one chiefly responsible for the Church's philanthropic work, administered considerable sums of money. But lesser sums also passed through the hands of presbyters and other clerics in the bishop's entourage.[76] It was therefore important for them to be completely disinterested.[77] Otherwise, how could a greedy man honorably fulfill the work of philanthropy?[78] The best guarantor of disinterest is the spirit of poverty with which clerics, especially priests, must be endowed, as the Gospel teaches. If the people themselves are exhorted to despise wealth, how much more should the clergy! Christ's true minister should be able to say like Peter to the paralytic at the gate of the Temple: "Gold and silver I have none" (Acts 3:6). He should remember that the preachers of the kingdom were sent out without a staff or a bag, without sandals, or bread, or money (Matt 10:9-10). This means that he should not seek to acquire the good things of this world, but should trust in divine providence, reckoning that the less he seeks worldly goods, the more they will be put at his disposal. He should not be ashamed of his poverty, because for the priest this is a mark of glory (*Off*. 1.50.246).[79] From Paulinus's *Life of Ambrose*[80] we know that Ambrose set an example in this matter too. When he was ordained, he donated all his wealth to the Church and the poor (*Vit. Ambr*. 38).

It is a good indication of a priest's impartiality if he refuses to claim at law what he is entitled to when it is to somebody else's disadvantage, even if he is sure that judgment would be given in his favor. Apart from the fact that legal costs often exceed the amount claimed, by forgoing his rights the priest will win the respect and sympathy of all. He will be seen as a friend and promoter of peace (*Off*. 2.21.106; 3.9.59). Writing to a Bishop Marcellus, who had entered into litigation with his brother and sister over some property, St. Ambrose declares that suffering loss is more beneficial for priests than the gains of this world (*Ep*. 82.6). It is not fitting for a priest to try to vindicate himself in this way, even if he wishes to benefit the Church and the poor with what he gains (*Ep*. 82). It would be entirely contrary to the disinterest expected of him to pursue an inheritance. Such conduct is inappropriate even in a layman. What should he therefore say to those whose constant concern should be the service of all in the greatest measure possible without ever causing an injustice to anyone (*Off*. 3.9.58)? Unfortunately there were abuses and the civil authority was obliged to intervene to limit the inheritance rights of clerics. St. Ambrose expresses his regret that these measures operate to the disadvantage of the Christian clergy, while pagan priests can inherit without hindrance anything anyone cares to leave to them. "We do not reckon that there is any injury done to us," he writes, "and therefore we are not upset at the loss; we prefer to possess less rather than to be less well regarded" (*Ep.* 18.13-14).[81]

Contempt of riches is only an aspect of the ascesis, or denial of worldly satisfactions, which the priest must undertake if he is to serve God properly. St. Ambrose, who became a bishop at a time of great political unrest and had fiercely attacked the vanities of worldly life, appears very sensitive to the need to flee this world.[82] To the priests gathered around the altar he applied the saying: "Where the corpse is, there the eagles will be gathered together" (Matt 24:28), which he interpreted: "Wheresoever the body shall be, there shall the eagles also be, who are accustomed to fly so as to escape the earthly and to seek the heavenly" (*Sacr.* 1.2.6).[83] And in the Gospel parable of the wise and faithful steward, as opposed to the unfaithful and indolent one (Luke 12:41-48), Ambrose finds a severe warning to those priests who neglect the government of the people of God to devote themselves to worldly pleasures (*Exp. Luc.* 7.131). By his own excellent example, he exhorts the priests to distinguish themselves by the austerity of their lives (*Valent.* 7). Paulinus assures us that he spared himself neither vigils nor labor. He mortified the body by daily fasting. Indeed it was his custom to take no food at midday except for Saturday, Sunday, and the feasts of the more important martyrs. He prayed without ceasing during the day and also for much of the night (*Vit. Ambr.* 38). In putting forward the ideal life of one dedicated entirely to God, Ambrose appeals to the Old Testament image of the Levite. God raised up the Levites from amongst the people because he did not want to see them sharing in the ordinary activities of other men. To please God, the Levites suppress their passions and forgo the things of this world. They abandon country, parents, children, and their whole families to cleave to him alone. He who has vowed himself to the service of God must not be concerned with anything apart from God. He must devote himself unreservedly to his service. The priest must separate himself even from those who are his closest relatives and dearest friends (*Cain* 2.2.7ff.; *Fug.* 2.6-8). This of course means that he must not prefer his parents to his priestly office (*Off.* 1.50.257). He must be prepared to say with the Levite to his father and mother: "I regarded him not" (Deut 33:9). That is what St. John did when he left his father as soon as he heard Christ's call (Matt 4:21-22; *Exh. virginit.* 5.32-33). And that is also what Acholius of Thessalonica did, whom St. Ambrose praises in a letter written a little after his death. When he was still a young man, Acholius dedicated himself to the eremitical life and went to Achaia, where he enclosed himself in a small hut. While he was living there, he was informed that he had been elected to the metropolitan throne of Macedonia. His disciple and successor Anysius had also spent his youth in the desert without allowing himself to be deflected from his purpose, in spite of the insistent entreaties of his relations (*Ep.* 15.11-13; 16.3). Two influences thus come together to persuade Ambrose to include in his ideal picture of the priest the principles of both austere asceticism and the most perfect possible self-denial: the Levitical ideology of the Old Testament and ideas drawn from Eastern monasticism.[84] In spite of this, the monastic and the priestly ideals do not coincide in Ambrose's mind. The priestly life and the monastic life remain two distinct ways of living, each of which is pursued in a different manner:[85]

> The former is accustomed to being constricted and restricted, the latter to being denied and hardened. The former is like a kind of theater, the latter is practiced in seclusion. The former is exposed to public gaze, the latter is hidden. The one life is led in the world, the other in the cave. The one struggles against the profligacy of this world, the other against the desire of the flesh. The one is more outgoing, the other more reserved. The one is governed, the other is tamed. But both deny themselves so as to belong to Christ....The former, then, accepts the challenge, the latter withdraws. The former conquers seductive errors, the latter avoids them. The former is victorious over the world, the latter exiles itself from it. The former is crucified to the world and the world to it (cf. Gal 6:14), the latter does not wish to know the world. The former is subject to numerous temptations and consequently its victory is more obvious, the other rarely falls and protects itself more easily. (*Ep.* 63.71-72, 74)

In the monastic life, flight from the world is understood literally. In the priestly life it is understood metaphorically, which makes such a life more difficult and more praiseworthy.

Chastity

A basic virtue, which must shine its special light on the priest, is chastity.[86] Whether married or unmarried, the priest is exhorted by Ambrose to practice perfect continence. Some have embarked on the ministry of the altar "with bodily integrity and incorrupt modesty, without ever having entered into the bond of marriage."[87] Others have had a wife and children (*Exh. virginit.* 4.24).[88] Both, however, must emphatically deny the flesh and practice continence. This is one of the reasons why a son rarely follows his father's profession when his father is a cleric. The opposite is the case when the father follows a different profession. Continence seems a difficult burden to the young.[89] Why this demand? One would have expected that here too a comparison would be drawn between monastic and priestly spirituality. But this does not seem to be the case. Again, the influence of the Old Testament seems to be strong, as the following passage suggests. Ambrose says that a man who exercises the office of priesthood should not be defiled by sexual relations:

> I have not omitted to mention this too, because in many remote places those who exercise a ministry, even the ministry of priesthood, have children. They defend this, appealing to ancient custom, from the time in which the sacrifice was offered on different days after intervals. And even the laity observed the rule of continence for two or three days in preparation for participating in the sacrifice in purity, as we read in the Old Testament, and washed their clothes (Exod 19:10-11, 14-15). If so much reverence was demanded in the type, how much more is needed in the reality? Learn, priest and Levite, what the washing of your clothes represents: it is the presentation of your body purified for the celebration of the mysteries. While the people were forbidden to approach the sacrifice without having first washed their

clothes, you who are polluted in body and soul have
the audacity to supplicate on behalf of others, you have
the audacity to serve others. (*Off.* 1.50.249)[90]

Clearly what Ambrose is praising here is not the celibate
life or virginity but continence. Even though he regarded
virginity as an advantage in those dedicated to the
Lord through ordination, he never insisted on it for the
clergy. What he emphasizes is the avoidance by priests
of actions which lead to bodily pollution. Some appeal
to ancient custom to establish a contrary habit. But Ambrose replies that the sacrifice was not offered every day.
Moreover, in the Old Testament the people themselves
practiced continence for two or three days before the
sacrifice, to be ready for it in a state of purity. All the
more reason, then, for the priests of the true sacrifice to
be obliged to keep their bodies chaste for the celebration of the mysteries. Influenced by the Old Testament,
Ambrose regards conjugal relations as productive of a
bodily pollution that does not permit the celebration of
religious rites. Now that the sacrifice is celebrated daily,
priests must abstain from them permanently. If they are
married, this means abstinence from marital relations
(*Exh. virginit.* 4.24). If they are unmarried, Ambrose does
not explicitly forbid them to enter into marriage, without
this implying an open consent to contract the marriage
bond in the present circumstances. As a result, at least
in the West, the prohibition of marriage for unmarried
priests is regarded as a natural consequence.[91] Young
clerics in particular had to take all necessary measures
to preserve their chastity, for this is more difficult in the
young. The safest guardian of chastity is *verecundia*.[92]
This virtue is a combination of moderation, modesty,

a sense of decorum and shame. In all circumstances, clerics must maintain an attitude which is dignified and most decorous (*Off*. 1.18.71-75; 1.50.255). They will pay no attention to immoral talk and will certainly not engage in it (*Off*. 1.18.76). They will decline invitations to dinner parties, where the flow of wine encourages salacious conversation (*Off*. 1.20.86).[93] The younger clergy will not visit the homes of widows or young women, unless the visit is to do with philanthropic work. In such circumstances they must be accompanied by an older person, that is, by the bishop, or otherwise by one of the presbyters.[94] Why should they give pagans an opportunity to defame them? How many strong characters were not taken by surprise by the strength of the passions (*Off*. 1.20.87)?[95] In the Old Testament, the priests are commanded to wear a skirt to cover their nakedness when they are engaged in the service of the altar (Exod 28:42-43). Although it seems that certain celebrants of Christian worship always apply this literally, most interpret it spiritually to protect their chastity. This they succeed in doing through constant vigilance against any danger (*Off*. 1.18.80).

In connection with the theme of priestly chastity, the strict sense Ambrose gives to the impediment of digamy should be noted. Unlike St. Jerome,[96] he regards a marriage contracted before baptism as valid. Consequently, a second marriage contracted after baptism carries with it a prohibition on entering the clergy. Ambrose asks: How can someone who has twice enjoyed the companionship of marriage counsel widows to renounce marrying a second time? And what difference would there be between laypeople and priests if both were governed by the same laws? The priest must surpass the laity in his manner of life, just as he surpasses them in grace, because anyone who binds others by what he lays down should keep those rules himself (*Off.* 1.50.248; *Ep.* 63).

Humility

The Lord's ministers, especially priests, must be humble, meek, kind, and patient (*Off.* 1.20.89). They must not resemble those whose seats the Lord overturned in the Temple, who pride themselves on their status and demand the highest honors (*Enarrat. Ps.* 1.23). Nor should the grace of priesthood become a source of pride for those who have received it (*Exp. Luc.* 7.83; *Off.* 2.24.122). That is precisely why the Apostle Paul forbids the ordination of recent converts (1 Tim 3:6).[97] Even though this rule was ignored in Ambrose's own case, he emphasizes his strong personal resistance to the imposition of ordination by force.[98] Consequently, if the required humility is absent from such a priest, it is not he who is at fault but those who imposed ordination on him (*Ep.* 63). A priest should be free from all ambition. No one should be promoted to the higher grades of priesthood without diffidence or by using dishonorable means.[99] On the other hand, a cleric entirely indifferent to the immense responsibilities attendant on joining the ranks of the clergy would give a bad impression (*Off.* 2.24.119). Moreover, a priest should always be trying to the best of his ability to accomplish more than the populace. And on the subject of dispensing alms,[100] Ambrose repeats his advice to follow the rule of moderation, that priests should distribute alms in the interest of justice, not for show (*Off.* 2.16.76). They should not abandon the poor to the mercies of the powerful, naturally if this can be done without causing civil disturbance, lest they appear arrogant rather than generous (*Off.* 2.21.102). Charitable funds should not be expended without being carefully controlled "for the sake of promoting good will" (*Off.* 2.21.110). The priest should not try to appear magnanimous in front of strangers, "lest he should seek to win the goodwill of strangers to the detriment of the poor" (*Off.* 2.21.111). It is good for someone to do something which attracts praise as long as it is done without any desire to boast (*Off.* 2.24.122). The repeated condemnation of *iactantia*—boastfulness and a concern for personal advancement—encourages us to suppose that this failing was not at all rare in the readers of the *De officiis*. Priests should always bear in mind that they are disciples of a Teacher who was "gentle and lowly in heart" (Matt 11:29). Ambrose reprimands those who make the authority invested in them useless by abusing it:

> The apostles are bidden not to carry staffs in their hands, for thus Matthew thought it should be written [cf. St. Matthew 10:10]. What is a staff if not a sign of the exercise of power and an instrument for inflicting pain? Therefore, the disciples obey the precept of their humble Lord—for *in his humilation his judgement was taken away* [Isaiah 53:8]—their humble Lord, I say, through the obligations of his humiliation; for he sent them to sow the faith, not to enforce it, but to teach it, and not emphasize the force of power, but extol the dotrine of humility. (*Exp. Luc.* 7.59)[101]

The Apostle Paul threatened the Corinthians with the

rod, but did it in a spirit of love and gentleness (1 Cor 4:21; *Exp. Luc.* 7.60-61). The use of the rod should not be set aside, only its abuse. Although the first approach would have been a mark of negligence in the fulfillment of duties, the second would have given the impression of spiritual despotism (*Off.* 2.24.120).[102] For their part the laity should not be deceived. The priest's deep humility has great power, the consequences of which are immense (*Ep.* 63.58). Always following the example of the Lord, who was the embodiment of humility, the priests must make this virtue their own. Its outward expression is in the washing of feet immediately after baptism.[103] If a priest is worthy of respect, this is in no way the result of his personal virtues. It is the result of the priesthood vested in him. And if he is able to accomplish something useful, this is due entirely to the intervention of the divine power whose instrument he is. Humility is an indispensable requirement as long as he is a servant of God's grace (*Enarrat. Ps.* 38.25; *Sacr.* 1.2.7; *Exp. Ps. 118* 20.13).

Other Patristic Testimonies

Among the many other patristic testimonies from the fourth and fifth centuries, the most important are scholia on relevant passages in the New Testament. I shall deal briefly with some representative testimonies from ecclesiastical writers of the period to demonstrate the unified mind of the local churches in different regions.

John Chrysostom

John Chrysostom's treatise *Priesthood* has already been discussed at some length. Some mention, however, should also be made of his exegetical works on the Pauline Epistles. In his explanation of the passage "If anyone aspires to the office of bishop" in 1 Timothy (3:1ff.), Chrysostom gives a clear picture of the qualifications required for episcopal office. He examines the motive for desiring ordination, which should be a wish not to exercise authority but to give "support" (*Hom. 1 Tim.* 10.3). On the phrase "husband of one wife" (1 Tim 3:2), with an eye on the prevailing Jewish practice, he thinks that the Apostle was legislating "to prevent lack of moderation" (*Hom. 1 Tim.* 10.3).[104] By the term "above reproach" (1 Tim 3:2) he shows that the bishop must possess all the virtues, so that as a ruler he should be "brighter than any lamp" (*Hom. 1 Tim.* 10.3)[105] and "be leading a spotless life" (*Hom. 1 Tim.* 10.3). He will thus be a model for all who look to him to follow (*Hom. 1 Tim.* 10.3). By "temperate" (1 Tim 3:2) he emphasizes the bishop's discernment and sharpness of vision which banishes the listlessness, preoccupations, and disturbances that can cloud the mind's clarity. He must be vigilant, not only for himself but also for the flock, like an alert general inspecting his forces day and night and taking whatever measures are necessary (*Hom. 1 Tim.* 10.3). "Sensible, dignified, hospitable" are qualities that the bishop must possess in the highest degree, since they are qualities which the faithful also should possess (*Hom. 1 Tim.* 2.1). Chrysostom regards it as a fundamental qualification that the bishop be "an apt teacher" (1 Tim 3:2). "No drunkard" (1 Tim 3:3) refers to those who are impertinent and insulting. "Not violent" (1 Tim 3:3) is one who does not harm the brethren's conscience, "not one who strikes with his hands" (*Hom. 1 Tim.* 10.3).[106] The teacher of souls is a physician, and a physician is not violent toward his patients but "raises them up and heals them" (*Hom. 1 Tim.* 10.3). Chrysostom gives a beautiful reply to the question he himself poses: When speaking about a bishop's qualities, why did the Apostle Paul not say "that the bishop must be an angel, subject to no human passion…he must already have left this earth"? (*Hom. 1 Tim.* 10.3). His response is that the Apostle put it in the way he did "because very few such men could have been found, whereas many bishops were needed to preside over each city. Since it would otherwise have hindered the progress of the churches, he prescribed a limited virtue, not that sublime one which belongs above. For to be temperate, sensible, and dignified belongs to many" (*Hom. 1 Tim.* 10.3). Then he stresses that if a bishop is unable to manage his own household, it is highly unlikely that he should be able to lead the Church (*Hom. 1 Tim.* 10.3).[107] The word "neophyte" (1 Tim 3:6) means the newly catechized person who has recently received baptism (*Hom. 1 Tim.* 10.3). The phrase "well thought of by outsiders" (1 Tim 3:7) is explained by Chrysostom that in addition the candidate should have a good reputation among the enemies of the faith. This is not unattainable, since anyone who really does lead a life "above reproach" is respected even by the pagans: "truth silences even one's enemies" (*Hom. 1 Tim.* 10.3). In another exegetical homily on Titus, when commenting on the passage "and you shall appoint presbyters in every city" (Titus 1:5), he explains that this refers to bishops (*Hom. Tit.* 2.1). Finally, in the eleventh homily on

1 Timothy he says that after Paul spoke about the characteristics of bishops, "he omitted the order of presbyters and went straight on to deacons" (*Hom. 1 Tim*. 11.3). He explains that the difference between these is not great because presbyters are also appointed as teachers and leaders of the Church, and consequently what he said about bishops also applies to them. The bishops surpass them only as regards ordination (*Hom. 1 Tim*. 11.3).[108] As for the qualifications of deacons, Paul says much the same as he does for bishops, which Chrysostom explains briefly because he has already dealt with them at length in other homilies.

Gregory of Nyssa

Even though Gregory does not deal specifically with this theme, a number of testimonies can be drawn from his writings. I give a few examples. Like earlier fathers, Gregory regards the fundamental virtue and qualification for entry into the clergy as being "above reproach" (*Ep*. 17). He emphasizes that in choosing a candidate, no attention should be paid to his "ancestry" or "wealth" or "worldly standing" but, as "the apostolic word has laid down," "to aim at the best in selecting him, that the man appointed should have the appropriate leadership qualities" (*Ep*. 17). In particular, in his letter to Letoius, Gregory stresses that "nobody inquires into the candidates for the clergy to see whether they have been polluted by idolatry of this kind" (*Ep. can*. 6), meaning cupidity, or love of money, which Paul too regards as idolatry and the root of all evil (1 Tim 6:10). He also tells Letoius that even a man who has "accidentally become guilty of murder" (*Ep. can.* 5) is to be regarded as "ineligible for the grace of priesthood." And in his letter to the Church of Nicomedia he explains that he who controls "the Church's rudder," and is anxious to bring the souls sailing with him safely into God's harbor, should be an "expert helmsman" to avoid any mishap: "for how many ships have gone down with all hands through the inexperience of those guiding the Churches!" (*Ep.* 17). Finally, he emphasizes especially that a pastor who is the teacher of all must be humble in the greatest degree possible, morally restrained, moderate, eager to attain the most profit, wise about the things of God, "trained in the ways of virtue and forbearance" (*Ep.* 17).

Cyril of Alexandria

Cyril of Alexandria was a prolific author and an excellent exegete. In his exegetical work *On Worship in Spirit and in Truth* he stresses generally that the priesthood of the Old Testament was a type of the Christian priesthood (*Ador.* 11 [PG 68:728A]). He notes that the letter of the Old Testament has been abolished through the spirit, and that the Law and the prophets have been fulfilled. The worship of the Jews is continued now in a spiritual manner, for the Jewish precepts were an image and shadow of the new worship (*Ador.* 11 [PG 68:728A]). The Old Testament has influenced the shaping of the Christian tradition in an important way.[109] It forbids from approaching the altar a man who is blind, lame, with his nose mutilated, or his ears cut off, or humpbacked or bleary-eyed, or with an inflammation in his eyelids, or who has lost a testicle, or has an ulcer, or an eruption of the skin, or a deformed foot or hand, or generally has any defect (Lev 21:17-21). This tradition was also adopted by the Church, but in Christian usage a more spiritual significance is attached to these impediments. In explaining the word "blind," Cyril says it means not merely someone deprived of sight but a person handicapped because his "mind and wits are maimed" so that he cannot discern the truth (*Ador*. 12 [PG 68:785CD])... Similarly by "lame" what is emphasized is someone who shows apathy and lack of spirit in facing his duties (*Ador*. 12 [PG 68:785D]). People with mutilated noses or ears are not only physically damaged but more importantly are unable to sense the spiritual smell and sound of the divine mysteries, "and according to the most wise Paul, those with itching ears, turning them away from the truth and devoting themselves to the spirits of error, have fallen headlong into profane nonsense" (*Ador*. 12 [PG 68:788CD]).[110] Also unfit for the priesthood are the humpbacked and those with eye diseases. But "humpbacked" for Cyril means, more than the literal sense, "a person bent and looking downwards in the mind," one whose thoughts are fixed on what is earthly and carnal (*Ador*. 12 [PG 68:789B]). The spiritual sense of "bleary-eyed" is "indecent," meaning someone who is unchaste, profane, and obscene. And the spiritual sense of having "an inflammation of the eyelids" is "someone whose vision has almost completely gone" (*Ador*. 12 [PG 68:792A]). These spiritual faults are regarded as impediments of equal weight to the physical ones. If someone lacking a sensory organ is denied access to the priesthood, how much more so someone who lacks the corresponding spiritual organ. By the Old Testament expressions "uncircumcised," "foreigner," "leper," and "having a discharge" (*Ador.* 12 [PG 68:840D]),[111] Cyril understands the deeper sense as indicating that the cleric must not be "impious and unbelieving" but "pious and devout" (*Ador.* 12 [PG 68:840D]). A cleric must be the husband "of one wife" (1 Tim 3:1). And his wife, according to the law, should not be "a prostitute," "defiled," or "divorced," but irreproachable not only in body but also in spirit, that is to say, a woman who fully accepts the correct tradition of the Church's teaching (*Ador.* 12 [PG 68:812Dff.]).[112] Special emphasis is laid on the virtue of humility in clerics, which combats arrogance that provokes unseemliness, weakness, and proud thoughts: "The divine celebrant sanctified for my liturgical service should aim at humility and should not leap up to the heights. He should renounce arrogance so as not to behave in an indecent and unseemly way. For a boastful attitude gives rise to what is unseemly and indecent, and a weakness of the mind very difficult to correct" (*Ador.* 12 [PG 68:820A]). "Faith," "hope," "love," "patience," "gentleness" and "love of the poor" are described by St. Cyril as sacrifices "perfumed with a spiritual fragrance" belonging to the evangelical mode of life of those who serve God (*Ador.* 13 [PG 68:877B]). In his commentary on Joel he emphasizes "the grace of the Holy Spirit" and the faith which adorn the Church's spiritual teachers: "For it was necessary that the Church's spiritual teachers and those to be trained under the sun should have been adorned more than the others with the gift of the Holy Spirit, and, as if decorated from the outset with faith for holiness, should have been made splendid by divine and heavenly grace" (*Comm. Joel.* 2.2.34-35). Commenting on the prophet Micah, he emphasizes that the priesthood should not be a source of commercial gain (*Comm. Mich.* 3.36). Finally, a basic qualification for the priesthood, in Cyril's view, is the candidate's call from above: "No one should seek to serve God as a priest of his own accord; he should await a call" (*Ador.* 11 [PG 68:728A]). The Lord chooses and sends forth the servants of his divine mysteries: "Our Lord Jesus Christ ordained the guides and teachers of the whole world and the stewards of his divine mysteries, whom he commands to glow like lamps and shed light all around" (*Comm. Jo.* 12) according to the text: "one does not take the honor upon oneself, but one is called by God" (*Comm. Jo.* 12).[113]

Theodore of Mopsuestia

Theodore of Mopsuestia was also a notable exegete. An innovative interpreter, he followed the principles of the Antiochene school. Of particular interest to us is a fragment from his commentary on 1 Timothy. In this he gives a very clear explanation of the Pauline passage: "A bishop must be...the husband of one wife" (1 Tim 3:2). Like other fathers, Theodore regards "the husband of one wife" as one who lives with his wife chastely, as well as one who "has lived in such a way, that having divorced his first wife and legally married a second, he lives the same manner of life with her" (*Fr. 1 Tim.* 3). He therefore believes that "he should not be excluded, in accordance with Paul's legislation, from access to the episcopacy" (*Fr. 1 Tim.* 3). Theodore goes on to maintain that baptism does not make "a man who has lived with two wives…as if he had lived with one, as everybody assumes" (*Fr. 1 Tim*. 3). All the more reason that a man who has lived legally with one wife, but has become entangled with many others in a licentious manner "is not rightly admitted to the episcopate…on the grounds that he happens to have received baptism" (*Fr. 1 Tim*. 3). Theodore also emphasizes that Paul makes no mention in his pastoral epistles of subdeacons and readers because these were not regarded as degrees of priesthood: "It is worth adding that one should not wonder that neither subdeacons nor readers are mentioned; for these are outside the degrees of ministry in the Church, having developed later in response to need" (*Fr. 1 Tim*. 3).

Theodoret of Cyrus

Theodoret of Cyrus's commentaries are a rich mine of testimonies. In these he deals very clearly with the different grades of priesthood. He notes that after mentioning bishops, Paul passes directly to deacons, "omitting the presbyters" (*Comm. 1 Tim*. 3) because "these were sometimes called presbyters and sometimes bishops. Those who are now called bishops were termed apostles" (*Comm. 1 Tim*. 3). In time, however, the name "apostle" was applied "to those who were really apostles," and the name "bishop" "to those who were once called apostles" (*Comm. 1 Tim*. 3). Theodoret uses the same argument in his exegesis of Paul's Epistle to the Philippians (*Comm. Phil*. 1). He interprets the phrase "husband of one wife" more or less as Theodore of Mopsuestia does, to mean that for Paul "a man who lives chastely with one wife is worthy of episcopal ordination" (*Comm. 1 Tim.* 3). But immediately afterwards he says: "he did not forbid a second marriage, but laid down that which often happens...if a man has necessarily been separated from his first wife by death, nature compels him to marry a second time, not in a willful way but out of force of circumstances. On this basis I accept those who have interpreted the passage in this way" (*Comm. 1 Tim.* 3).[114] Paul's "dignified" is applied by Theodoret to all the cleric's activities, to his conversation, his outward dress and bearing, "that he might manifest the chastity of his soul in a bodily way too" (*Comm. 1 Tim.* 3). "An apt teacher" means not an eloquent one, but "one who is trained in the things of God and is able to recommend what is related to them" (*Comm. 1 Tim.* 3). "Neophyte" similarly means not someone young in years but someone "who has recently come to belief," who is without sufficient preliminary instruction in divine matters and has not had the necessary training in virtue, and can therefore be blinded by the passion of arrogance (*Comm. 1 Tim.* 3). In his discussion of Paul's list of qualifications for the diaconate, Theodoret stresses the same virtues (*Comm. 1 Tim.* 3).

Isidore of Pelusium

In his many letters, Isidore of Pelusium,[115] whom Photius called "our court's muse" (*Ep.* 2.44) addressed exegetical and dogmatic questions, engaged in polemics with pagan and Jewish ideas, refuted Christian heresies, and taught morality. He praised virtuous clerics and censured unworthy ones outspokenly, especially Bishop

Eusebius of Pelusium and his circle, rightly thinking that it was silence and hushing up what was evil rather than exposing it and punishing it that damaged the Church (*Ep.* 26).[116] To Eusebius Isidore emphasized that the priesthood is "awe-inspiring and difficult to attain" (*Ep.* 28)[117] and that the clergy should be primarily an example to imitate, not people who "teach one thing but do another" (*Ep.* 112). He regards the priesthood as a supreme honor, an angelic state, and forbids it "to be bought or sold for money" (*Ep.* 113).[118] He severely reprimands those who "love the priesthood unworthily" (*Ep.* 22) censuring especially those who "unworthily attain ordination by the bishop" (*Ep.* 104), for the bishop should be a type of the great shepherd, who is Christ: "For since a bishop is a type of Christ, he fulfills his work, and through his position shows everyone that he is an imitator of the great and good shepherd, put forward to bear the weaknesses of the flock" (*Ep.* 136). He severely censures priests "who live an evil life" (*Ep.* 38) and those "who are negligent about the care of the poor" (*Ep.* 44). The priest should be a "lamp" which "God lights" and "sets on a lampstand of his own light-bearing chair, to shed light in the Church" (*Ep.* 32).

Ambrosiaster

A commentary on the thirteen Pauline epistles once attributed to Ambrose of Milan is now agreed to be the work of a contemporary known as Ambrosiaster.[119] His commentaries on 1 Timothy and Titus contain a number of discussions of the qualifications required in clerics. In particular, he comments perceptively on the

phrases "husband of one wife," "not a neophyte," and
"well thought of by outsiders" (*Comm. 1 Tim.* 4.1-8) as
applied to the bishop. He then goes on to comment on
the qualifications required for deacons, "that they might
be chosen for God's ministry" (*Comm. 1 Tim.* 4.9-17).

Jerome

Finally, we shall deal briefly with testimonies drawn
from Jerome's commentary on Paul's Epistle to Titus.
After clarifying the meaning of the terms presbyter and
bishop, Jerome notes that "the presbyter and bishop
are candidates for ordination" (*Comm. Tit.* 1). In referring to and explaining the bishop's qualifications, he
compares the passage from Titus with a similar one in
1 Timothy. He considers the basic qualification for a
bishop to be Paul's requirement that he should be blameless and "without fault" (*Comm. Tit.* 1). On the phrase
"husband of one wife" St. Jerome declares that the truly
monogamous man is one who teaches monogamy and
continence by his example (*Comm. Tit.* 1). On the phrase
"not given to much wine," which Paul addresses to
Timothy to emphasize that drunkenness is licentiousness and the source of many evils, St. Jerome presents
a vivid picture of those who "vomit in order to drink,
and drink in order to vomit" (*Comm. Tit.* 1). He insists
that the qualifications Paul mentions are virtues which
must adorn every believer, and therefore must distinguish the shepherd of the faithful in a much greater
degree. In speaking of the bishop's duty of hospitality, he
reminds him that considering that everybody wants to
hear those words: "I was a stranger and you welcomed

me" (Matt 25:35), how much more the bishop, whose house should be open to all. And considering that a layman has the duty of giving hospitality, how much more the bishop, who "is inhuman if he does not receive all people" (*Comm. Tit.* 1).

Conclusion

From our examination of patristic texts of the fourth and fifth centuries it is apparent that the authors were eager to uphold the privileged position that the cleric had in the Church's structure, and at the same time to emphasize the basic qualifications expected in a candidate for ordination. All the fathers who address the subject stress above all the fundamental need of a "call from above." The candidate thus called by God receives ordination and through it is endowed with divine grace, which is a spiritual authority enabling him to fulfill his priestly duties. The exalting of the priestly office and the privileged status of the clergy, who are to be true shepherds of Christ's spiritual sheep, demands a deep sensitivity to the great responsibilities of the work to be undertaken and the capacity to achieve its goals. The cleric must be crowned with all the virtues in their fullness, and must possess religious, moral, and intellectual qualifications exceeding those of others, that he may exercise leadership "in the household of God, which is the Church of the living God" (1 Tim 3:15). Paul's exhortation to Timothy that "a bishop must be above reproach" (1 Tim 3:2) is emphasized especially by the fathers. The expression "above reproach" refers to the cleric's moral integrity. It is the most basic virtue, encapsulating many others. In the works of the fathers the virtues most emphasized are piety, chastity, humility, kindness, justice, faith, discretion, gentleness, self-denial, hospitality, love of the poor, patience, endurance, forbearance, and many others. But above all there is love for God, which is the crown of all the virtues and the chief characteristic of those who minister to God. From this springs the cleric's love for the faithful of the Christian community. He is the shepherd and the faithful are the sheep, for whom the shepherd sacrifices himself. These virtues, of course, should grace the life of every Christian who wishes to be placed "at the right hand" of the Lord when he comes "in glory" and hear him say: "Come, O blessed of my Father, inherit the kingdom prepared for you from the foundation of the world" (Matt 25:34). It is therefore obvious that as the spiritual shepherd of the faithful a cleric must be adorned with all the above virtues and in the highest degree humanly possible. In order to establish whether these virtues are present in the candidate and whether he is suitable for the assumption of priestly office, the fathers regard his detailed examination as indispensable. They require him to be "well thought of by outsiders," as a consequence of his moral probity. The testing of the candidate for some time in the lower grades of the clergy will enable the bishops to assure themselves of his quality and decide on his suitability. Many of the fathers also stress the need for the candidate to be educated. If every trade and profession, they say, demands special skills as a basis for practicing it, it is natural that special skills should be required of those undertaking the government of the Christian community. Paul, besides, in his Epistle to Timothy urges that the bishop be "an apt teacher" (1 Tim 3:2). Both a secular and an ecclesiastical education render the shepherd capable of performing his duty to teach with greater ease, especially if he is also gifted with eloquence.

As will be shown in the remainder of this study, most of the presuppositions emphasized and discussed by the fathers were taken up by the Church councils. The insistence of the councils on the chastity, the education, the testing and examination of aspirants to the priesthood is an indication of the direct influence of the relevant patristic teaching on the councils and the common interest of both fathers and councils in resolving the same issues. The councils, in defining doctrines and formulating canons, express patristic teaching, often using the phrase: "Following the holy fathers."[120]

Notes

1. The *Ecclesiastical Canons of the Holy Apostles* and the *Canons of Hippolytus* are exceptions.

2. For interpretations of 1 Tim 3:2-7 (on bishops), 1 Tim 3:8-13 (on deacons), and Titus 1:6-9 (on presbyters), see the hermeneutical works of John Chrysostom, Theodore of Mopsuestia, Theodoret of Cyrus, etc. Patristic authors and legislators frequently went to the Pauline epistles for their descriptions of the model cleric.

3. Besides Ephraim the Syrian (*On Priesthood*), Gregory of Nazianzus (*Apologia*), and John Chrysostom (*Priesthood*), patristic authors who deal with pastoral matters include Athanasius (*Letter to Dracontius*), Basil (many letters [especially *Ep.* 28], ascetic works, and a commentary of doubtful authorship on Isaiah), Gregory of Nyssa (*Letter to Letoius*),

Isidore of Pelusium (*Letters*), Cyprian (*Letters*), Ambrose (*De officiis ministrorum*), Jerome (*Epistula ad Nepotianum*), and Gregory the Great (*Liber regulae pastoralis*). See Christou 1960, 9ff.

4. For the literature on priesthood in this period, see Michel 1932, 1278-1281.

5. On his life and works see Altaner 1958, 308ff. The *Priesthood* numerical references are to page numbers in Assemani 1732-1746, vol. 3.

6. Cf. Matt 10:41.

7. Cf. John Chrysostom, *Hom. 2 Tim.* 2: "What then, you say, does God ordain all, even the unworthy? God indeed doth not ordain all, but he worketh through all, though they be themselves unworthy, that the people may be saved" (trans. *NPNF*[1] 13:481-482).

8. Cf. Balanos 1930, 233ff.; Quasten 1950-1986, 3:20ff.

9. Epiphanius, *Pan.* 68.7.

10. Foremost among the critics of the past would be Edward Gibbon, but, more recently, Barnes 1993. Barnes's portrait of Athanasius is so cynical that it caused one reviewer to describe Barnes's Athanasius as "a calculating and mendacious mastermind, who used violence, intimidation and intrigue to defeat ecclesiastical and imperial enemies" (Teeter 1994, 398-401).

11. See Brakke 1995.

12. "The crowning achievement of Athanasius's effort was to articulate an asceticism that cohered with his political goals" (Brakke 1995, 270).

13. Cf. Stephanidis 1959, 145-146, 149, 188.

14. See Mouratidis 1962, 50.

15. Ibid.

16. Cf. Mouratidis 1962, 51.

17. See Mouratidis 1962, 51.

18. See Mouratidis 1962, 52.

19. Cf. Mouratidis 1962, 52.

20. Cf. Mouratidis 1962, 52-53.

21. Cf. Mouratidis 1962, 53.

22. See Mouratidis 1962, 53; Mouratidis 1956, 41ff.

23. Cf. Phytrakis 1950, 25ff.

24. Cf. Mouratidis 1962, 54.

25. See Mouratidis 1962, 54.

26. See Mouratidis 1962, 55.

27. Cf. Mouratidis 1962, 67.

28. Cf. Mouratidis 1962, 68ff.

29. Cf. Mouratidis 1962, 68ff.

30. Cf. Mouratidis 1962, 55.

31. Cf. Mouratidis 1962, 55.

32. On his life and works, see Altaner 1958, 266ff.; Gallay 1943; McGuckin 2001.

33. See Papadopoulos 1912, 7.

34. Cf. Volk 1895; Menn 1904.

35. Other sources with information on Gregory's ordination are: *Od.* 11 (*Vit.*); *Or.* 1 and 3; Basil, *Ep.* 225. Cf. Gallay 1943, 72-74; McGuckin 2001, 107-110; Fleury 1930, 125-133.

36. St. Jerome, too, is among those who, aware of the burden of the priesthood and the duties and dangers of the office, counsel avoidance of it. In his letter to the newly ordained Paulinus he advises a life of seclusion (*Ep.* 58).

37. Cf. *Or.* 2.21; *Theol. Or.* 1.3.

38. On the persecutions generally, see Stephanidis 1959, 131ff.; Frend 1965; Lane Fox 1987, 419-492.

39. See *Or.* 2.8; *Or.* 43.58. Cf. John Chrysostom, *Sac.* 3.10; 4.1. On the clergy in the time of St. Gregory of Nazianzus and his contemporaries, see Giet 1941, 299-300; Fleury 1930, 124-125; Phytrakis 1968, 41ff.

40. Elsewhere St. Gregory, referring to the case of Eusebius, St. Basil's predecessor on the episcopal throne of Caesarea, who had been elected in the midst of popular disturbances while he was still a catechumen, complains of such *ad hoc* ordinations which no doubt occurred frequently (*Or.* 18.33; cf. *Od.* 12, in which he gives a vivid description of the situation). As bishop of Constantinople, he himself had as his successor an elderly senator, Nectarius, who was still an unbaptized neophyte when Theodosius proposed him for the vacant see: Sozomen, *Hist. eccl.* 7.8; Theodoret of Cyrus, *Hist. eccl.* 5.9. Jerome (*Ep.* 69, *To Oceanus* 9) expresses a similar opinion

when he writes that no one applies Paul's precept of 1 Tim 3:6 anymore: someone who was a catechumen yesterday becomes a *pontifex* today.

41. In *Or.* 2.16-22 St. Gregory gives many similar examples from the medical profession. This is a reminder that his brother Caesarius was a distinguished doctor at the time and exercised his profession at the imperial court.

42. On Amphilochius's relations with Gregory, see Holl 1904, 158-196; Bonis 1953; McGuckin 2001, 133-134.

43. Cf. John Chrysostom, *Hom. 2 Tim.* 2.

44. On the christocentric orientation of pastoral work, see Mouratidis 1962, esp. 96ff.

45. Cf. Matt 10:9ff.; Mark 6:8ff.; Luke 9:2ff.

46. On the calling, the sanctity, and the ministry of the priest, see Guillet 1948; Volk 1895; Menn 1905.

47. See Christou 1960, 13. Altaner (1958, 292) dates Chrysostom's *Priesthood* to 386.

48. See Christou 1960, 9.

49. Cf. Zizioulas 1965, 160-169.

50. Cf. pp. 24-26 above.

51. In his three books *Adversus oppugnatores vitae monasticae* (*Against Those Who Attack the Monastic Life*) he defends the monks and presents a picture of the monastic ideal. Cf. *Hom. 1 Tim.* 14. For Chrysostom's views on monasticism, see Heiss 1928; Stiglmayr 1929; Dumortier 1955. On monasticism generally in the fourth century, see Chitty 1966; Burton-Christie 1993; Gould 1993a.

52. Gregory of Nazianzus also mentions Paul as a model ecclesiastical pastor (*Or.* 2.51ff.).

53. Cf. Fleury 1930, 124-125; Giet 1941, 299-300.

54. See p. 120 above.

55. Cf. Isidore of Pelusium, *Ep.* 2.50. About 150 years before Chrysostom, Origen describes clerical abuses in similar terms. But convinced that the effectiveness of priestly authority depends on the personal holiness of those who exercise it (*Comm. Matt.* 12.14; *Or.* 28.8), he fiercely attacks those who do not live up to his ideal image of the cleric: *Comm. Matt.* 15.26; 16.21-22; *Hom. Ezech.* 10.1; *Hom. Num.* 22.4.

56. Cf. 1 Cor 14:34. Starting with St. Paul, the tendency to limit the role of women in the Church is often expressed very clearly. Thus Tertullian opposes the involvement of women in sacramental acts (*Bapt.* 17). In his Montanist period, he forbids women to preach in ecclesiastical assemblies, baptize, or perform any priestly duties (*Virg.* 9): " 'It is not allowed for a woman to speak in church, but also neither to teach, nor to baptize, nor to offer [sacrifice at the altar], nor to claim a share of any male function, much less of priestly office, for herself" (trans. Dunn 2004, 153). Origen takes a similar line in *Hom. Isa.* 6.3. But although Origen forbids women to preach in public, he does allow them to teach members of their own sex, especially young girls. See also *Didasc. ap.* 3.5.2: "Indeed, a widow should care for nothing else except this, to pray for those who give, and for the whole church" (trans. Vööbus, 144).

57. On the virtue of obedience, see Mouratidis 1956.

58. On relations between the laity and the clergy, see Ephraim the Syrian, *On the Priesthood*, and pp. 102-104 above.

59. Cf. Col 3:16; 4:6; 1 Thess 5:11. John Chrysostom, *Hom. Col.* 9 and 11.

60. Cf. Isidore of Pelusium (*Ep.* 2.52 and 125), where the priesthood is also exalted. Cf. also Phytrakis 1936, 14ff.

61. Chrysostom has in mind here the factions and civil disturbances that sometimes accompanied the election of bishops. To restrict the abuses to which the free participation of the laity in the election of bishops led, the Council of Laodicea laid down in Canon 13 that "the crowd should not be permitted to effect the election of those who are to be ordained to the priesthood." As Poulitsas emphasizes, "on the basis of this canon forbidding the participation of the crowd, but not of the laity as a whole, the custom prevailed that only reputable members of the laity should participate in the election of bishops" (1946, 284). Cf. Trembelas 1955, 18ff.

62. Cf. *Can. eccl.* 16, where the compiler, relying on 1 Tim 3:7, requires among other things the favorable testimony of those

outside the Church. Nevertheless, another piece of evidence a century later, together with this text of John Chrysostom, clearly reveals the beginning of the restriction of lay participation in the election of clerics. This piece of evidence comes from Athanasius, *Defense against the Arians* 30. Here Pope Julius (d. 352) protests the uncanonical election of Gregory the Cappadocian as bishop of Alexandria because the consent of the laity was not sought: "For what canon of the Church, or what apostolic tradition warrants this, that when a Church was at peace, and so many bishops were in unanimity with Athanasius the bishop of Alexandria, Gregory should be sent thither, a stranger to the city, not having been baptized there, nor known to the general body, and desired neither by presbyters, nor bishops, nor laity—that he should be appointed at Antioch, and sent to Alexandria, accompanied not by presbyters, nor by deacons of the city, nor by bishops of Egypt, but by soldiers?" (trans. *NPNF*[2] 4:115-116).

63. Cf. *Hom. 1 Tim.* 5. St. Basil also speaks about the use of short-term tactics in the election of clerics: "It also demonstrates the factious state of affairs during the sedition, that neither in concord nor in unanimity they all hurry on the selection of one able to rule them, but each seizes the first person he meets and chooses not one who is worthy, but one who is related to himself; neither one able to save, but one who is distinguished by birth" (*Enarrat. Isa.* 3.112; trans. Lipatov, 126).

64. St. Basil also deals with the president (*proestos*) as preacher of the Gospel (*Moral.* 70).

65. In Chrysostom's time preachers were highly valued.

66. Cf. Basil (*Ep.* 2) and Isidore of Pelusium (*Ep.* 3.96), where the need for preparing preachers is discussed.

67. On the beginnings of individualization, see Mouratidis 1962, 68ff.

68. Mouratidis 1962, 69. Cf. p. 117 above.

69. Cf. *Hom. 2 Tim.* 6.

70. See also Chrysostom's exegesis of this passage in *Hom. 2 Cor.* 4.3.

71. Cf. Gregory of Nazianzus, *Or.* 2.37.

72. See Altaner 1958, 343.

73. Cf. Thamin 1895, 201-217; Gryson 1968, 295-316.

74. Cf. Thamin 1895, 365-366.

75. See also *Off.* 1.30.158.

76. Cf. Stephanidis 1959, 46.

77. Cf. Achelis 1912, 1:104; Gaudemet 1958, 16ff.

78. Referring to Titus 1:7, Ambrose writes: "[T]he Apostle has provided a pattern, saying that a bishop must be blameless, and elsewhere he says: 'For a bishop must be blameless as being the steward of God, not proud, or ill-tempered, or a drinker, or a brawler, or greedy for base gain.' How can the compassion of one who distributes alms and the greed of a covetous man agree with one another?" (*Ep.* 63; trans. Beyenka, 343).

79. Cf. *Ep.* 10.2 and *Ep.* 61.3.

80. A translation of this biography by J. A. Lacy may be found in Fathers of the Church 15, 27-66.

81. Cf. *Cod. theod.* 16.2.20 of the year 370, in which women are forbidden by a rescript of the Emperor Valentinian I (addressed to Pope Damasus) to leave a legacy to a cleric. On this subject, see also Gaudemet 1958, 159, 164, n. 2, and 167. On St. Ambrose's relations with the government generally, see also Palanque 1933.

82. On the ordination of St. Ambrose, see among his works *Paen.* 2.8.72; *Off.* 1.1.4. See also Paulinus, *Vit. Ambr.* 6; Balanos 1930, 444; Palanque 1933, 1-3, 18, 484-487; Quasten 1950-1986, 4:144-145.

83. Trans. Deferrari, Fathers of the Church 44, 271.

84. Cf. Bickel 1916; Roberti 1940; Phytrakis 1945, 36ff.

85. See Chrysostom's comparison between monk and priest, pp. 129-130 above.

86. Cf. Thamin 1895, 365-366.

87. *Off.* 1.50.249: "But you are quite aware that you have this obligation to present a ministry that is blameless and beyond reproach, and undefiled by any marital intercourse, for you have received the grace of the sacred ministry with your bodies pure, with your modesty intact, and with no experience at all of marital union" (trans. Davidson, 1:261).

88. Here the preference for the celibate over the married life is very marked. For Ambrose's views on this topic, see Perini; Audet, 130-133.

89. *Off.* 1.44.218: "In the office of the church, however, you find nothing more unusual than the case of a man who follows in his father's footsteps. This is either because the severity of the work is off-putting, or because abstinence is more difficult at a treacherous age, or because the way of life appears too obscure to youth with all its energies, and so young men turn to the kind of pursuits which they believe will win them greater applause" (trans. Davidson, 1:243).

90. Cf. Cyprian, *Ep.* 55.8, where perfect continence is also proposed.

91. In the Old Testament period, the prophets fasted before their divine revelations; and when they prophesied, they abstained from marital relations. The same rule was applied by bishops and presbyters before they celebrated the Eucharist. Consequently, the custom in the West of a daily celebration of the Eucharist obliged bishops and presbyters to practice perpetual continence.

92. St. Ambrose discusses this virtue at length in *Off.* 1.17.65-1.20.89.

93. We have already noted a similar precept in the *Apostolic Tradition* of Hippolytus and the *Apostolic Constitutions* (see pp. 79-80 and 84-85 above), in which the need for vigilance at memorial meals is emphasized.

94. Cf. Carthage, Canon 38, which lays down the same precautionary measure.

95. This observation is reminiscent of Jerome's fatherly advice to Nepotianus, in which he urges him not to abandon the continence he practiced in the past: "A woman's foot should seldom or never cross the threshold of your humble lodging. To all maidens and to all Christ's virgins show the same disregard or the same affection. Do not remain under the same roof with them; do not trust your chastity in the past" (*Ep.* 52, *Ad Nepotianum* 5; trans. Wright, 203). The reason for this advice is given below: "Beware of men's suspicious thoughts, and if a tale can be invented with some probability avoid

giving the scandalmonger his opportunity" (ibid., 203-205).

96. Jerome sets out his views on the possibility of the ordination of a man who has married twice in *Ep.* 69, *To Oceanus*. In his judgment, a second marriage is not an impediment so long as the aspiring cleric who contracted it was a widower who had previously married before his baptism. Cf. Jerome's *Comm. Tit.* 1.6. Cf. also pp. 166-168 and 170 above.

97. Cf. Pontius, *Vita Cypriani* 3, where the principle of the postponement of a neophyte's ordination is upheld, in spite of the fact that it was not applied in Cyprian's own case, as his biographer informs us.

98. In his detailed refutation of Celsus's accusations, Origen emphasizes that good leaders are pressed by Christians to accept ecclesiastical office, even though because of their great humility they are reluctant to be appointed hastily: "But we know of the existence in each city of another sort of country, created by the Logos of God. And we call upon those who are competent to take office, who are sound in doctrine and life, to rule over the churches. We do not accept those who love power. But we put pressure on those who on account of their great humility are reluctant hastily to take upon themselves the common responsibility of the Church of God. And those who rule us well are those who have had to be forced to take office, being constrained by the great King who, we are convinced, is the son of God, the divine Logos. And if those who are chosen as rulers in the church rule well over God's country (I mean the Church), or if they rule in accordance with the commands of God, they do not on this account defile any of the appointed civic laws" (*Cels.* 8.75; trans. Chadwick, 510).

99. Cf. Achelis 1912, 2:11: "The model provided by Christ calls for humble conduct and friendliness in dealing with other people. It is a serious reproach against the bishop if it can be said he mounted the episcopal throne out of vainglory."

100. See pp. 148-149 above.

101. Trans. Tomkinson, 257.

102. Cf. Gregory of Nazianzus, *Or.* 2.54.

103.   Cf. *Sacr*. 3.2.4-7. No doubt here St. Ambrose was defending the liturgical practice of the Church of Milan, which retained the washing of the feet.

104.   Cf. *Hom. Tit.* 2.1.

105.   Cf. *Hom. Tit.* 2.1.

106.   Cf. *Hom. Tit.* 2.1.

107.   Cf. *Hom. Tit.* 2.1.

108.   Cf. pp. 128-129 above.

109.   See, e.g., *Can. ap.* 18.

110.   Cf. 2 Tim 4:3-4.

111.   Cf. Lev 15:1ff.

112.   Cf. Lev 21:7, 13-14.

113.   Cf. Heb 5:4.

114.   Cf. *Comm. Tit.* 1.

115.   Cf. Phytrakis 1936, 14ff.

116.   Cf. *Ep*. 30, *To Bishop Eusebius*. Cf. also Balanos, 388-389.

117.   Cf. *Ep*. 45, *To Bishop Martyrios*.

118.   Cf. *Ep*. 119, *To Bishop Eusebius*; *Ep*. 111, *To the Presbyter Zosimus*.

119.   See Balanos, 448.

120.   See Karmiris, 1:175-176, 223 and passim.

The Councils of the
Fourth and Fifth Centuries

The points we have noted in the teaching of the fathers on the qualities desirable in the clergy came to be incorporated into the canons of ecumenical and local councils.[1] These councils laid the foundations for the development of canon law. Rules that had arisen through tradition or custom came to be enshrined in established law. Although in the beginning this law was only applied locally by the bishops who had come to a common agreement, with the passage of time it became acceptable to other bishops through their participation in councils. The peculiar significance of the Church's councils lies in their preserving the purity of dogmatic teaching, their issuing pardons through court decisions, their imposing punishments on clerics, and finally their regulating Church order and governance.[2]

The qualifications examined in the previous chapter, as they appear in patristic texts of the fourth and fifth centuries, chiefly express the Church's teaching. In the present chapter we shall examine those qualifications which were officially canonized by the Church councils. The councils began in the first half of the fourth century when local synods were convened to resolve points of controversy that had arisen in dogma, administration, or

law, and to legislate for the Church.[3] No legal decisions
are preserved from the earliest local synods in the East.
By Canon 2 of the Quinisext Ecumenical Council (691),
the Eastern Church accepted the validity of the canons of
the local synods examined by the council. To these should
be added the canons of successive ecumenical councils
and the imperial legislation on Church matters.

   Considering that the canons of the Eastern Church
do not constitute a systematic body of law, but were
regulations usually produced in response to specific
historical situations,[4] I shall confine my examination of
the qualifications required for the clergy to the explicit
rulings in the sources. The important work of the precise definition of the regulations and prohibitions of the
Bible, together with their completion, was left largely
unfinished by the Orthodox Church. There are many
gaps in the sources. For some matters a canonical ruling has to be deduced from the Church's practice. For
example, on the baptismal status of those who are to be
ordained, no source of canon law says explicitly that the
ordinand's baptism is an absolutely necessary precondi-
tion. Yet this was regarded as self-evident from earliest
times.[5] In his work *On the Authority of the Priesthood*, I.
Eutaxias lists those qualifications which are "absolutely
necessary" and must be met for an ordination to be
valid.[6] But despite their importance, they are of little
concern to the ecclesiastical legislator. The Church's
practice holds that a candidate for ordination must be
male and baptized.[7] Yet with regard to those qualifications that are not "absolutely necessary," they have attracted such interest from the ecclesiastical legislative

organs that they have been the subject of much detailed canonical legislation.[8] Thus two groups of qualifications have been identified: the first concerns the validity of the ordination and contains matters so self-evident that they have not been dealt with explicitly in the written rulings; the second the legality of the ordination, and gives detailed lists of qualities that confirm the calling of the ordinand. It is this second group that will concern us in what follows.

The Council of Ancyra

The local synod held in 314 at Ancyra, the provincial capital of Galatia, was convened to heal the wounds inflicted on the Church by the last persecution of Maximinus (313) and resolve the problems that had resulted.[9]

The problem of the lapsed

One of the questions addressed by the synod was how to deal with those who, unable to endure the tortures during the persecution, had sacrificed to idols, but afterwards had repented and returned to the Church.[10] Such men were unsuitable for the priesthood because they had denied the true faith. They were apostates and their impiety was to be punished with the severest penalties of the Church.[11] Also described as apostates are those who had converted to paganism or Judaism for whatever reason. All these people, together with those who had participated in pagan customs, were to perform public penance.[12] The duration of the penance could be long or short, according to the gravity of the offense. It was precisely because of this that such people were excluded from the priesthood.

The measures imposed by the Church on clerics who had gone into heresy or schism were naturally applied with even greater severity to apostate clergy. These rules had been laid down in 256 by the Council of Carthage. According to this council, presbyters or deacons who had been ordained within the catholic Church and had then fallen into heresy or schism, or had been ordained by heretics and then repented, were to be received back as laymen.[13] Impediments to priesthood were heresy, schism, or ordination by heretics, which is why the Church imposed such a severe penalty on clerics who returned to the fold from heresy or schism. According to the order then prevailing, such clerics were no longer considered worthy, and consequently had no right to remain any longer in their office. Because of their disregard for the true faith, they had shown contempt for the essence and authority of the Church, which by endowing them with priestly authority for the spiritual good and salvation of the faithful had clearly expected an exemplary life from them. Moreover, their impiety had as a consequence the loss of many other people. It was their sacred duty not only to keep the faith pure and undefiled themselves, but to keep their brethren free from the pollution of heresy. But by embracing heresy they showed themselves unworthy servants of Christ. In so doing, they voluntarily offended against the faith that they had professed at their ordination before God and the Church. Instead of using their sacred authority for the good of the faithful and the glory of God, they abused it to the destruction of many. This was an offense which stained the priestly office.[14] They therefore no longer had any right to belong to the clerical order appointed by God to proclaim his eternal verities and lead the faithful in the way of truth.

Even those apostates who repented quickly after their fall, and resumed the struggle to defend the Christian faith against its pagan persecutors, were no longer able to return to the ranks of the clergy.[15] The Council of Ancyra permitted them to retain the honor attached to their office but forbade them completely from exercising it:

> Presbyters who have offered sacrifice and afterwards resumed the struggle, not hypocritically but sincerely, and have not planned beforehand or used subterfuges or persuasion that they may be thought to have endured torture, when it was only applied apparently and in pretense—it is decreed that these may enjoy the honor of their seat. But it shall not be lawful for them to make the offering, or to preach, or to exercise any priestly function whatsoever. (Ancyra 1)[16]

Deacons were treated more leniently, because bishops were allowed discretion in imposing a heavier or lighter punishment according to their assessment of the work offered and the deacon's conduct in the Church:

> Similarly, deacons who have sacrificed, and afterwards resumed the struggle, shall keep their other honor but shall cease from every sacred function, from bringing up the bread or the chalice and from proclaiming [the Gospel]. But if any of the bishops observe them performing some [penitential] labor or showing a profound humility and wish to add something or take something away, they shall have the authority. (Ancyra 2)

It now remains to examine the position which the synod took on those who only sacrificed or performed some other idolatrous act under compulsion. With regard to clerics, so long as after having been forced to do this they persisted in confessing their faith and devotion to Christ throughout the duration of the persecution, they were not to be dismissed from office. Even though they succumbed momentarily, they were not in a worse state than those whose faith had not been tested by torture. They therefore should be classed with the confessors.[17] On the entry into the clergy of laymen who had undergone a similar ordeal, the synod permits it on condition that their previous life was otherwise irreproachable:

> Those who fled and were arrested, or were betrayed by their servants, or have otherwise had their property confiscated, or have endured tortures, or were thrown into prison declaring that they were Christians, and were dragged about, or things were forcibly put in their hands by those compelling them, or they were made to receive some food, professing all the time that they were Christians, and have always expressed their sorrow at what had happened, by their whole sobriety, demeanor and humility of life—these, as being without sin, are not to be excluded from communion. But if they have been excluded by any, out of greater strictness, or even through the ignorance of some, they are forthwith to be admitted. This shall apply equally to the clergy and to the laity. It has also been considered whether laymen who have fallen under the same compulsion may be promoted to the clerical order. It has been decreed that these too, since they have not sinned at all, may be ordained if their former manner of life is found to have been upright. (Ancyra 3)

As the Church readmitted those who had sacrificed to the pagan gods under duress and had continuously maintained that they were Christians, how much easier it was for her to admit those who had sacrificed before their baptism. Since baptism washes away all sins committed previously to it, a man who has sacrificed before his baptism is not thereby prevented from entering the clergy: "It is decreed that those who sacrificed before baptism and subsequently were baptized may be promoted to the clerical order, since they have been cleansed" (Ancyra 12).

The Council of Neocaesarea

After the local synod of Ancyra, another was held at Neocaesarea in Pontus.[18] This synod also issued canons referring directly or indirectly to the qualifications required in candidates for the clergy. The qualifications drawn from these canons are examined in what follows.

The chastity of the clergy[19]

After the denial of the faith, the most grave sin, constituting an impediment to ordination, was the loss of chastity. The Church regarded chastity as a virtue which endows a person with moral power and substance. This virtue, when practiced out of religious conviction, is productive of an exemplary Christian life. By contrast, the moral dangers and spiritual ruin that the contrary vice brings about are catastrophic. Therefore the Church, in her vigilant concern to guard the moral integrity of her members, punishes with the severest penalties those who do not keep the virtue of chastity.[20]

Since the Church has such a strong interest in maintaining chastity in her body, it is not surprising that she has taken every care to ensure that the clergy are chosen from her best members. The absence of chastity in a cleric's life can darken his personal reputation and diminish or even destroy the standing of the clergy in the estimation of the people. St. Irenaeus typically proclaims that only in the true Church are there priests who are not only guardians of the true and pure faith, but at the same time are living examples of chastity and blameless conduct. It is these the faithful must follow, shunning those who are ruled by the passions and have put the fear of God out of their hearts, since it is the former who are the priests of the true Church (*Haer.* 4.26.2ff.). Therefore a man who after baptism has given himself over to an immoral life is regarded by the Church as unworthy to assume priestly office. Clerics who have deviated from the virtue of chastity are not only to be deposed from their priestly office, but are sometimes to be excommunicated.[21] This penalty was imposed by the Council of Neocaesarea on fornicating or adulterous presbyters: "If a presbyter...commits fornication or adultery, let him be expelled altogether and brought to penance" (Canon 1).[22] The synod is milder toward clerics who have sinned sexually before their ordination. A presbyter who after his ordination voluntarily confesses earlier sexual transgressions is forbidden only to offer the sacrifice: "If a presbyter is promoted after having committed carnal sin and confesses that he sinned before ordination, let him not offer the oblation but let him continue in his other duties because of his zeal in other respects" (Neocaesarea 9). If the person who has committed such sin was a deacon, he was demoted to a lower grade:[23] "Likewise with a deacon, if he falls into the same sin, let him have the rank of a subdeacon" (Neocaesarea 10).

It was not only the clerics themselves who had to remain undefiled by such sin, but also people with whom they came into close contact. Considering that the Church insisted strongly on an impeccable moral standard in her ministers, she could not tolerate the esteem in which they were held being endangered by their being married to a partner guilty of carnal sin. The lack of chastity in the spouse of a cleric or ordinand, both before his ordination and in some circumstances after it, was a serious impediment to the exercise of his priestly and pastoral duties. Accordingly, the Council of Neocaesarea forbade the ordination of a candidate whose wife was guilty of adultery. If she committed adultery after his ordination, his continuation in the clergy depended on his divorcing her.[24] "If the wife of a layman has committed adultery and has been clearly convicted, such a man cannot be admitted to the ministry. If she has committed adultery even after his ordination, he must divorce her, he cannot retain the ministry entrusted to him" (Neocaesarea 8). The reason for the Church's position on this matter of a person whose wife has committed adultery lies in the essential nature of the conjugal relationship. The immoral conduct of a cleric's wife could not but have an adverse effect on her husband's good standing. His good name was thus lowered in the public esteem and did not allow him to be numbered among those chosen, even though he himself had not committed any sin. If a cleric whose wife was guilty of adultery did not want to divorce her, he was also reckoned to share in some degree in her guilt. A cleric, however, was obliged to divorce his wife only if her adultery became known to the community. It appears that it was only then that a wife's adultery became a serious impediment to her husband's entering the ranks of the clergy or remaining in them.[25]

The age requirement for presbyters[26]

The synod laid down the age of thirty for a presbyter. Before that age ordination was not permitted. The grounds given for this requirement were that the Lord himself had begun his divine apostolate at that age: "Let no one be ordained presbyter before the age of thirty, even though the person is very worthy, but let him wait. For the Lord Jesus Christ was baptized in his thirtieth year, and began to teach" (Neocaesarea 11).[27] The reason why the Church laid down this age requirement was her concern that she should have in the ranks of the clergy men who possessed well-developed spiritual and moral qualities, which are not easily found in the young. Indeed, that is why St. Cyprian did not ordain a confessor called Aurelius to a rank higher than reader (*Ep.* 38).

We cannot determine with any certainty what the age requirements were for each rank of the clergy. The *Didascalia* prescribes the age of fifty for the assumption of episcopal office (2.1), while the *Ecclesiastical Canons* requires that presbyters "have attained experience in the world" (*Can. eccl.* 17). As the vagueness of this last phrase suggests, it seems that the rules relating to age were not laid down with any precision.[28] It is clearly stated in the *Didascalia* that younger men may be ordained to the episcopate, when older and more mature men are not available.[29] This concession is made with reference to the Old Testament, citing the examples of Solomon, who was only twelve when he became king of Israel, and Joash and Josiah, who were seven and eight respectively (*Didasc. ap.* 2.1.4).[30] Of course these examples were not meant to suggest that a bishop could be ordained at a similar age, but to show that relatively young men could be ordained if the circumstances required it. To be sure, the Church wished from the outset to select men, especially for the higher ranks of the clergy, who were of mature years. But since she could not make this wish an inflexible rule, she had to adapt to the prevailing conditions.

"Clinical" baptism

"Clinical" baptism refers to seriously ill people confined to bed, whether or not catechumens, who are baptized by sprinkling with an abbreviated baptismal rite.[31] Among these were many who through no fault of their own or ulterior motive received baptism on their deathbed. But there were others who deliberately put off their baptism for unworthy reasons. We learn from a letter of St. Cyprian that the word "clinics" (*klinikoi*) was used instead of "Christians" for those baptized during an illness, which gave the impression that they were second-class Christians. Cyprian rules against the term to remove any stigma from them.[32] But in spite of this, a second category of "clinics" gradually emerged who deliberately postponed baptism after the end of their period as catechumens.[33] They hoped in this way in the event of a fatal illness to receive forgiveness at the last moment through the grace of baptism. However, there were doubtless those who delayed being baptized out of a zealous concern to be as perfectly prepared as possible for their Christian rebirth in baptism. The majority, afraid through laziness or cowardice of losing the grace acquired through baptism, postponed the rite until the last moment before death. They thus hoped that at the hour of death they would be forgiven all the sins they had previously committed through "the bath of regeneration."[34]

The "clinically" baptized were barred from any grade of priesthood whatsoever. This principle was laid down by the Council of Neocaesarea in Canon 12: "If anyone is baptized during illness, he cannot be promoted to the presbyterate, for his faith has come not by free choice but by necessity" (Neocaesarea 12). The reason for this exclusion is obvious: to bar those who postponed baptism out of an ulterior motive. By such behavior they manifested the superficiality of their faith, and their lack of a self-denial essential to the pursuit of perfection. There was consequently no doubt that they were unfit to assume priestly duties. How could they have attracted others to imitate Christ when they themselves were unable to provide a personal example of imitation?

But if there was no doubt about the unworthiness of such candidates, the same could not be said of others who had accepted "clinical" baptism without any ulterior motive. With regard to these the question was put whether their decision to receive baptism was sincere. There was genuine uncertainty about their conversion, given the conditions under which it had come about. Could their faith be relied upon as secure? The decision to exclude them from the ranks of the clergy is understandable. Nevertheless, Canon 12 allows for exceptions to be made. These are, on the one hand, evidence of perseverance in a genuine Christian life and, on the other hand, the lack of suitably qualified candidates: "unless perhaps on account of subsequent zeal and faith and through the scarcity of men" (Neocaesarea 12).

The case of Novatian provides us with a historical example. He received "clinical" baptism on account of a serious illness.[35] Nevertheless, he was later ordained a presbyter, probably by Pope Fabian, in spite of the protests of the clergy and a large number of the laity "because it was not lawful for a man such as he who had been sprinkled on his bed to enter the clergy."[36] The ordination was carried out after the ordaining bishop had appealed to the clergy and laity to consent to this single case. It is inconceivable that he would have done this if he had known of any suspicious conduct in Novatian incompatible with the priesthood. Information to the contrary is later, coming from Pope Cornelius whose election Novatian had strongly opposed. But even Pope Cornelius portrays Novatian as a person from whom one would not have expected any evil.[37]

The First Ecumenical Council (Nicaea)

Convened in 325 to put an end to the Arian heresy that was troubling the Church, the First Ecumenical Council held at Nicaea also addressed questions relating to the ordination and promotion of clerics.

The ordination of eunuchs

The Mosaic law excluded from the service of the altar those who had a physical disability that could be considered unclean (Lev 21:17-23). In the early Church, among the bodily impediments that limited or prevented the exercise of ecclesiastical office, the most important were those that affected a person's physical appearance. Serious physical disabilities were a reason for exclusion from the clergy.[38] Every instance of physical defect accompanied by a corresponding external deformity was subjected to ecclesiastical scrutiny. And indeed so long as congenital or other physical defects did not affect a candidate's moral integrity or prevent him from exercising his ecclesiastical office, the Church did not exclude him from the priesthood.

Among the physical defects defined by the early Church was eunuchism. Eunuchism was an impediment to ordination because it was seen not so much as a physical defect as the result of a loathsome and sinful act. But if this act had not been carried out with the consent of the one on whom it had been inflicted, it did not exclude him from entry into the clergy. Consequently, those who had been castrated by a doctor for medical reasons, or by barbarians after having been taken prisoner, or by their master if they had been slaves were not excluded.[39] This is laid down by Canon 1 of Nicaea:

> If anyone has had an operation performed on him in sickness by doctors, or has been castrated by barbarians, let him remain among the clergy. But if anyone in good health has castrated himself, even if he is already enrolled in the clergy, he should resign, and henceforth no such person should be promoted. But as it is evident

> that this is said of those who willfully carry out the act
> and presume to castrate themselves; thus if any have
> been made eunuchs by barbarians or by their masters
> and are in other respects found to be worthy, the canon
> admits such men to the clergy.

By this enactment the synod did not introduce anything new, but simply confirmed existing tradition. The fathers of the council appeal to an existing canon. This "canon"[40] has been identified with a canonical tradition formed by ecclesiastical practice.[41] We see this ecclesiastical tradition reflected in the well-known case of Origen.[42] Taking the passage on eunuchs in Matthew (19:12) literally, he applied it to himself while still a young man. Later he was ordained a presbyter by Bishops Alexander of Jerusalem and Theoctistus of Caesarea, but was censured by his own bishop, Demetrius of Alexandria, on whose initiative a synod was held in Alexandria in 228, which judged Origen's ordination to be uncanonical. We must assume that it was cases like this that led the fathers of Nicaea to arrive at the same judgment and issue Canon 1. Origen, for example, was imitated by Valesius, whose followers constituted the Valesian heresy. Epiphanius describes the Valesians as "castrated" (apokopoi) (Pan. 58.1). We also know of a certain eunuch called Hyacinthus who was a presbyter in Rome in the time of Commodus, and another eunuch called Dorotheus who was a presbyter in Antioch at the end of the third century.[43] The frequent repetition of such instances probably contributed to the synod's adoption of Canon 1.

From Justin Martyr (1 Apol. 29) we learn of a young man who asked Felix, the prefect of Alexandria, for permission to castrate himself. He hoped in this way

to counter the pagan slander that Christians led profligate lives. The civil authority denied his request but
the Church did not. Consequently, it is difficult for us
to maintain that even without canonical enactment
the Church had been hostile to self-mutilation from
the beginning.[44] An examination of the deeper reason
for the synod's legislation leads us to concur with this
judgment. As already mentioned, the Council of Nicaea
regarded voluntary castration only as an impediment to
entry into the clergy. Earlier, however, there were different opinions as to whether this constituted a grave
impediment. According to Origen himself, those who
interpreted literally the Lord's words "eunuchs are
those who have castrated themselves for the kingdom
of heaven" (Matt 19:12) accepted the act of castration
for religious reasons as permissible (*Comm. Matt.* 15.1).
Even when after his earlier literal reading of the real
meaning of the Matthaean text, Origen turned against
voluntary castration, he judged it a "presumptuous act"
rather than a transgression to be condemned. Indeed,
Origen's own bishop, Demetrius, when informed of the
youthful Origen's self-castration, praised him for his
zeal and true faith.[45] It would appear from this that the
need to draw up the canon on eunuchism arose from
the absence until that time of any general rule, whether
written or oral, regulating the matter.

The ordination of neophytes[46]
    According to the Council of Nicaea it sometimes
happened that persons who had only recently been
baptized were promoted to the highest ranks of bishop

and presbyter. This custom was censured by the synod as against good ecclesiastical order. The first to define the position to be taken with regard to neophytes was the Apostle Paul. One of the reasons why he opposed their ordination as bishops was the fear that they would fall into the condemnation of the devil (1 Tim 3:6). What Paul wanted to guard the neophyte against was the loss of his own soul. Calling the episcopal office "a noble task" (1 Tim 3:1), Paul informs all who aspire to it that they must possess all the qualities that render them capable of exercising the office worthily. Persons are therefore required who are sufficiently experienced to be able to bear the burden of their task. He then goes on to list the negative characteristics which must be absent if the noble apostolate of the episcopal office is not to be hindered or rendered totally ineffectual (1 Tim 3:2-7). At this point we can discern another reason, doubtless more important than the first, for why a neophyte should not be ordained. Not being yet established in the faith and Christian morality, he ran the risk of backsliding, with catastrophic consequences for the souls of the faithful entrusted to him.

Although no Christian is immune from temptations, and the possibility of backsliding cannot be ruled out for anyone, the danger to the recent convert is much greater. Because as a person newly initiated into the Christian faith it was not possible for him to have sufficiently developed the spiritual means for combatting sin, there was a strong fear of his falling. In particular, with regard to the assumption of priestly duties, the question was asked: Can a person who has recently converted to the

Church from paganism, and has not yet been nourished by the spirit of humility and self-denial, put into effect as a cleric those supreme virtues that are indispensable to his calling? Besides, his necessarily limited knowledge, as a neophyte, of the deeper aspects of the Christian faith would inevitably lead to a depreciation of the clergy's standing. For this reason, the Church felt it necessary to insist firmly on preserving this apostolic injunction concerning neophytes.

Tertullian gives typical expression to the lack of confidence in neophytes. Satan is all the more enraged when he sees humanity completely freed by baptism, with his previous sovereignty collapsing and his authority nullified. That is why he battles against the neophyte using every means he has at his disposal. He attempts to assault the eyes with carnal desires, to seduce the spirit with earthly delights, or to destroy its faith through fear of the powerful of the earth (*Paen.* 7). Elsewhere, he describes with contempt the arbitrary ways of the heretics, how freed from all discipline and order they receive neophytes into the ranks of their clergy (*Praescr.* 41). And he concludes that such conduct is not tolerated in the catholic Church.[47] There the only people ordained are those who have been tested in faith and morals in such a degree that ecclesiastical office can be entrusted to them without fear.

Relying on the Pauline injunction mentioned above, Canon 2 of the Council of Nicaea categorically forbids the ordination of neophytes. Nevertheless, we learn from the same canon that "in spite of the ecclesiastical canon" neophyte bishops and presbyters had already been ordained:

Since many things have been done contrary to the ecclesiastical canon, either through necessity or otherwise
because men are impetuous, in bringing at once to the
spiritual font men who have recently come over to the
faith from a pagan life, and have been catechumens
for a very short time, and then as soon as they have
been baptized promoting them to the episcopate or the
presbyterate, it has seemed right to us that henceforth
nothing of this sort should be done. For both time is
needed for the catechumen and a longer probation after
baptism. For the apostolic rescript is clear which says:
"not a neophyte, or he may be puffed up with conceit
and fall into the snare of the devil." But if in the course
of time any carnal sin is discovered concerning the
person and he is convicted by two or three witnesses,
let him resign from the clergy. He who acts otherwise
shall imperil his clerical status as one who daringly
opposes the great Synod. (Nicaea 2)[48]

It seems, however, that this Nicene canon was not strictly
observed, for the same prohibition was repeated by the
synods of Sardica (Canon 10) and Laodicea (Canon 3).[49]
The exceptions to the general rule on the ordination of
recent converts mentioned from the first half of the third
century would have led to abuses. In the 80th Apostolic
Canon, which allows exceptions only in certain rare
cases, "unless perhaps this takes place by divine grace,"[50]
we see an attempt to legitimize them. The first exception
known to us is the famous case of Cyprian, who was
elected bishop while he was still a neophyte. His biographer, Pontius, says that Cyprian received the two grades
of presbyter and bishop at the same time.[51] Although
his background was purely pagan, he showed from the
beginning more maturity in faith than most people attain in a lifetime.[52] According to Pontius, Cyprian was

the first and perhaps the only person who showed by his example that a firm and fervent faith can sometimes substitute for a long period of probation before promotion to the ranks of the clergy.[53]

Another celebrated exception to the rule against the ordination of neophytes was that of St. Ambrose. While he was still a catechumen he heard to his surprise and consternation the shouts of the people calling for his election as their bishop. Faced with such pressure, he tried to decline, insisting on his unfitness for the post. Twice he tried to resolve the problem by flight. But finally he bowed to the enthusiastic wishes of the people, to which were added those of the Emperor Valentinian I. After receiving baptism, he was ordained bishop within eight days. This was in 374. As equally well-known as Ambrose's ordination in the West was that of Nectarius in the East. The Emperor Theodosius the Great himself recommended to the fathers of the Second Ecumenical Council the election of Nectarius to the throne of Constantinople after the resignation of St. Gregory of Nazianzus. The fathers at first demurred because Nectarius was still a catechumen, but eventually elected him unanimously.[54]

Another of the better known examples is that of Synesius of Cyrene. He was elected bishop of Ptolemais and metropolitan of Pentapolis in about 410 in spite of his protest that he lacked the necessary qualifications. But in the face of pressure from the clergy, the people, and Theophilus of Alexandria, he withdrew his objections after first laying down certain conditions. These were two: continuity in the married state with his Christian wife, and the retention of some philosophical convictions at variance with Christian dogma. In spite of these conditions, Theophilus, who valued the esteem in which he was held and his culture and goodness, bowed to the people's wishes and ordained Synesius bishop, in spite of his recent baptism and the conditions he had laid down.[55]

These examples do not exhaust the list of ordinations in exceptional circumstances. But they suffice to show that the Church consented to it only when the candidates were considered outstanding in their virtue and moral integrity.

The preliminary investigation[56]

Ordination was preceded by a careful examination of the candidate's life and fitness for office.[57] Although the details of the procedure are inadequately known, there is ample evidence that it did exist.[58] As in so many other matters where a custom is confirmed by tracing it back to Paul, so too in this case the authority of the Apostle is often invoked not only to justify its origin but also to establish the procedure itself. Paul himself not only insisted on certain necessary qualities in a bishop (1 Tim 3:2; Titus 1:7), but also counseled extreme caution to his disciple Timothy before proceeding to ordain anyone: "Do not be hasty in the laying on of hands, nor partici-pate in another man's sins" (1 Tim 5:22). Such reserve is indispensable if the unworthy are to be sifted out. In this way the bishop too is protected from participating in another's guilt.

St. Cyprian provides us with important evidence of the discipline observed in Carthage in the mid-third century. In a letter addressed to the presbyters, deacons and people of his Church he mentions, among other things, that in the ordination of clerics it was the custom that the bishop should consult the flock beforehand and with it examine very carefully the character and virtues of each candidate.[59] According to the general rule prevalent throughout the Church, the opinion of the clergy and people was sought before the election of a bishop. The same took place in the election of a presbyter. This procedure was carried out under the bishop's supervision to determine the candidate's fitness for office.[60] In the case of the ordination of the Spanish bishops Basilides and Martial, Cyprian and his African fellow bishops emphasized the need for a preliminary examination before proceeding to ordination, because the episcopal office demands men of good reputation without any blemish: "For this reason there ought to be elected to the office of bishop, with great care and after sincere examination, men who are sure to be heard by God" (*Ep.* 67). There follows a clear description of how bishops are to be chosen, with special mention of the advice of the people, who would be well-acquainted with the life of the candidates.[61] In the same letter, St. Cyprian remarks that this was the prevailing custom in most of the African dioceses. For it to have been so widespread we may safely assume that it had been the practice for some time.[62]

The fathers of Nicaea say the following about the examination that should precede admission to the clergy: "If any have been promoted presbyters without examination, or on being examined have confessed their sins, and after they have confessed, persons acting contrary to the canons have laid hands on them, these the canon does not admit. For the catholic Church defends only what is irreproachable" (Nicaea 9). This preliminary examination is regarded by the synod as a means of restricting entry into the ranks of the clergy only to those persons who have a blameless reputation.[63] Consequently, no negligence is permitted in establishing a candidate's capabilities, and any oversight constitutes a grave offense which is condemned by the Church without regard to motive. The primary reason for a careful examination is to avoid ordaining people whose previous life was unknown.[64] But the canon also contains the following safeguard: the examination would have been inadequate if no report needed to be given of its results. Otherwise its purpose would have been defeated....If, then, it resulted in a voluntary confession, or even in proof of past sins, the guilty were excluded from the priesthood. The Church explicitly repudiates such ordinations. But the canon does not reveal in any detail what sins the synod had in view. No doubt serious offenses were meant which would have demanded public penance and excluded the guilty person from the priesthood.

The document containing the fullest information on the examination of ordinands that has come down to us is St. Basil's letter to the *chorepiscopi*.[65] Written in 371, this letter was addressed to country bishops whose episcopal seats were large villages. Complaining about the lapse of ancient custom Basil writes:

It gives me great pain that the canons of the fathers have lately fallen into neglect, and that all discipline has been banished from the churches. I fear that, as this indifference proceeds, the affairs of the Church will gradually come to complete ruin. The practice that has long been followed in God's churches was to accept subdeacons for the service of the Church only after a very careful investigation. Their conduct was inquired into in every detail, to learn if they were not railers, or drunkards, or quick to quarrel, and whether they so controlled their youthful spirits as to be able to achieve that "holiness without which no man shall see God." Now while this examination was conducted by priests and deacons living with the candidates, these would then refer the matter to the *chorepiscopi*, who, after receiving the votes of those who were in the strict sense of the word witnesses, and giving notice to their bishop, then enrolled the subdeacon as a member of the sacred orders.

But now you, in the first place, thrusting me aside, and not even consenting to refer such matters to me, have arrogated to yourselves the entire authority. In the second place, becoming careless in the matter, you have allowed priests and deacons, selecting whomso-ever they pleased, without examining into their lives, through motives of partiality based either upon kinship or upon some other friendly relationship, to introduce into the Church unworthy men. Consequently, though there are many numbered as subdeacons in every vil-lage, yet there is not one worthy to conduct the service at the altar, as you yourselves testify, since you have difficulty in finding candidates at the elections.

Therefore, since I perceive that the situation is already approaching the incurable, especially now that vast numbers are forcing themselves into the subdiaconate through fear of the conscription, I have been compelled to resort to the renewal of the canons of the fathers;

and I bid you by this letter to send me the list of the subdeacons in each village, stating by whom each has been introduced, and what is his mode of life. Do you also keep the list in your own possession, so that your records may be compared with those deposited with me, and that no one may be able illegally to enter his own name at will. With this proviso, however, that if any of the names on the list have been introduced by priests after the first year of the indiction, these persons are to be cast back among the laity. Let them all be examined by you anew; and if they are worthy men, let them be accepted by your vote. Purge the Church by excluding those who are unworthy of her, and henceforth examine and accept only worthy candidates; but do not enrol these men before you have referred them to us. Otherwise rest assured that he who has been received into the subdiaconate without my approval will be still a layman. (Basil, *Ep.* 54)[66]

In this letter we have an excellent description of the procedure followed in Cappadocia in the period immediately after the First Ecumenical Council. Referring to the custom that had prevailed generally in the Church, but had been circumvented in his own time, Basil seeks to bring it back into force, at least in the diocese of Caesarea. Although he gives a detailed description of the manner in which the examination is to be conducted, he does not specify to whom this is directed. The whole procedure of examination leads us to believe that this concerned more the lower clergy, especially laymen who were seeking to enter the priesthood.[67]

According to St. Basil, the stages in the examination of candidates for the clergy are as follows: (i) The presbyters and deacons who live in the candidate's community are authorized to carry out the examination. (ii) The result of this examination is reported to the *chorepiscopus*, who also collects other evidence submitted to him. This evidence no doubt derives from those best acquainted with the candidate's life. Considering that it has been submitted by people living in small villages, it is evident that they knew him well. (iii) The bishop finally reviews the results of the examination and the testimonies that have been submitted and communicates his decision to the *chorepiscopus*. (iv) On receiving a positive response from the bishop, the *chorepiscopus* enrolls the candidate in the ranks of the clergy. Basil instructs the *chorepiscopi* to send him a list of those already serving as clergy in each village and keep a copy. On the basis, then, of the inquiry the list of clergy is drawn up. Apart from the stages of the examination of candidates, St. Basil also mentions some of the more common sins to which special attention should be paid by those conducting the inquiry. These are railing against others, drunkenness, a tendency to quarrelsomeness, and an inability to discipline their youthful indulgence (*Ep.* 54). He also mentions some unworthy motives for seeking entry into the clergy which should be the object of inquiry. These are the ordination of the ordainer's friends and relations, regardless of their suitability, and also the desire to avoid military service (*Ep.* 54).[68]

Particularly relevant here is Canon 6 of Theophilus of Alexandria on the examination of candidates for ordination. It is part of a letter adopted by the Council of Constantinople in 394:

> With regard to candidates for ordination, the prescribed form is the following: when the entire priesthood has agreed and made its choice, the bishop is to test the

candidate, and with the consent of the priesthood ordain him in the body of the church. The laity should be
present, and the bishop should address them to see if
they, too, can also testify in his favor. Ordinations are
not to be carried out in private. When the Church is at
peace, it is fitting that ordinations should be carried out
in the churches in the presence of the saints. Moreover,
candidates should be ordained in their home district,
where there are people familiar with their opinions.
They should not be ordained unless they have been
examined by truly orthodox clergy, with the bishop
himself present, who addresses the laity, who are also
present. This is to prevent any canvassing of favors
becoming a means of obtaining ordination.[69]

In a letter addressed to the bishops of Libya and
Pentapolis, Cyril of Alexandria (bishop 412 to 444) also
insists on the examination of those who offer themselves
for ordination. He writes that he has been informed by
some abbots of abuses practiced by monks. There are
some who have taken wives and, without renouncing
their conjugal rights, have gone to bishops unaware of
their domestic situation and been ordained presbyters.
Others who have been thrown out of their monasteries
because of their lack of discipline have succeeded in being ordained by some bishop, no doubt through deception. Then they have returned to their monasteries and
insisted on celebrating the sacred services. The whole
import of the letter addresses the problem of delinquent
monks. But Cyril also applies his strictures to candidate
clergy in general:

Since, therefore, as I said, all things must be done on
our part toward the edification of the people, let your
reverence look to these matters and, if anyone is about
to be ordained a cleric, let your reverence thoroughly

investigate his life, both as to whether he has a wife or not, and how and when he married her, and if he is not one of those expelled either by another God-fearing bishop, or from a monastery, then let him be ordained after he has been found blameless. Thus we will preserve both our own conscience clean and the holy and august ministry blameless. (*Ep.* 79)[70]

The Synod of Hippo (393) issued a canon for the African region which emphasized the need for investigation.[71] The Synod of Seleucia (410) did the same for the Church of Persia (Canon 16). Whatever the form of the investigation, the need to carry one out with regard to people seeking ecclesiastical office was felt very early on, so that gradually the practice became general throughout the Church.

The question of the lapsed

In contrast to Canon 2 of the local synod of Ancyra,[72] which deals with lapsed deacons leniently, Canon 10 of Nicaea demands the expulsion of the lapsed without exception: "However many of the lapsed have been ordained through the lack of knowledge or even with the full awareness of those who ordained them, this does not prejudice the Church's canon, for if they become known they shall be deposed" (Nicaea 10).

The Council of Sardica

This synod, convened in 343, adopted and confirmed the teaching of the First Ecumenical Council held in Nicaea.

The examination of the clergy[73]

Ecclesiastical legislation of the fourth and fifth centuries that imposed on the clergy a certain length of time in the lower grades as a period of probation before proceeding to the higher ones did not introduce any new custom into the Church.[74] On the contrary, it continued an unwritten tradition which began with the teaching of the Apostle Paul and culminated in the decisions of the fathers of the First Ecumenical Council. Gradual promotion within the ecclesiastical hierarchy was a suitable way of cultivating the personal development of clerics. Although the beginnings of this custom can be traced back to Paul, its practical application can nevertheless not have appeared at the outset, because the apostles originally could address themselves only to laypeople. But in the course of time, as the number of clerics grew considerably, the tendency appeared to choose people for the higher ecclesiastical offices from clerics of the lower ranks.

As already noted, Paul was the basic authority for this tradition. The principles governing this early legislation relating to the promotion of the clergy to the higher ranks are the following: (i) Neophytes are barred from the higher ranks of the clergy (cf. 1 Tim 3:6). The Apostle's precept that the danger of arrogance threatened any neophyte assuming a leadership role in the Church constituted a basic rule in selecting future bishops (Nicaea 2 and Sardica 10). (ii) A period of probation, extending throughout the lower grades of the clergy, is also imposed on future bishops (cf. 1 Tim 3:10).[75] (iii) No one should hasten to have hands laid on him, for fear that men as yet unready would thereby assume episcopal office and involve those who had ordained them in the sin (1 Tim 5:22).

As we have seen, the main authority mentioned for

the testing of the clergy is Paul. But between him and the fourth-century synods which legislated on the matter, Church organization underwent development. Of special relevance is the fact that during this period the ground was prepared for the appearance of the minor orders.

We are given further details about the gradual promotion of clerics by Cyprian. He mentions the office of reader as the first grade of the clergy. This office was preceded by a trial period during which candidates carried out the duties of a reader on probation (*Ep.* 29).[76] Cyprian himself received into the clergy those who had confessed their faith bravely during the persecutions, but initially only into the lowest rank, that of reader. Examples of such cases are those of Aurelius (*Ep.* 38), who was still a mere youth, and a certain Celerinus (*Ep.* 39.4). Cyprian says explicitly that even in exceptional cases he was following the ecclesiastical practice that was in force at least locally.[77] Elsewhere Cyprian is eager to defend the legality of the election of Cornelius as bishop of Rome also because he had canonically ascended through the grades of priesthood.[78] There are nevertheless situations in which the exercise of the intermediate grades can sometimes be omitted, when people of virtuous conduct and spiritual integrity are to be promoted to the higher grades. Thus there are occasions on which deacons have been raised to the episcopate,[79] and, more rarely, those on which laymen have been made bishops.[80] More often laymen are promoted to the office of presbyter without spending the customary period in the lower ecclesiastical grades. Classic cases of laymen promoted immediately to the office of presbyter are those of Origen, Cyprian, and Novatian.[81]

Even though the usual mode of promotion in the clergy was to remain for a while in each grade, starting with the lowest, no legal text from the first three centuries prescribing this has come down to us. The survival of this custom is therefore probably due to oral tradition. The period of the councils, whose canons regulate the life of the Church, begins mainly in the fourth century. But we cannot believe that until this period there was no official line governing matters of this kind. The Church's firm practice, reflected in the term "ecclesiastical canon" or "rule" in Canon 2 of Nicaea, clearly indicates the existence of an established guideline in the matter of the promotion of neophytes to the higher ranks of the clergy. The fathers of Nicaea reveal that the rapid promotion of neophytes was contrary to customary Church discipline, being "against the ecclesiastical rule" (Nicaea 2). We therefore have good reason to believe that until the canonical rule was formulated regulating the probation of clerics through their rising step by step through each of the lower ranks of the clergy, there was an unwritten tradition governing the matter.

The written conciliar regulation of Church practice with regard to the probation of the clergy begins in the fourth century. In the First Ecumenical Council premature ordinations are the object of frequent and severe censure. They are regarded as an abuse of apostolic precept, customary Church practice, and ecclesiastical legislation in general. The extant documents do not precisely define the duration of the clergy's probation. They simply demand a long probationary period. It is not easy to determine whether the councils were relying on a widespread custom, or whether they were concerned to leave the duration of the probationary period to the discretion of each bishop. Canon 2 of Nicaea simply says: "Time is needed for the catechumen and a longer probation after baptism."[82] Since neophytes were being promoted without the expected preparation to the higher ranks of the clergy, including the episcopate, the synod censures this abuse. But it is not content simply to censure; with the Council of Sardica it also prescribes the practice of testing clerics. Through such testing a period of learning is made available in which the cleric acquires the necessary qualifications for higher office and gives evidence of his abilities through the fulfillment of tasks allotted to him.[83] This principle is stated in Canon 10 of the Council of Sardica in the lively words of Hosius of Cordoba, one of the leading participants in the council:

And here is something else I think necessary. It should be examined in a most detailed and careful way, that if some rich man or advocate of the law courts should be wanted as bishop, he should not be appointed unless he has fulfilled the ministry of reader and deacon and presbyter, that by passing through each grade, if he is considered worthy, he should advance progressively to the culmination of the episcopate. The time to be spent in each grade should not be of short duration, so that his faith, his virtuous manner of life, his steadfastness and his forbearance can become known, and, having been considered worthy of the divine priesthood, he may enjoy this supreme honor. For it is not fitting, nor does discipline and good order allow, to embark on this rashly or lightly, so as to appoint a bishop or a priest or a deacon in a casual manner. For in this way he would be rightly considered a neophyte. Moreover, the most blessed Apostle, who also became teacher of the Gentiles, appears to have forbidden these appointments to be made hastily. For a probation of even the longest period will not easily be able to give an adequate impression of the character and mode of life of each candidate. All gave their approval and said that these rules must not be repealed. (Sardica 10)

According to this canon, the period of testing allows the candidate's moral probity to be established. The likely candidates mentioned are rich men and lawyers, who because of their social status enjoyed certain privileges which they could use to embark on an ecclesiastical career: (i) A "rich" man was one who had access to the good things of this world. This category very likely included landowners, who not infrequently oppressed the poor to increase their wealth and enlarge their estates.[84] (ii) An "advocate of the law courts" was a lawyer who had received a rhetorical and legal education fitting him for high office in the civil administration.[85] The rich man, on account of his economic power, and the lawyer, on account of his education, could as bishops support their clergy and people with greater effectiveness. As a result they were preferred by both the clergy and the laity, who had an eye on their own interests.[86]

The claim that Canon 10 rested on Pauline authority is correct. For the Apostle forbids a neophyte to be ordained a presbyter. But the appeal to his authority does not necessarily mean that the only issue was that of the ordination of neophytes. Besides the neophytes, Church members included the catechumens, on the ordination of whom the Council of Nicaea had already

pronounced,[87] and the laity. The latter, having gradu-
ated from the neophyte stage, now lived in the world as
baptized believers. Canon 10 does not make it explicit
whether it addresses candidates who are catechumens,
neophytes, or laymen. Neophytes are mentioned only
with regard to the reason for enacting the canon. The
main point is to ensure that favor is not shown to rich
men and lawyers, making it easy for them to enter the
ranks of the clergy. Because of their social status, it was
generally felt that the people's interests vis-à-vis the civil
authorities would be better served by clergy coming
from the higher social classes. Special mention is made
of them to avoid the danger of promoting them without
observing a period of probation in each of the clerical
orders. The justification given for this legislation by the
mention of Paul's prohibition does not limit the canon
only to neophytes. The named representatives of the
higher social classes could have been catechumens, neophytes, or established laymen. It appears that the canon
has in mind all three categories. Moreover, by this canon
the Council of Sardica obliges candidates to rise through
the orders of reader, deacon, and presbyter before ordination as bishops without prescribing how much time
they should spend in each grade. Advancement to the
office of bishop only came about after passing through
all the grades and devoting an appropriate number of
years to exercising the ministry proper to each. The aim
of the canon is clear: the period clerics remain in each of
the grades allows those responsible for electing a bishop
to satisfy themselves of the orthodox faith and moral
qualities of possible candidates.[88]

The Council of Laodicea

The content of the canons of the local synod of Laodicea, which dealt for the most part with administrative, moral, and liturgical matters, suggests that the synod was convened in a peaceful period for the Church. This consideration leads us to date the synod to the second half of the fourth century, between 343 and 381.[89] Many of its canons take the same line as Nicaea, but without explicit mention of the council.[90]

The ordination of neophytes

Canon 3 of Laodicea is without doubt to be included with those canons which reaffirm the position of the First Ecumenical Council. The canon briefly lays down: "It is not fit that those recently baptized should be promoted to the priestly order" (Laodicea 3). Together with Canon 10 of Sardica[91] it forms part of the Church's legislation regulating the matter of clerical probation.[92]

The education of the clergy[93]

It is obvious that the work and ministry of a cleric whose life does not conform to the true faith and Christian morality is bereft of all success.[94] Nevertheless, a virtuous life and the possession of the true faith are not sufficient in themselves for the successful pursuit of his high calling. According to his position in the hierarchy, a cleric must possess the learning indispensable for the accomplishment of his work. Certainly, greater learning is expected of the bishop than of the presbyter, who in turn must possess greater learning than the deacon.

Canon 12 of Laodicea lays down the spiritual qualities

required in a bishop as follows: "That bishops...be appointed...who are long tested both in the word of faith and in leading an upright life" (Laodicea 12). We may conclude from this that knowledge of the content of faith was an indispensable requirement at least of the bishop. Before the Council of Carthage (419)[95] there is no other mention of a demand that the clergy should be learned or what such learning should consist in. But Canon 18 of Carthage requires that "when a bishop or cleric is ordained, before they are ordained what has been laid down by the synods should be brought to their notice, that they should not regret having acted contrary to the synod's canons" (Carthage 18).

Among the qualities that should grace an aspiring bishop or presbyter, Paul mentions attachment to the teaching that has been handed down so that they may be able to instruct the faithful in sound doctrine (Titus 1:9; 2 Tim 2:2). A bishop or presbyter should be experienced above all in teaching the true faith, without this implying that the pastoral care of his spiritual children should be underestimated (Titus 2:1; 2 Tim 4:2). Moreover, even deacons should be examined not only for moral worthiness but also for their capacity to exercise their office (1 Tim 3:9-10). Apart from her concern for the spiritual development of the faithful, the Church also had to combat powerful and dangerous heresies which disturbed her, particularly from the post-apostolic period onwards. Anticipating these, Paul calls on bishops, in the person of his spiritual child, Titus, to defend the true word of the faith and hold firm to it so that they can refute those who oppose it (2 Tim 4:2-4; Titus 1:9).

To be qualified in this way, it was necessary for the clergy, whose responsibility it chiefly was to defend the orthodox faith, to be adequately prepared. Since the Bible was the heretics' chief weapon in propagating their doctrines, a thorough knowledge of Scripture was indispensable to the clergy, and particularly to bishops.[96] One of their most important duties was the preaching of the word, which presupposes the reading and study of the Bible, that they might not proclaim their own thoughts and ideas but what was taught by the Holy Spirit.[97]

A suitable education was therefore required in candidates for the clergy. In apostolic and post-apostolic periods this could have been found in Jews who had turned to Christianity after having studied with rabbinic teachers, as in Paul's case.[98] Otherwise the clergy were either autodidacts or had a Greek education. A special preparation for clerics, apart from their general culture and their introduction to the spirit of the Christian faith, was not yet needed within the simple conditions of early Church life.[99] Whenever there was need for greater education and ability, the charisms of the Holy Spirit were added, or else the bishops themselves were especially gifted or received assistance and support from others more gifted than themselves.[100] From the end of the second century, an important role in the education of the clergy was played by private schools (*didaskaleia*)[101] and eventually by the catechetical schools (of Alexandria,[102] Caesarea in Palestine,[103] Antioch,[104] etc.), even though their aim was different.[105] Nevertheless, the chief means of acquiring a relevant education remained private study, or attending the lectures of learned clerics who taught in the manner of the pagan philosophers, or indeed entering a monastery.[106] Some, such as St. Basil[107] and Gregory the Theologian, acquired a philosophical education at pagan centers of learning before studying theology. Knowledge of liturgical practices and worship was transmitted to them through participation in worship in their communities, and also through gaining experience in the lower grades of the clergy.[108]

Although the Church in the first centuries sought educated laymen for her clergy, her primary concern was to attract only those who led a moral life.[109] We learn elsewhere that if the bishop was not a learned man, at least he should be steeped in the word of God.[110] There is no lack of examples in this period of bishops who were learned and those who were not. Papias of Hierapolis is referred to as a richly cultured man with a deep knowledge of Holy Scripture (Eusebius, *Hist. eccl.* 3.36). Polycrates of Ephesus was famous for having diligently studied the whole Bible (Eusebius, *Hist. eccl.* 5.24). Peter of Alexandria was also renowned for his familiarity with Scripture (Eusebius, *Hist. eccl.* 9.6). On the other hand, Hippolytus thought ignorance of Scripture the cause of grave errors in some of the bishops of his time (*Comm. Dan.* 4.18ff.). The election, however, of craftsmen, miners, shepherds, and others to episcopal office indicates that a formal education was not considered absolutely necessary for the clergy, at least in the early period.[111] We can therefore say that for the first centuries of the Church's life the clergy relied on the favorable testimony of the people, by whom they were also elected.[112] After a brief practical training, with learning acquired especially through studying with other learned clerics, they assumed the duties of priestly office.

The good esteem of clerics

If the post-baptismal life of an aspiring cleric was the object of close scrutiny by the Church, there was even more reason for the examination of his earlier life, particularly if he had come to Christianity from paganism. To the list of sins which barred an applicant from the priesthood were added certain professions and disreputable occupations. This principle was founded on the Apostle to the Gentiles himself, who expressly requires candidates for the office of bishop and presbyter to be held in good repute by the pagans (1 Tim 3:7). There is no mention of deacons in this regard, probably because a good reputation with the pagans was regarded as an obvious requirement for all the ranks of the clergy.[113] Even conversion to Christianity could not eliminate the bad reputation of a former pagan, if he had previously practiced a trade or profession incompatible with the character of a cleric. Such a candidate could not have a fruitful ministry either among existing Christians or among formerly pagan catechumens, who would have known better than anybody else what his life had been before. Moreover, so long as the Church sought to avoid anything that would provoke contempt or lack of esteem in the pagans, she could not afford to entrust ecclesiastical office to people who did not enjoy a good reputation. For the same reason it was unwise for the Church to retain in her body already ordained clerics who had practiced trades or professions regarded by the pagans as dishonorable.[114] This prohibition is clearly expressed by Canon 36 of Laodicea: "Priests and clerics must not be magicians, or enchanters, or mathematicians, or astrologers, or makers of so-called amulets, which are snares of their own souls. And those who wear them we order to be expelled from the Church." Magic practices carried on outside the Church were condemned from the time of Simon Magus to the present day (Acts 8:8-24). Even in Old Testament times magic and sorcery were punishable by death (Exod 22:18). In his commentary on this canon, Balsamon describes magicians as those who invoke Satan for whatever reason,[115] and enchanters as casters of spells who utter incantations to draw down satanic power to further their own desires. Mathematicians are those who believe that the heavenly bodies have authority over the universe and that their movements regulate and govern the cosmos. Astrologers are those who by a demonic activity study the stars and foretell all things from them. By the phrase "makers of so-called amulets which are snares of their souls," and especially the word "amulets" (*phylakteria*)[116] we should understand superstitious charms. These amulets were various objects hung around the neck, the wearers of which believed that they were able to protect them from all hostile influences because of the magic power they contained. This pagan practice was followed by many Christians, even clerics. The Council of Laodicea therefore condemned such people.

Apart from prohibiting disreputable occupations, the Council of Laodicea issued a series of canons designed to protect the good reputation of the clergy (Canons 4, 24, 30, 54-55). He who contravened these canons was undoubtedly unable to win for the Church the appropriate respect and esteem of pagans. Besides, he became a stumbling block for Christians. Moreover, unseemly behavior in the clergy would lend support to pagan charges against Christianity, leading to the clergy being held in contempt. Consequently, so long as the Church endeavored to avoid anything that the pagans could exploit to her disadvantage, she was obliged in choosing her clergy to take cognizance of pagan prejudice against her and protect the reputation of clergy already ordained.

The Council of Carthage

This council was convened in 419 at Carthage, the metropolis of Roman Africa. The canons it issued included a series from earlier local synods held in the same region from time to time. Together they form the so-called African Code.[117]

The assumption of secular responsibilities

The less tied a person is to worldly concerns, the more he can devote himself to God's service without distraction. And the more he must communicate with the divine, the less he can afford to be distracted by worldly interests. Since it belongs to the cleric to be concerned with the service of God and the spiritual guidance of others as his unique and divine mission, all his activity must be directed toward that end. For this reason a cleric must be free from attachment to the worldly concerns that can hinder him from the perfect realization of his mission. Evidently such thoughts motivated the fathers who framed Canon 16 of the Council of Carthage: "It has likewise seemed good that bishops and presbyters and deacons should not become contractors or financial agents, or earn a living from any shameful or dishonorable trade. For they should pay heed to the text: 'No one serving God involves himself in worldly business.' "[118] By "contractors" (*eklêptoras*) is meant lessees of rented farms, by "financial agents" (*prokouratoras*) administrators or stewards, by a "shameful" trade living off the earnings of prostitutes or the like, and by a "dishonorable" trade engaging in commerce.[119]

The Church could not demand a complete detachment from worldly affairs. She had to take account of the conditions of the times. She could not, for example, ignore the obligations of a married cleric toward his family, for he had to provide for them to some extent. Clerics in fact had the right to live on the voluntary offerings of the faithful (cf. 2 Thess 3:8-9; 1 Cor 9:6ff.). But often these were insufficient for the needs of a family.[120] By force of circumstances, many clerics, like Paul himself, fell back on a means of earning a living parallel to their priestly duties (Acts 19:3; 1 Thess 2:9; 2 Thess 3:8).[121] Thus they were allowed to follow a limited number of trades and professions to gain a livelihood. But if these hindered the performance of their priestly duties, they had to be considered impermissible.[122]

Posts in the civil service were forbidden to the clergy. In the early days such posts would have been a problem for the Church, for Christians were unable to fulfill one of the basic requirements, which was to offer sacrifice to the emperor (Eusebius, *Hist. eccl.* 7.15). There was therefore all the more reason for forbidding them to clerics. Besides, posts in the civil service had altogether a pagan coloring, which was a further reason why a cleric who was presumptuous enough to accept secular office was to be deposed,[123] or a layman who accepted it was excluded from the clergy. In time, however, especially when the Christian religion, benefiting from official toleration, began to receive state privileges, Christians could participate freely in the civil government. A desire by clerics to take up state appointments probably followed. But it is not difficult to see that the involvement of the clergy in the machinery of government would have had undesirable consequences for the Church. A cleric bound in this way could not have fulfilled the demands of his office in the manner expected.[124] One of Cyprian's letters informs us of what seems to be the first official ban on clerics being appointed guardians or trustees (*Ep.* 1).[125] In all probability, this marks the beginning of the Church's prohibiting clerics to take up secular offices. An offender against this rule is threatened with excommunication.[126] The ban no doubt includes guardianship. Until the second century this was purely a family matter and came under private law. But since then guardianship had evolved into a public office under state control.[127] At any rate, it seems from Cyprian's letter that it was not easy to abolish the custom of the faithful making clerics guardians.[128] Once a guardian had been nominated, it was not possible for him by law to refuse the office.[129] However, a cleric who sought appointment to secular offices was to be deposed.[130]

Another category excluded from entry into the clergy were the *curiales*, the members of the town councils. Apart from the taxation of private property, these officials were responsible for the collection of local taxes.[131] The reason, then, for the Church's unwillingness to accept *curiales* into the ranks of the clergy was her fear of coming into conflict with the policy by which *curiales* were personally responsible for any sums they failed to collect. The Church in that case would have suffered economic damage.[132]

In 315 clerics were freed from the obligation they had until then to take up public services assigned to them.[133] But this measure put an even heavier burden on the remaining *curiales*, who then bore the whole weight of taxation. They therefore sought to become clerics themselves, not for religious motives but to escape the pressure put upon them.[134] In spite of this, the Church insisted on the ban. Such men had no right of entry into the clergy.

The Fourth Ecumenical Council (Chalcedon)

Convened in Chalcedon in 451, the Fourth Ecumenical Council issued canons dealing generally with ecclesiastical discipline and administration.

The assumption of secular responsibilities

Canon 3 of Chalcedon goes further than the Carthaginian canon[135] in regulating the matter of the assumption of secular responsibilities:

> It has come to the knowledge of the holy council that some of those enrolled in the clergy, [have] for the sake of sordid gain, become lessees of estates and apply

themselves to secular business, neglecting the service of God while they frequent the houses of secular people and, out of avarice, take on the management of property. The holy and great council has therefore ruled that in future no bishop or cleric or monk is to lease estates or involve himself in the secular administration of business, unless he is strictly required by the laws to take on the compulsory guardianship of minors or if the bishop of the city entrusts him with responsibility, out of the fear of God, for church property or orphans and destitute widows and people who especially need the help of the church....If anyone in the future attempts to transgress what has been laid down, he is to be subject to ecclesiastical penalties. (Chalcedon 3)[136]

Although Canon 16 of Carthage forbids the undertaking of secular business in general, Canon 3 of Chalcedon makes two exceptions:[137] (i) when the cleric is summoned by law to undertake the guardianship of minors; and (ii) if the bishop entrusts him with ecclesiastical matters such as the care of needy persons, orphans, and widows.[138]

Notes

1. Cf. Lafontaine 1963.
2. Hefele deals with the councils at length in the introduction to his classic work on the subject (1907-1952, volume 1). See also Schwartz 1910. For English translations of the conciliar canons see *NPNF*[2] 14, Tanner 1990, and Price and Gaddis 2005.
3. See Christophilopoulos 1954, 30-31.
4. See Eutaxias 1872, 45.
5. Regarding the problems occasioned by the Paulianists (the followers of Paul of Samosata) and their return to the catholic Church, Canon 19 of Nicaea lays down the way

they are to be received. It regards the Paulianists' baptism as invalid. If they are simply laymen, they are obliged to be rebaptized on admission to the catholic Church. If they have received ordination from heretics, they are obliged not only to be rebaptized but also to be ordained by an orthodox bishop, since heretical ordination was regarded as invalid. The only canon of the Carthaginian council of 256 also refers to the baptisms performed by heretics. It rejects such baptism, requiring those entering the catholic Church after abjuring their heresy to be rebaptized.

6. See Eutaxias 1872, 39. Cf. Milasch 1906, 361.

7. Some Orthodox scholars have questioned the permanence of the all-male priesthood on theological and historical grounds. Much of this debate has centered on the theological significance of the distinction between male and female, and on the exact nature of the female diaconate as an institution in the early Church. The most comprehensive study of this latter issue is FitzGerald 1998. More generally, a series of conferences have addressed the role of women in the Church, including a theological consultation organized by the Ecumenical Patriarchate in Rhodes in 1998 that called for the restoration of the female diaconate. For reflection on these meetings, as well as an introduction to this debate's ecumenical setting, see FitzGerald 1999; 2002; Kollontai 2000. For a collection of introductory essays on this subject written from a variety of Orthodox perspectives, see Hopko 1999. For a shorter and more recent collection of essays, see Behr-Sigel 1991 as well as Behr-Sigel and Ware 2000. Finally, for a convenient collection of primary sources and commentary, see Madigan and Osiek 2005.

8. In contrast to the "absolutely necessary" qualifications, the absence of those which are not "absolutely necessary" does not render the ordination invalid, but is a reason for deprivation of the priestly authority that has been validly transmitted. See Eutaxias 1872, 39.

9. Cf. Hefele 1907-1952, 1:219.

10. On the lapsed, see Poschmann 1940, 368-397; Kotsonis 1952, 87-93; Richert 1901, 47ff.

11. Cf. Gaudemet 1958, 621.

12. See Ancyra 4-9; Nicaea 11. On the sins which were subject to public penance, see Stephanidis 1959, 107-109; Gaudemet 1958, 674-675.

13. See Cyprian, *Ep.* 72.2, which contains the decisions of a local Carthaginian council of 256 (not to be confused with another council held in Carthage in the same year). Cf. Christophilopoulos 1954; Hefele 1907-1952, 1:118. The case is known of one of the three bishops who ordained Novatian to the episcopate, thus originating the schism bearing Novatian's name. These bishops were consequently deposed and excommunicated by the Church. After the earnest entreaties of the people, one of them repented and was received back into the Church, but only as a layman (Eusebius, *Hist. eccl.* 6.43).

14. Cyprian, *Ep.* 72.2.2-3: "What greater sin can there be, what blemish can be more disfiguring, than to have rebelled against Christ, to have scattered his Church which He bought and established with his own blood, to have been heedless of the peace and charity of the gospel, going into battle with all the fury of enmity and discord against the people of God who are of one heart and one accord? And even if they do subsequently return to the Church themselves, they still cannot restore and bring back with them those who were led astray by them and were then overtaken by death outside the Church; there they perished, deprived of peace and communion within the Church....That is why it is sufficient if pardon is granted to them on their return: in the household of faith infidelity ought to be given no advancement" (trans. Clarke, 53).

15. Peter of Alexandria, Canon 10: "That clergymen, who run themselves into persecution, and fell, though they did afterward recover themselves, and suffer torments, yet are not to be admitted to perform the sacred offices" (trans. *NPNF*[2] 14:601).

16. Cf. *Can. ap.* 62; Nicaea 10; Athanasius 3. Cyprian deals at length with the Church's attitude toward the lapsed in his *De lapsis* (14ff.).

17. Peter of Alexandria, Canon 14: "That they who endured tortures, and afterwards, when they were deprived of speech and motion, had their hands forced into the fire, to offer unholy sacrifice, be placed in the Liturgy [i.e., in the diptychs] among the confessors" (trans. *NPNF*[2] 14:601). On the confessors, see Stephanidis 1959, 86ff.

18. Although this synod is usually thought to have been held immediately after the Council of Ancyra, Hefele (1907-1952, 1:242-243) dates it somewhat later, before Nicaea, when the lapsed were fewer and the rules dealing with the problem had already evolved.

19. Cf. Lafontaine 1963, 155ff.

20. Canons 16 and 20 of Ancyra, and most of the canons of Elvira.

21. Applying the principle "you shall not take vengeance twice for the same thing" (Nah 1:9), *Apostolic Canon* 25 is against excommunicating an already deposed cleric.

22. Elvira 18 is similar: "Bishops, presbyters, and deacons, if—once placed in the ministry—they are discovered to be sexual offenders, shall not receive communion, not even at the end, because of the scandal and the heinousness of the crime" (trans. Laeuchli, 128).

23. Later, the First Ecumenical Council abolished the penalty of degradation, making it impermissible (Nicaea 9).

24. The same ordinance for the West is found in Canon 65 of Elvira: "If the wife of a cleric has committed adultery, and her husband knew of it but did not immediately throw her out, he shall not receive communion even at the end, lest it appear as though instruction in crime is coming from those who should be the model of a good life" (trans. Laeuchli, 133).

25. The demand that the spouse of an aspiring or already ordained cleric should be chaste goes back to the age of the Church's foundation. Since the Old Testament lays down precise rules for the conduct of the wives of Jewish priests (Lev 21:7, 14; Ezek 44:22), it was scarcely likely that the New Testament would fail to touch on a similar theme (1 Tim 3:11). The same rule is emphasized in *Didasc. ap.* (2.2).

26. Cf. Lafontaine 1963, 121ff.

27. Cf. Carthage 16, where it is prescribed that the deacon at his ordination should be at least twenty-five years old. A century later, the Council of Seleuceia (410) in Persia adopted the decisions of Neocaesarea and laid down the same age requirement for presbyters. See Canon 16 of Seleuceia in Chabot 1902, 269.

28. According to Gaudemet, the disparity between the legislation and its application in this matter deprives the canonical prescriptions of much of their interest (1962, 189). But there were also cases in which breaking the rules on age provoked a reaction from certain ecclesiastics, such as Bishop John of Jerusalem. He protested against the ordination of Jerome's brother Paulinian to the priesthood while he was still a youth. But Jerome defends his brother against the charge, maintaining that Paulinian was thirty years old (see *Ep.* 82, *Ad Theophilum* 8; *Comm. Ezech.* 14.47).

29. From the first century AD there are cases of exceptions to the general rule on the ordination of young men. Thus St. Paul writes to his spiritual child, Timothy: "Let no one despise your youth" (1 Tim 4:12). Nor did Ignatius hesitate to urge the Magnesians to respect their young bishop (*Magn.* 3). We also have the examples of Gregory Thaumaturgus and his brother Athenodorus, who "made such progress in divine things, that while they were both young men they were deemed worthy of the episcopate in the churches of Pontus" (Eusebius, *Hist. eccl.* 6.30). Many young bishops were likewise present at the First Ecumenical Council at Nicaea (Eusebius, *Vit. Const.* 3.9). See Achelis 1912, 2:7. Cf. Dvornik 1933, 48, n. 48, where examples are given of young clerics in the early Church, which could be invoked by those who broke the canonical rules on age.

30. Cf. 3 Kgdms 2:12 [1 Kgs 2:12], 4 Kgdms 12:1 [2 Kgs 12:1], 4 Kgdms 22:1 [2 Kgs 22:1].

31. Cf. Leclercq 1914b; Bareille 1923, 209-211; Richert 1901, 54ff.; Eutaxias 1872, 132ff.

32. Cyprian, *Ep.* 69.13: "And what is more, there are some who actually dub those who have thus obtained the grace

of God through His saving water and lawful faith 'clinics' instead of Christians. I can find no source for their use of this term....And so, insofar as it is vouchsafed to us through faith to perceive and understand the matter, my verdict is this: whosoever by the law and rights of faith has obtained within the Church the grace of God shall be judged to be a legitimate Christian. But if anyone is of the view that such people have obtained nothing on the grounds that they have only been sprinkled with the water of salvation, if they are, in fact, empty and without grace, then let them not be misled; if they recover from their serious illness and regain their health, let them be baptized. But if it is not possible for those who have already been sanctified with the baptism of the Church to be baptized, why should they lay a stumbling block before those who have acted in all good faith, reliant upon God's loving-kindness? Or is it that they are arguing that while they have indeed obtained the Lord's grace, they have gained the Holy Spirit and the gifts of God only in a smaller and lesser measure: they are certainly to be reckoned as Christians but not to be put all the same on an equal level with other Christians" (trans. Clarke, 42-43).

33. Cf. Gaudemet 1958, 57.

34. Bardy (1949, 206-207) suggests as a reason for delaying baptism the desire to complete the period of adolescence, which was the critical coming of age. Cf. Bareille 1923, 209-211.

35. Cf. Dölger 1930, 258-267.

36. Letter of Pope Cornelius (251-253) to Fabius (in Eusebius, *Hist. eccl.* 6.43).

37. Eusebius, *Hist. eccl.* 6.43: "How extraordinary a change and transformation, dear brother, we have seen take place in him in a short time."

38. The lack of legislation on this subject during the first three centuries is understandable, since they were naturally unable to perform priestly duties.

39. Cf. Eutaxias 1872, 237-238.

40. Hefele (1907-1952, 1:377) identifies this canon with *Apostolic Canons* 21-22. He regards it as not improbable that the

motive for repeating its import was provided by the notorious Arian bishop Leontius, who had castrated himself. See Socrates, *Hist. eccl.* 2.26.

41. See Funk 1891, 183.

42. See Eusebius, *Hist. eccl.* 6.8. Cf. Hefele 1907-1952, 1:377; Eutaxias 1872, 237-238.

43. On Hyacinthus, see Hippolytus, *Haer.* 9.12; and on Dorotheus, see Eusebius, *Hist. eccl.* 7.32.

44. See Hefele 1907-1952, 1:377.

45. Eusebius, *Hist. eccl.* 6.8.

46. Cf. Richert 1901, 54; Eutaxias 1872, 124ff.

47. He would surely not have mentioned this practice if it had been common in the catholic Church.

48. Cf. *Can. ap.* 80.

49. See Hefele 1907-1952, 1:378-379.

50. Some regard this canon as dependent on Nicaea 2 (see Funk 1891, 201), while others regard it simply as a later copy (see Hefele 1907-1952, 1:824, n. 5).

51. *Vit. Cypr.* 3: "Finally, with regard to God's grace there was no delay, no postponement. I have said too little; he immediately received the orders of the presbyterate and the priesthood" (trans. Müller and Deferrari, 8).

52. *Vit. Cypr.* 3: "The letters of the apostles say that neophytes should be excluded [from religious discussions], lest in their uninstructed new state they commit some offense against God, should the stupor of paganism still cling to their unconfirmed minds....Cyprian, coming from ignorant pagans, begins with as mature a faith as that with which few, perhaps, have finished" (trans. Müller and Deferrari, 7-8).

53. *Vit. Cypr.* 3: "Cyprian was the first and, I think, the only one to show that more can be accomplished by faith than by time" (trans. Müller and Deferrari, 7-8).

54. For the sources of the Nectarius affair, see Gedeon 1885, 134, n. 88; Michel 1959, 29; Hefele 1907-1952, 2:8.

55. See Evagrius Scholasticus, *Hist. eccl.* 1.16. Cf. Balanos 1961, 113; Alivizatos 1949, 74; Liebeschuetz 1986.

56. Cf. Lafontaine 1963, 103ff.

57. Cf. Achelis 1912, 2:30. St. Cyprian declares that he has

carried out an examination of the reader Saturus and the subdeacon Optatus to make sure that they had the necessary qualifications (*Ep.* 29.1.2): "You should know, therefore, that I have made Saturus a reader and Optatus, the confessor, a subdeacon. Some time ago we all agreed together to place both of them in a rank next to the clergy. In the case of Saturus, we gave him the reading several times on Easter day; and as for Optatus, when we were recently putting under careful examination readers for the teacher-presbyters we appointed him one of the readers for the teachers of catechumens. We have therefore tested whether they possessed all the qualities which ought to be present in those being prepared for clerical rank" (trans. Clarke, 25).

58. The disciples of the apostles were already subjected to "testing" (1 Tim 3:10), and the *Apostolic Tradition* of Hippolytus (*Trad. ap.* 68) and *Apostolic Constitutions* (*Const. ap.* 8.4) preserve a very ancient Christian tradition and testify to the examination of candidates by those who are to ordain them. Cf. Pheidas 1969, 44-45, 85.

59. Cyprian, *Ep.* 38.1.1: "Dearest brethren, it is our custom when we make appointments to clerical office to consult you beforehand, and in council together with you to weigh the character and qualities of each candidate" (trans. Clarke, 52).

60. According to the *Ecclesiastical Canons of the Holy Apostles,* for episcopal office it was necessary "that three chosen men be present and test [the candidate] to establish his fitness" (Canon 16), while for the office of presbyter "the bishop who has been appointed…shall appoint as presbyters those whom he has tested" (Canon 17).

61. Cyprian, *Ep.* 67.5.1: "Hence we should show sedulous care in preserving a practice which is based on divine teaching and apostolic observance, a practice which is indeed faithfully followed among us and in practically every province. And it is this: when an episcopal appointment is to be duly solemnized, all the neighboring bishops in the same province convene for the purpose along with the people for whom the leader is to be appointed; the bishop is then selected in

the presence of those people, for they are the ones who are acquainted most intimately with the way each man has lived his life and they have had the opportunity thoroughly to observe his conduct and behavior" (trans. Clarke, 24).

62. Cf. Botte 1962, 87.

63. Such an examination was found so useful that it was brought into the civil administration by the Emperor Alexander Severus (222-235), as mentioned in his biography by Aelius Lampridius. The emperor determined that the period of probation and examination of public officials should last from their appointment to their confirmation: "[W]henever Alexander desired to name any man governor of a province, or make him an officer in the army, or appoint him a procurator, that is to say, a revenue-officer, he always announced his name publicly and charged the people, in case anyone wished to bring an accusation against him, to prove it by irrefutable evidence, declaring that anyone who failed to prove his charge should suffer capital punishment. For, he used to say, it was unjust that, when Christians and Jews observed this custom in announcing the names of those who were to be ordained priests, it should not be similarly observed in the case of governors and provinces, to whose keeping were committed the fortunes and lives of men" (trans. Magie, 2:271).

64. It was to deal with such a situation that Canon 24 of the Council of Elvira forbade the ordination of persons baptized outside the diocese in which they were to serve as clerics, because their personal lives would be little known: "All those who have been baptized away from home, since their life has scarcely been examined, shall not be promoted to the clergy in foreign provinces" (trans. Laeuchli, 129). See Achelis 1912, 2:15, n. 1. Christodoulos (1896, 170) also gives other sources which have the same end in view. Commenting on the Elviran canon, W. Ülhof (1962, 9ff.) maintains that it was occasioned by the Church's concern that the suitability of the person be ensured by familiarity with the candidate's earlier life in his own diocese. Gaudemet (1962, 186) agrees, because the issue of examining aspirants to the clergy was

one reason for observing and respecting the jurisdiction of each bishop.

65. On *chorepiscopi*, see Stephanidis 1959, 98ff.; Gillmann 1903; Leclercq 1914a; Scholten 1992.

66. Trans. Deferrari, 1:343-347. Cf. Giet 1941, 300. Basil perhaps has in mind the abusive ordinations performed by Arians. Cf. *Ep.* 34; 47; 70; 92, etc. Cf. also Pheidas 1969, 136ff. The same situation caused concern to Athanasius (*H. Ar.* 3).

67. See Gaudemet 1958, 128.

68. On Basil's testimony to the clerical abuses of his time, see Giet 1941, 299ff. See also p. 175, n. 39 above.

69. Trans. Russell 2007, 86-87.

70. Trans. McEnerney, 97-98. Cf. Theophilus of Alexandria, Canon 7.

71. That is, no one was to be ordained who had not been approved either by examination of the bishops or by the testimony of the people (Canon 20).

72. See p. 187 above.

73. Cf. Lafontaine 1963, 235ff.

74. G. Le Bras (1949, 380) maintains that the requirement that clerics should advance through the minor orders and spend some time in each was formed on the model of the *ordo promotionis* of Roman jurisprudence, which lawmakers and emperors upheld strictly. Cf. *Cod. theod.* 8.7.1. But G. Dix (1947, 284) sees in this custom an administrative measure rather than evidence of an organic concept of the Church. Cf. Bihlmeyer 1951-1956, 1:108; Achelis 1912, 2:32; Croce 1948.

75. In the first two centuries this cannot refer to promotion from a grade lower than that of a deacon, for the diaconate was the lowest grade of the clergy until the beginning of the third century. Cf. Wieland 1897, 18ff.

76. Cf. Tixeront 1925, 231; Baus 1962, 394; Hess 1958, 107-108. The Council of Elvira (Canon 30) seems to mark the beginning of ecclesiastical promotion from the rank of sub-deacon.

77. This practice cannot have been followed everywhere throughout the Church in this period, for the minor orders

had not yet been created. Cf. Wieland 1897, 42ff., 52ff., 106ff., 125ff.; Gaudemet 1962, 194; 1958, 104.

78. Cyprian, *Ep.* 55.8.2: "Cornelius did not get to the episcopate by one sudden step; rather, having advanced through all the successive clerical offices and having served the Lord honorably in these services of religious administration, he reached the lofty pinnacle of the episcopacy by climbing up through every grade in the Church's ministry" (trans. Clarke, 37). Cf. Harnack 1924, 863; Achelis 1912, 2:32.

79. Eusebius, *Hist. eccl.* 7.11. Cf. *Can. eccl.* 22: "Those who have served well as deacons may also aspire to episcopal office without reproach." H. Achelis (1912, 2:419-420) mentions as deacons who were promoted to the episcopate: Eleutherus, a deacon of Anicetus of Rome; Eusebius, a deacon of Alexandria who became bishop of Laodicea; Caecilian, archdeacon and later bishop of Carthage; and Athanasius, who was elected bishop while still a deacon. Cf. Lebreton and Zeiller 1942-1949, 4:977; Gaudemet 1958, 336.

80. Eusebius, *Hist. eccl.* 6.29.

81. See, respectively, Eusebius, *Hist. eccl.* 6.8; Pontius Diaconus, *Vit. Cypr.* 3; Eusebius, *Hist. eccl.* 6.43.

82. See pp. 200-201 above.

83. The same things are prescribed by *Apostolic Canon* 80: "It is not right to ordain him bishop presently who is just come in from the Gentiles, and baptized; or from a wicked mode of life: for it is unjust that he who has not yet afforded any trial of himself should be a teacher of others, unless it anywhere happens by divine grace" (trans. *ANF* 7:505). Cf. Hess 1958, 104; Gaudemet 1958, 150.

84. Cf. Piganiol 1947, 361-364.

85. Cf. *Cod. theod.* 8.10.2 and 1.29.3, where a lawyer is called a *scholasticus*.

86. Cf. Zeiller 1938a, 429ff.

87. See pp. 200-201 above.

88. See Hess 1958, 105ff.

89. See Hefele 1907-1952, 1:746-747.

90. See Hefele 1907-1952, 1:747.

91. See pp. 214-215 above.

92. See pp. 211-216 above.

93. See Lafontaine 1963, 217ff.

94. On these qualifications see pp. 185-192 above.

95. In the West, the Council of Hippo of 393 (Canon 2) made it an indispensable requirement that clerics should know the canons. Canon 2 was later adopted by the Council of Carthage and included among the canons of the African Code (Canon 18). See Hefele 1907-1952, 2:126. In about 410 the Council of Seleucia required the knowledge of the Psalms of David by heart before becoming a subdeacon (Canon 16). This no doubt refers to a formal knowledge of the text rather than the ability to expound it. See Chabot 1902, 269. The *Statuta Ecclesiae Antiqua*, on the other hand, provide more detail on the learning required in a bishop. A private collection published pseudonymously in the West in the second half of the fifth century, the document states that he should be a man of letters, a careful exegete, instructed in the law of the Lord, and well-trained in matters of Church doctrine (Mansi 1901-1927, 3:949-950).

96. On the bishop as the bearer of the "charism of truth," see p. 54, n. 34 above.

97. Origen, *Hom. Ezech.* 2.2. In Alexandria in the fourth century the presbyters also began to preach. In Africa this custom appears with St. Augustine, who as a presbyter was invited to preach by the aged bishop of Hippo, Valerius (Possidius, *Vita Augustini* 5). See Gaudemet 1962, 192. The Council of Ancyra (Canon 1) presupposes the giving of homilies ("*homilein*") as one of the duties of presbyters. See Achelis 1912, 2:417.

98. See Probst 1873, 65.

99. According to Achelis (1912, 2:6), the Church was protected in the period of Gnosticism by the relative lack of education in the clergy. It was through the presence of mild and stable clerics that the Church was able to preserve and develop the teaching of the Christian faith.

100. Nelz 1916, 10; Bihlmeyer 1951-1956, 1:108.

101. Some scholars criticize Eusebius's account of an illustrious catechetical school at Alexandria as mere fancy and argue that the school did not take shape until the time

of Origen at the very earliest. See Broek 1995, 39-47; Wilken 1984, 15-18. Nevertheless, Annewies van den Hoek (1997) has presented a compelling case that partially vindicates Eusebius's account. In particular, she reminds us that "*didaskaleion*" does not refer only to a school building, but also to a more loosely organized tradition of instruction, or "school tradition." Thus, "*didaskaleia*" in Alexandria may have been less than fully streamlined in structure and location but still significant and longstanding.

102.   The Catechetical School of Alexandria began in the last decade of the second century and flourished until the end of the fourth century. Cf. Bihlmeyer 1951-1956, 1:107; Bardy 1937a; 1942.

103.   The School of Caesarea was founded by Origen (d. 254), but we do not know whether it was a private *didaskaleion* for a limited circle of students or a public institution.

104.   The School of Antioch, which was directed by the martyr Lucian, dated from the mid-second century to the beginning of the fourth century.

105.   Their chief aim was the study of sacred Scripture and the scholarly support of the Church's dogmatic teaching. They served the needs of interested cultured Christians in general. Hence mention can be made of the education of clerics only in relation to the education offered to all who studied in such schools. Among these students there would naturally have been clerics or aspirants to the clergy. L. Bréhier (1941, 42) regards such schools as the precursors of the foundations which would later be dedicated to the education of future clergy.

106.   See Gennadius of Heliopolis 1953, 97 and 438. Cf. Bréhier 1946-1950, 3:456.

107.   The study of ancient Greek literature was considered indispensable by St. Basil (see *To Adolescents*).

108.   See Baus 1962, 395. For the purpose of training in the minor orders, see Harnack 1924, 860-866; Jouassard 1959, 117-118. See also pp. 211-216 above.

109.   "If he has received an education, he will be able to interpret the Scriptures. But if he is uneducated, he will be

meek" (*Can. eccl.* 16).

110.   "But if it is possible, let him be instructed and able to teach: but if he does not know letters, he shall be capable and skilful in the word: and let him be advanced in years" (*Didasc. ap.* 2.1.2; Vööbus, 44). Cf. *Const. ap.* 2.1.2.

111.   See Nelz 1916, 24, n. 86 with references to sources.

112.   According to Origen, the presence of the people was required at the election of a cleric, so that all should know that he was not chosen without having been tested (*Hom. Lev.* 6.3).

113.   The *Ecclesiastical Canons of the Holy Apostles* (16) repeat this requirement for a good reputation among the pagans for bishops, but not for deacons, of whom they say simply that they should be "testified to by the multitude" (*Can. eccl.* 20).

114.   See Richert 1901, 53-54.

115.   Balsamon's commentary on Laodicea 36.

116.   On the precise meaning of this word in the New Testament (Matt 23:5) there is disagreement among the Church fathers. Chrysostom takes the *phylakteria* to be the small books containing God's wonders on behalf of Israel which the Jews held in their hands (*Hom.* 72). Epiphanius seems to be more accurate when he says that the *phylakteria* were the purple strips sewn onto their outer garment. These were thin or broad according to the social status of the wearer (*Pan.*15). See Papaevangelos 1967, 1227-1228.

117.   Cf. Hefele 1907-1952, 2:125.

118.   Cf. *Can. ap.* 7; 81; 83.

119.   Zonaras's commentary on Carthage 16.

120.   Cf. Cyprian, *Eleem.* 9ff.

121.   The historian Socrates tells us that in the first half of the fourth century the holy Cypriot bishop, Spyridon, continued out of humility to practice his earlier occupation of shepherd (*Hist. eccl.* 1.12). Similarly, in the same century, Zeno, bishop of Maiouma, wove "linen clothing" to maintain himself and help support the poor (Sozomen, *Hist. eccl.* 7.28). The clergy under St. Basil practiced various professions as a means of earning a living (Basil, *Ep.* 198.1). Moreover,

Epiphanius knew of many similar cases (*Pan.* 80.6). See Bright 1882, 156.

122.   The Council of Elvira (Canon 18) laid down rules for taking up commercial occupations with certain restrictions. The *Statuta Ecclesiae Antiqua* require a cleric to have some profession, thus making manual labor obligatory (Canons 51-3; Mansi 1901-1927, 3:955). Although agricultural work is permitted, large-scale farming for profit is forbidden (Chalcedon 3; Carthage (397) 15) as is lending capital on interest (Nicaea 17; Arles 12; Carthage (348) 13, (397) 16, (419) 16; *Can. ap.* 44; Laodicea 4). See Gaudemet 1962, 196-197; 1958, 168ff.; Jonkers 1942, 294.

123.   Paul of Samosata would have been summoned to account for his assumption of secular office, had he not already been excommunicated (Eusebius, *Hist. eccl.* 7.30). See Bright 1882, 149.

124.   Cf. 1 Tim 2:4. The ordination of former judges or state officials was forbidden because these offices were linked to practices incompatible with the priesthood. The reason for excluding judges was that they might have participated in unjust judgments or imposed the death penalty. State officials were excluded because they would necessarily have participated in idolatrous practices or attended indecent spectacles. See Gaudemet 1958, 42.

125.   Cf. Jerome, *Ep.* 52.5 and 16. St. Cyprian regards it as a sign of the Church's secularization during the long period of peace that bishops had become "administrators of worldly affairs." He censures the marked cupidity of certain bishops. See *Laps.* 6. Cf. Achelis 1912, 2:417.

126.   "The bishops who preceded us after holy deliberation on this question decreed the following salutary provisions for the future: no brother should nominate on his death one of the clergy as guardian or trustee, and should anyone do this, the offering should not be made on his behalf nor should the sacrifice be celebrated for his repose. For he does not deserve to be named at the altar of God in the prayer of the bishop seeing that he was prepared to distract away from that altar bishops and ministers of religion" (Cyprian, *Ep.* 1; trans.

Clarke, 52). Cf. Bright 1882, 149.

127.   See Sohm 1949, 535ff.

128.   As an example to the laity, Cyprian excommunicated the dying Geminius Victor, who had made a cleric his heir. See Cyprian, *Ep.* 1.

129.   See Sohm 1949, 542ff.

130.   *Can. ap.* 6 (the content of which belongs to an earlier age). See Hefele 1907-1952, 1:802, n. 1.

131.   See Gaudemet 1958, 144ff. Cf. Declareuil 1935, 50-52.

132.   See Jonkers 1942, 299ff.

133.   Constantine the Great was responsible for this concession. He expressed his unwillingness that clerics should be burdened with obligations of a secular nature which took them away from their sacred duties: "Those persons who devote the services of religion to divine worship, that is, those who are called clerics, shall be exempt from all compulsory services whatever, lest, through the sacrilegious malice of certain persons, they should be called away from divine services" (*Cod. theod.* 16.2.2; trans. Pharr, 441). In 349 Constantius renewed this order dispensing clerics from secular obligations: "All clerics must be exempt from compulsory services as decurions and from every annoyance of municipal duties" (*Cod. theod.* 16.2.9; trans. Pharr, 442). Cf. Eusebius, *Hist. eccl.* 10.7; Batiffol 1911, 226.

134.   The government took measures to counter the avoidance of unwanted state offices through entry into the clergy and forbade this tactic. See Jonkers 1942, 299ff. Later it also tried to hinder the ordination of the wealthy (*Cod. theod.* 16.2.17 and 19). The motive for this action was fear that resources would be absorbed by the Church rather than the *curia*. See Gaudemet 1962, 196; 1958, 144.

135.   See pp. 223-224 above.

136.   Trans. Price and Gaddis 2005, 3:94-95. Cf. Canon 7 of the same council, which expands Canon 3. Canon 7 refers to the assumption of administrative positions in the "army" (*strateia*). A cleric who acquires such office or assumes any kind of civic dignity in general is anathematized by this

canon. Cf. *Can. ap.* 83 and the commentary on these canons by the canonists Zonaras and Balsamon.

137.   Cf. Gaudemet 1958, 169-170.

138.   On the premise that the trade would supply adequate means for the maintenance of a cleric and the support of his charitable works, state legislation facilitated the clergy's participation in such activity by remitting the "gold and silver" tax which was levied on merchants (*Cod. theod.* 16.2.8 (343), 14 (357), 15 (360), 16 (401). This privilege was finally withdrawn from the clergy, the Eastern Emperor Arcadius obliging them in 399 to choose between a commercial or an ecclesiastical career (*Cod. theod.* 13.1.16), and the Western Emperor Valentinian III in 452 abrogating entirely the exemption from taxation of clergy engaged in commerce (*Novels* 35.4). See Gaudemet 1962, 197-198; 1958, 170-172.

The Marriage of the Clergy and Relevant Legislation

The Christian View of Celibacy

In the Bible the first appearance of humanity is as a human couple (Gen 2:18-24). By his presence the Lord blessed the marriage at Cana in Galilee (John 2:1-11), sanctifying this natural institution and rendering it sacred, legitimate, and at the same time indissoluble. But in spite of this the Lord opens up another path, the higher path of celibacy, not only permitting it, but exalting the celibate life and advocating it. He teaches explicitly that this life is a privilege only for the few, for those who are able to receive it: "Not all men can receive this precept, but only those to whom it has been given. For there are eunuchs who have been so from birth, and there are eunuchs who have been made eunuchs by men, and there are eunuchs who have made themselves eunuchs for the sake of the kingdom of heaven. He who is able to receive this, let him receive it" (Matt 19:11-12). By these words the Lord does not mean the physically mutilated, either naturally or by human intervention, but those who by a firm and irrevocable decision have suppressed their own urges by the indwelling of divine grace and remained celibate. We understand by this that celibacy is a charism, a special gift of God granted only to certain people, which is why celibacy is considered higher than marriage and superior to conjugal life.

The Apostle Paul, being himself celibate, developed a detailed teaching on marriage but also stressed the value of celibacy. Although during the foundation of the Church of the Gentiles by Paul and his collaborators there was never any question of forbidding the institution of marriage, there is nevertheless in some of his teachings a definite tendency towards asceticism.[1] He clearly proclaims that "it is well for a man not to touch a woman," that for the unmarried and widows "it is well for them to remain single" as he is, and yet because of the danger of carnal passion, that is, to protect themselves from sexual sins, it is better that they should marry (1 Cor 7:1-2, 8-9). He urges them to marry if they cannot otherwise exercise self-control, "for it is better to marry than be aflame with passion" (1 Cor 7:9). He also emphasizes that "he who marries does well, but he who refrains from marriage does better" (1 Cor 7:38). By bearing children a woman can be saved from the consequences of Eve's transgression (1 Tim 2:14-15). And to avoid any misunderstanding he adds explicitly that "the unmarried man is anxious about the affairs of the Lord, how to please the Lord; but the married man is anxious about worldly affairs, how to please his wife" (1 Cor 7:32-34). In giving his reasons for this preference he says: "I say this for your own benefit, not to lay any restraint upon you, but to promote good order and to secure your undivided devotion to the Lord" (1 Cor 7:35). Paul's interest in the subject of marriage and celibacy shows that a strong ascetic movement had already emerged.[2] This raised questions that would not have been easy to answer without, on the one hand, dampening the ardor of useful disciples, and, on the other hand, imposing difficult burdens on recent converts. Paul no doubt feared that the former would quickly go beyond the bounds of what was reasonable. He therefore condemned the heresies which forbade marriage (1 Tim 4:3), but it was already the case that certain believers had tendencies in that direction. In this period few would have joined the new religion if they had not regarded the things of this world as inferior to the inestimable treasures of paradise. Besides, the more the believers were fired with religious ardor, the more they sought to express it in the mortification of the body and the passions, and in the renunciation of worldly goods. Thus the tendency of the stronger was given prominence, while the admiration of the populace for their higher virtue and strength endowed them with a reputation for sanctity which was able to influence other people.[3]

Although the ideal of virginity received support from the Savior and the Apostle to the Gentiles, it is nevertheless strange how exalted and praised it came to be by Church writers immediately after the apostolic age. Athanasius the Great says that the Savior "granted virginity as well as everything else as an image of angelic holiness for us to have on earth" (*Apol. Const.* 33). In his work *On the Praise of Virginity* Gregory the Theologian regards virginity as God-given, "a noble gift, brighter than gold, or electrum, or ivory" (*Od.* 1, *Virg.* 3-4) and proclaims the Holy Trinity as the first virgin. In his funerary oration on Basil the Great, he praises the great teacher and archbishop of Caesarea because nobody else "honored virginity more than he, or laid down laws for the flesh, not only by his own example, but in what he studied" (*Or. Bas.* 62). John Chrysostom maintains in his preaching on virginity that it is superior to marriage "as heaven is higher than earth, or angels superior to men." For "it makes those dwelling on earth live the same kind of life as those living in heaven. It does not let those who are clothed in bodies be left behind the incorporeal powers, but though they are men leads them to the same zeal as the angels." And with rising fervor he asks: "What is more pleasant, or more beautiful, or more luminous than virginity? For it emits a radiance brighter than the sun's rays, detaching us from all ordinary things in life, and enabling us to gaze directly with the naked eye at the sun of righteousness" (*Virg.* 10, 11, 21). Also worth noting is Gregory of Nyssa's vigorous praise of virginity, although he himself was a married man. He believed that the only adequate way to praise virginity was to manifest it personally, since this virtue was beyond praise (*Virg.* 1). Similar testimonies to the supreme value of virginity may be found in many other ecclesiastical writers.

The presuppositions of Christian celibacy, or virginity, were considered to be the following: (i) the personal choice of celibacy in absolute freedom without its being imposed by others;[4] (ii) complete devotion to the Lord "for the sake of studying the law," as Ignatius of Antioch says (*Phld.* 4); and (iii) the virtue of humility (*Pol.* 5.2). To these may be added perfect and absolute love for God, as Clement of Alexandria says.[5]

From these considerations it would appear that from the very beginning of Christianity the celibate life was established in the Church as a highly valued institution destined to endure with her for all eternity.[6]

Both the Church's teaching and her relations with the pagan environment contributed to shaping and establishing these ascetic tendencies.[7] Many early Christian writers felt that the surrounding culture was immoral and profligate, but the Christians were not alone in their assessment. Pagan philosophers had been making many of the same criticisms for centuries. Self-discipline, frugal living, and freedom from emotional attachments were common motifs in various pagan philosophical schools.[8] In fact, the first-century Stoic philosopher Epictetus even called on mankind to engage in *askesis*.[9] Of course, such clarion calls were not always heeded, and Christian writers found ample reason to emphasize the moral life. It is worth noting that in the New Testament the avoidance of adultery is given special emphasis, especially when Christianity began to spread beyond the narrow boundaries of Judea. The first Christians appear as an ascetic community, explicitly applying injunctions to daily life.[10] Their conduct bore permanent witness against a licentiousness perceived to predominate in society.[11] It was therefore natural that proselytes should have gone to the opposite extreme, regarding even legitimate and natural instincts as illicit and liable to condemnation. In spite of occasional exaggerations, civilization owes much to the moral reformation which Christianity brought to human life.

The imposition of the Church's will in matters concerning the chastity of the clergy was not achieved without difficulty. The practice of virtue admittedly comes up against innate difficulties arising from the weakness of human nature (cf. Rom 7:14-23). The Apostle Paul shows cognizance of this when he requires that bishops and deacons be husbands of only one wife (1 Tim 3:2, 12; Titus 1:6).[12] His exhortation marks the beginning of a long legislative tradition concerning the marriage of the clergy. This tradition reached its climax in the East at the Quinisext Ecumenical Council, the Council in Trullo (692), which officially adopted earlier Justinianian legislation[13] forbidding the election and ordination of married clerics to episcopal office (Quinisext 48). During its long history, the legislation restricting the marriage of clerics naturally encountered opposition. Yet through gradual imposition it has endured to the present day.

By the famous edict of Galerius, Licinius, and Constantine (312), as well as the decisions of Milan (313), the persecution of Christianity was ended and the era of toleration was inaugurated, though Christianity was not yet recognized as the official religion of the empire.[14] A consequence was that the Church from that time became linked to the state and inevitably came into closer relationship with the world. This contact between the Church and the world, the end of persecution, and the large numbers of new converts coming into the Christian faith contributed to a decline in the general moral standards of believers.[15] Not long afterwards came the fall of the Roman Empire and the barbarian invasions. The clash between a culture in decline and a superior moral and spiritual power that nevertheless met strong opposition could not bring about positive results in the attempt to secure the most outstanding qualities in ecclesiastical office holders. If it is true to say that in such circumstances the Church chose to demand from her clerics perfect abstinence from the occasions provoking moral decadence, the shortcomings and weaknesses we hear of should not surprise us. The frequent repetition of these prescriptions by the canons of the Church councils demonstrates both the Church's irrevocable decision and the difficulty of introducing severe restrictions into the private life of clerics.[16] What difficulties the Church encountered in imposing and maintaining a discipline that was strict but indispensable for the effective exercise of ecclesiastical office will be discussed in the next section.[17]

The Influence of Monasticism

The Church seeks able and morally irreproachable office holders who can easily attain a holy life. She is thus constantly concerned that only upright and ethically principled candidates should be admitted into the ranks of the clergy. Married men are not excluded, but the celibate are strongly preferred.[18] Since the virtue of virginity was exalted and praised by the sayings of the Lord, Paul, and most of the fathers, as we have noted above, it is not necessary here to analyze the origins of monasticism and the reasons for its growth, or the spread of its ascetic tendencies throughout the Church. A natural consequence was the organization of monasticism in the second half of the third century. Apart from the promise of rich spiritual rewards both in this world and in the next, monasticism offered a safe refuge far from the disturbances and disorders of an unstable

Roman Empire.[19] Christian monastic life is the result of
the moral tendencies of early Christianity and also of
the situation in which the Church found herself from
the age of Constantine the Great.[20] Many believers, fully
devoted to the Lord and living an austere life within the
Christian community, were nevertheless distinguished
from the majority by their asceticism, self-restraint, and
prayer. These were called the "continent" (*enkrateis*), as
opposed to the "encratites" (*enkratitai*), who held dualist
ideas. These Christians distinguished themselves by an
austere continence, non-possessiveness, celibacy, fasting, and prayer.[21] Either alone or sharing a common life,
they lived in special houses, often with men and women
living together for the sake of greater asceticism and continence. The women were called "the brought-in ones"
(*syneisaktoi* or *introductae*).[22] Later, from the middle of
the third century, the "continent" moved away from the
cities and lived permanently in uninhabited areas. They
came to be known as anchorites, hermits, or monks. This
was to facilitate the struggle against sin. The examples
and reputation of famous anchorites such as Antony the
Great, Pachomius, Macarius the Egyptian,[23] Ammonius,
and others attracted crowds of admirers to the desert.
The first monks had nothing to do with the clergy, nor
were they allowed to become clerics.[24] Sometimes their
enthusiastic tendencies became exaggerated, provoking
conflicts in the Church. Among extremists known to us
were "the followers of Eustathius," called Eustathians,
who among other things held that marriage rendered
salvation impossible and sought to impose the monastic
life on all Christians. They were condemned, however,

and anathematized by the local synod of Gangra. By condemning all manifestations of extremism in this respect, the Church succeeded in bringing together the monastic life and the clergy.[25] We thus see monasteries acquiring clerics or monks receiving ordination. At the same time, the life of the clergy of the Christian communities was influenced by monasticism and acquired many monastic characteristics. This convergence, we can say, even extended to mutual influence in matters of dress. The celibacy of bishops in the East proves to derive from monasticism. Monastic life, attracting the admiration of the majority of Christians, supplied the Church with many of her leaders and shepherds.[26]

Parallel to the celibate life led by clerics, there were also married clergy who practiced continence within marriage. This tendency had many adherents in both the West and the East. A man who had vowed himself to celibacy could, if he desired, return to his earlier secular life and contract marriage. Such conduct would certainly have been strongly censured by the Church, especially in the period of the persecutions, when the enthusiastic tendencies of Christians were at their height.[27] But even such an ardent supporter of celibacy as Epiphanius preferred that those who were unable to keep their vows should marry, and after repentance be reconciled with the Church, rather than sin in secret.[28] With regard to marriage after ordination, ecclesiastical tradition was firm and inflexible. A man who entered into marriage after he had already been ordained was prevented from exercising his priestly office.[29] In the Church of the first three centuries, the decision to live in a state of celibacy or continence was voluntary, and was supported more by widespread custom than by any known legal text.[30] Thus there were two parallel tendencies already formed in the early centuries, one favoring marriage, the other celibacy. We have a vivid example of the opposition between the two tendencies from the First Ecumenical Council. Hosius of Cordoba, representing the early preference in the Western Church for compulsory clerical celibacy, came into conflict with Paphnutius, an Egyptian bishop. Paphnutius, who was himself an ascetic, protested at the heavy yoke which Hosius sought to impose. There was no question here of East-West opposition in the one as yet undivided Church, for the Western fathers enjoyed the same veneration and esteem as their colleagues of the East. But apart from that, for many of the Eastern fathers, too, celibacy was a higher state than marriage and preferable to it.[31] In an address on this subject Eusebius believes that for priests the carnal begetting of children is a hindrance to their spiritual work because it does not allow them to give their undistracted attention to higher things. They should therefore abstain from marriage and embrace celibacy (*Dem. ev.* 1.9).

From the influence of monasticism and the high esteem in which the populace held many of the leading figures of the movement, we can see how celibacy was gradually imposed also in the East. No distinction is made between celibate and married bishops until the fourth and fifth centuries. By the time of the Quinisext Council it is decreed specifically that married men called to episcopal office must separate from their wives.

The reasons for the general imposition of celibacy on bishops in the East may be summarized as follows:[32] (i) The monastic ideal had already begun to be held in the highest esteem. Thus once the monks had been fully brought into obedience to the ecclesiastical adminis- tration, many of them went on to accept ecclesiastical office. (ii) The bishop was also the administrator of his church's property. Ecclesiastical and personal property could therefore have been confused by the heirs of a married bishop, especially if he had children. A general reason for the imposition of episcopal celibacy was also the fact that the bishop was expected to devote himself without distraction to the demanding work of the ministry of God. Accordingly, celibacy was imposed not in opposition to the apostolic tradition, but out of a concern to advance good order and improve the state of the Church.

The Council of Elvira

With regard to the marriage of clerics before ordi- nation, legislation in the East at the beginning of the fourth century permits it, while that in the West is more austere and restrictive.[33] From the beginning, Western legislation was inflexible in its aim to subjugate the natural urges of the flesh. It is therefore perhaps not entirely coincidental that the earliest recorded legisla- tion on this matter comes from the local synod held at Elvira in Spain in about 306. Canon 33 emphasizes that all who serve the altar are obliged on pain of deposition to abstain entirely from conjugal relations.[34] Moreover, the synod attempted to put an end to the scandal of *subintroductae* (Greek *syneisaktoi*), female companions of clerics, introducing a ban on a woman living with a cleric unless she was his sister or daughter, and even then on the understanding that she had taken a vow of virginity (Elvira 27).

Since this legislation had originated from a purely local synod, its canons were not binding outside the ecclesiastical province in which the synod had been held. It is not unlikely that this decision was the outcome of the overwhelming influence of one of the leading members of the synod, Hosius of Cordoba. The ruling was unable to influence the Church more widely, because about ten years later, synods were convened in the East at Ancyra (314) and Neocaesarea (315) which dealt with similar ecclesiastical topics. The lack of any reference by these two Eastern synods to the earlier synod held in the West suggests that in this period, the Spanish view did not correspond to the prevailing custom, at least in the East.

The Council of Ancyra

The Council of Ancyra made a notable contribution to the important question of clerical marriage. Canon 10 allowed deacons to marry after ordination, provided that they had revealed their preference for the married life at ordination itself. Deacons who married after ordination without having given the required notice were liable to deposition from their office: "If those who have been appointed deacons have testified at their appointment and said that they desire to marry because they are unable to remain as they are, and afterwards have married, let them continue in their ministry, because this has been permitted to them by the bishop. But if any have stayed silent and undertaken at their ordination to remain as they were, and afterwards entered into marriage, let them cease from the diaconate" (Ancyra 10).[35]

This canon was to be very important in the long history of canonical principles governing clerical marriage. If the fathers of the synod allowed deacons to marry after ordination, once they had declared their intention beforehand, there were all the more grounds for allowing married clergy to continue their marital life without any requirement for separation.[36] We do not know why the synod made this ruling. By allowing the marriage of deacons after ordination, the fathers showed forbearance in applying the prevailing canonical regime. Their adoption of the canon gave the candidate deacon the right to declare his attitude toward the question of marriage. His decision to accept celibacy,[37] regarded as a promise made before God to choose and practice the celibate life and devote himself fully to the service of God, was sealed, so to speak, by his ordination, just as a monk's commitment to celibacy was sealed by his monastic tonsure.[38] A marriage contracted after ordination was regarded as a renunciation of the promise of celibacy. As such it was punished by the dismissal of the deacon from his ministry: "let them cease from the diaconate." The essential point was the time at which the decision was made for either the celibate or the married life, not the decision itself.[39] Thus a decision for the celibate life made before the candidate's ordination bound him to a lifelong commitment, and the contraction of marriage after ordination was a renunciation of the promise for which the synod imposed a severe penalty.

The Council of Neocaesarea

Showing the same disposition toward married clergy as the Council of Ancyra, this synod forbids presbyters to enter into marriage after ordination on pain of deposition: "If a presbyter marries, he shall be deposed from office" (Neocaesarea 1). Celibacy for the presbyter is presented as a higher state than marriage. A man who takes a wife before his ordination to the higher clergy is not hindered from having marital relations with her. But if he entered into the higher ranks of the clergy as an unmarried man, he is permanently denied the right to contract a marriage.[40] According to the testimony of Bishop Paphnutius of the Thebaid, the rule prohibiting marriage after ordination dates from the third century. Speaking a century later, he refers to this rule as already established in the Church.[41]

It is evident that although the Eastern Church accepts that married men promoted to the higher ranks of the clergy may remain in the married state, she takes a very severe position on the marriage of celibates who are already ordained. We thus arrive at a disciplinary situation, as set out officially in the legislation dating from immediately before the First Ecumenical Council (Nicaea), which permits bishops and presbyters to continue in a marriage which they happen to have contracted before ordination, but forbids them to contract a marriage after it. Canon 10 of Ancyra is the sole exception. According to this canon, deacons and clerics in the minor orders, namely, subdeacons, readers, and cantors, have the right to contract marriage after ordination, provided that they have not been married before, and that their intended wives are not widows, divorcees, or concubines.[42]

The First Ecumenical Council (Nicaea)

The only reference to the subject of the marriage or celibacy of the clergy in the canons of Nicaea is an indirect one. According to Canon 3: "The great Synod absolutely forbids either a bishop, or a presbyter, or a deacon, or any of the clergy whatsoever to have a *subintroducta* living with him, unless she is his mother, or sister, or aunt, or only such persons as are beyond all suspicion."[43]

This canon reveals the limited extent of the austere party's attempt at the council to impose continence on the higher clergy.[44] According to the ecclesiastical historians Socrates and Sozomen, this attempt came up against the opposition of Bishop Paphnutius of the Thebaid.[45] At the time the council's canons were being discussed, certain fathers wanted to introduce a rule forbidding conjugal relations to married clergy. The saintly Bishop Paphnutius protested strongly against the difficult burden this would have imposed on the clergy, supporting his point of view by appealing to the passage in the Epistle to the Hebrews that describes the marriage bed as undefiled (Heb 13:4). Paphnutius's influence as a confessor and bishop of exemplary holiness was considerable. The loss of his right eye during the persecutions which bore witness to his suffering for the faith, and also his impeccable chastity which he had preserved from his youth, ensured that his motives were entirely above suspicion. The bishops, who sought his approval of the proposed canon, backed down and abandoned their attempt (Socrates, *Hist. eccl.* 1.11; Sozomen, *Hist. eccl.* 1.23).[46]

The Church's practice in the East in the matter of clerical marriage or celibacy is confirmed by Athanasius the Great, whose orthodoxy and Christian way of life were already acknowledged through his participation in the Ecumenical Council of Nicaea. An Egyptian monk called Dracontius had been elected bishop but, afraid that the assumption of episcopal duties would prevent him from keeping his monastic vows, he hesitated in accepting his election. To overcome his scruples, Athanasius wrote him a letter containing a number of persuasive arguments, among which is the assurance that his new role would not put any impediment in his way preventing him from keeping the self-imposed rules of his monastic way of life. He emphasizes that he knows bishops who have never been married and others who were already fathers of families.[47] The tone of the whole passage clearly reveals the lack of any canonical legislation regulating such cases. And although an austere asceticism was widely practiced, it was admired by the majority as the result of personal convictions, not the application of an established canonical tradition.

An equally persuasive testimony is provided by St. Gregory of Nazianzus. Gregory's father, who was also called Gregory, and was his predecessor as bishop of Nazianzus, had converted to Christianity at the time of the Council of Nicaea. Later he entered the priesthood and was elected bishop. The younger Gregory's pious mother, Nonna, prayed ceaselessly and earnestly for the birth of a male child. Before his birth she saw him in a vision and dedicated him to the service of God. The birth took place after the child's father had entered into the priesthood, as may be deduced from his words to his own son: "You had not yet so much as begun to measure out your life when the time came to me to offer the sacrifices" (*Vit.* [PG 37:1064]). The subsequent birth of a second son, Caesarius, proves that marital relations continued after the ordination of the elder Gregory. His son clearly never felt the slightest shame or inferiority because he was born after his father had become a priest.[48]

The Council of Gangra

A local council was convened at Gangra between 340 and 370. Its purpose was to examine the case of Eustathius of Sebaste in Cappadocia.[49] Eustathius, son of Eulalius, bishop of Caesarea in Cappadocia, was a zealot for purity. His extremist views on the baseness of marriage suggest Manichaean tendencies, though his rejection of fasting shows that in other ways his opinions were incompatible with Manichaean principles. His contempt for marriage and revulsion towards it led him to teach that it was impossible for married people to be saved. Moreover, he forbade even praying with them in their homes. Finally, he rejected blessings and sacraments performed by priests who were living with their wives. Such priests, he said, were beneath contempt.[50]

The Church recognized the urgent need to condemn

such views, which although contradicting her official teaching, were nevertheless dangerously similar to the enthusiastic tendencies of some of her zealots.[51] To combat this danger, a local synod was held in Caesarea, presided over by the heresiarch's father, Eulalius. But Eustathius's condemnation did not bring about the desired reining-in of his excesses, so the synod of Gangra was convened. Attended by fifteen bishops, including Eulalius, it quickly pronounced against Eustathius and his followers. The synod followed this up by drafting a series of canons which clarified orthodox teaching on the matter. These canons anathematize any who reject the mysteries celebrated by a married priest, and also those who maintain that marriage is an impediment to the celebration of the mysteries: "If anyone considers, with regard to a married presbyter, that one should not partake of the offering when he has officiated, let him be anathema" (Gangra 4). The canons also anathematize those who are proud of their supposed virginity and arrogantly despise their married brethren, regarding marriage as something incompatible with salvation: "If any one of those living in virginity for the Lord's sake should denigrate the married, let him be anathema" (Gangra 10).[52]

The whole affair provides a very clear record of the teachings then current. These reveal the lack of any explicit ruling which could have been understood as a general principle dealing with the marriage of the clergy. Eustathius's unsupported and absurd theories no doubt gave the Church the opportunity to discredit them officially and counter their growing influence. At

the same time, through her carefully measured conces-
sions to the ascetic spirit of the age, the Church followed
the royal middle way in dealing with the problem. This
is apparent in the epilogue of the Council of Gangra's
synodal letter: "We indeed admire virginity accompanied by humility, and we accept continence practiced
with dignity and piety."

Later Legislation

In the late fourth or early fifth century there appeared
the *Apostolic Constitutions*, as already noted.[53] The important influence they exercised on later ecclesiastical
legislation is reflected in the canon law of the Eastern
Church. They decree: "We say that bishops and priests
and deacons who have only been married once are to
be appointed, whether their wives are still alive or have
died, and after ordination they are not to be permitted,
if unmarried, to contract a marriage, or if they have
been married, to take other wives, but they are to be
satisfied with the state they were in when they were
ordained" (*Const. ap.* 6.17). The instruction to the higher
clergy that they should "be satisfied" doubtless refers
to the right of retaining the wife to whom they were
married before ordination. The *Apostolic Constitutions*,
although apocryphal, faithfully represent the practice
of the Eastern Church. Unlike later legislation referring
to bishops, which became progressively more austere,
this collection defines the subsequent attitude of Eastern
ecclesiastical law to clerical marriage.[54]

The *Apostolic Canons* forbade bishops and priests to
"release" (i.e., divorce) their wives on the grounds of

chastity, and threatened any transgression with excommunication: "Let not a bishop or presbyter or deacon put away his wife on a pretext of piety; but if he does put her away, let him be excommunicated, and if he persists, let him be deposed" (*Can. ap.* 5). The "pretext of piety" refers not only to the refusal to maintain a wife, but also to the grounds put forward of devoting oneself zealously to the exercise of perfect continence.[55]

Cases of breaking these canonical rules through falling into moral laxity were probably not rare, since the need was felt to legislate for the Church on such matters so as to preserve the standing of the Church's ministers. Thus a law of the Emperor Valentinian of 370 threatened severe penalties against clerics who visited the homes of widows or virgins (*Cod. theod.* 16.2.20). Fifty years later, the same issues were troubling the Church. In 420 the Emperors Honorius and Theodosius II repeated the provisions of the fifth apostolic canon, forbidding presbyters to divorce their wives on the pretext of continence (*Cod. theod.* 16.2.24). At about the same time (mid-fifth century), the historian Socrates refers to a new custom introduced into Thessaly, and prevailing also in Hellas, Macedonia, and Thessalonica: the compulsory separation of married priests from their wives. In the rest of the East such divorce was accepted only if mutually agreed. And there were many bishops who had no hesitation at all about continuing their marital relations (Socrates, *Hist. eccl.* 5.22).[56]

The prestige of well-known figures like Jerome and John Chrysostom and other important ecclesiastics, together with Western practice and the ascetic endeavors of the Origenists, no doubt contributed to the spread of this custom. But no less significant, as Socrates shows, was the fact that the ascetic movements that arose and developed locally did not succeed in spreading generally throughout the eastern provinces.[57] The Eastern Church thus preserved its earlier traditions intact that forbade marriage to those already ordained and firmly upheld the conjugal rights of those already married before ordination, as set out in the *Apostolic Constitutions* and *Apostolic Canons*.

Notes

1.   Cf. Lietzmann 1932-1944, 4:117-118.

2.   On the ascetic ideas of the early Church, see Lea 1884; Kourilas 1929; Lietzmann 1932-1944, 4:116ff.; Brown 1988.

3.   In his letter to Polycarp, St. Ignatius warns those who practice voluntary asceticism to guard against arrogance, or their asceticism will be lost (*Pol.* 5.2). Cf. Lietzmann 1932-1944, 4:121-123.

4.   "[T]he name *virgin* is given to a woman who voluntarily devotes herself to the Lord, renounces marriage, and embraces a life of holiness....Many girls are brought forward by their parents and brothers, and other kinsfolk, before they are of full age, and have no inner impulse towards a celibate life. The object of the friends is simply to provide for themselves. Such women as these must not be readily received, before we have made public investigation of their own sentiments" (Basil, Canon 18; trans. *NPNF*[2] 8:237).

5.   "[C]elibacy is not particularly praiseworthy unless it arises through love of God" (*Strom.* 3.6.51; trans. Ferguson 1991, 288). Cf. *Strom.* 3.7. See Bougatsos 1962a, 116.

6.   See Trembelas 1926, 82ff.

7.   For a contextualized study of this topic, see Brown 1988.

8. For a particularly relevant overview of one such school, see Sellars 2006, which includes a discussion of Stoic influences on late antiquity. Hellenistic philosophy and its understanding of asceticism exerted varying degrees of influence on early Christian writers. For a discussion of one well-known example, see Maier 1994. For discussion of some of the more subtle philosophical and cultural influences, see Krueger 1993.

9. Cf. Long 2002.

10. See Stephanidis 1959, 153.

11. On the immorality of the times Justin Martyr asks: "For what shall we say then of the countless multitude of those who have turned away from intemperance and learned these things?" (*1 Apol.* 15; trans. Barnard, 32).

12. It is wrong to interpret the phrase "husband of one wife" as implying the cleric's obligation to be married. See Vacandard 1905-1923, 1:73. In saying this, the Apostle counters lack of moderation. According to the traditional understanding of this passage, a cleric must be the husband of one wife if he has embraced the married life. This interpretation leads to the conclusion that the Apostle Paul was against the ordination of candidates who had married a second time (Achelis 1912, 2:18). Theodoret of Cyrus regards "a man who has lived chastely with only one wife" as worthy of the priestly office, but he does not exclude a man who has been led by circumstances to marry a second time (*Comm. 1 Tim.* 3; cf. Theodore of Mopsuestia, [*Fr. 1 Tim.* 3]). Jerome emphasizes chastity and continence in his commentary on the passage (*Comm. Tit.* 1). Some fathers regard these words of Paul as referring to chastity and the giving of an example of married trust beyond all suspicion, regardless of whether the husband had for some reason married a second time. See Gryson 1970, 1 (with bibliography). Cf. Zhishman 1913, 2:83; Trembelas 1926, 33ff., where it is stated that in the Eastern Church, only a second marriage contracted after baptism is an impediment to ordination. Those who were widowers before baptism and married again after having been baptized may be ordained without hindrance.

13. See Justinian, *Nov.* 6 (535) and 123 (546).

14. See Stephanidis 1959, 135-136.

15. Stephanidis 1959, 122. Cf. Balanos 1926, 22 and 26. Parallel to the occasional severe judgments of the moralists on the moral decline of their age, there are also examples of virtuous lives, as recognized by a later generation. See Labriolle 1938, 371-372.

16. See Gaudemet 1958, 148-149. Cf. Boissier 1909, 2:415-419.

17. This study could have been restricted to the first three centuries during which the prerequisites for entry into the clergy were being established. But I have preferred to extend my discussion to the fifth century, when the basic prerequisites received their fixed form. The period starting with the first decades of the fourth century, especially from 313, when the persecutions ceased and peace prevailed in the Church, was of decisive importance. This was when the Church began to give canonical expression to the ecclesiastical tradition on requirements for entry into the clergy which had been followed hitherto. No longer harrassed by the government, the Church needed to address the general moral laxity consequent on peaceful coexistence with the state.

18. This preference is reflected in the *Ecclesiastical Canons of the Holy Apostles*. For the election of presbyters it is necessary that the bishop should appoint "presbyters...who in some way abstain from marital relations with their wives" (*Can. eccl.* 17). With regard to the bishop himself, "it is good for him to be celibate, but if not, to have had only one wife" (*Can. eccl.* 16 [1 Tim 3:32]). Cf. Achelis 1912, 2:19.

19. Cf. Stephanidis 1959, 153ff.; Phytrakis 1945, 36ff.

20. See Stephanidis 1959, 153ff. Cf. Phytrakis 1960, 274ff.

21. Cf. Justin, *1 Apol.* 15.6; Athenagoras, *Leg.* 33; Herm. *Sim.* 9.11.3-7; Cyril of Jerusalem, *Catech.* 14.

22. On *introductae* see Achelis 1902; Labriolle 1921.

23. On the lives of these three great ascetics see Phytrakis 1945, 5-21; Chitty 1966, 1-19; Rubenson 1990; Rousseau 1999.

24. See Stephanidis 1959, 156. Cf. Phytrakis 1945, 58, where

it is suggested that Pachomius did not wish to have monks in priestly orders in his cenobium, so as to give no occasion for ambitious pride and quarrels among the monks.

25. On relations between the desert ascetics and the Church, see Phytrakis 1945, 57ff. Cf. Gould 1993b; Russell 2003.

26. Cf. Zhishman 1913, 2:168ff. Athanasius's *Letter to Dracontius* indicates that the custom of making monks into bishops had not yet become fully established. By mentioning the cases of Serapion, Apollo, Ariston, and Ammonius, who were appointed bishops from the monastic state, St. Athanasius tries to persuade Dracontius that he is not the first monk to be made a bishop. It would not have been an issue for Dracontius if it were permitted for monks to become bishops. See Trembelas 1926, 100; Russell 2003.

27. Cf. Laodicea 6, according to which a person who sets aside a promise of celibacy or virginity is treated like a digamist; if he is a layman, he becomes ineligible for ordination. Beyond this, there does not seem to have been any other penalty. Cf. also the commentaries of Balsamon and Blastaris. On the enthusiastic tendencies generally, see Holl 1898; Kotsonis 1952.

28. "If one drops out of the race it is better to take a wife openly, and in place of virginity do penance for a long time, and be readmitted to the church as one who has strayed and wept, and is in need of reinstatement" (*Pan.* 2.1.61 (7.6); trans. Williams 1994, 120). Cyprian takes up a similar position in his letter to Pomponius (*Ep.* 4).

29. See Pierre, Evêque de Chersonèse 1970, 32.

30. See Böhmer 1916. Böhmer attributes the early Church's tendency towards encratite attitudes to the idea that sexual relations make a man unfit to offer liturgical worship.

31. "It was fitting that he, most pure and a teacher of purity, should issue from a pure bride-chamber. For if one who fulfills well the priestly office abstains from women, how was Jesus himself to be born of man and woman? 'For thou art he,' he says in the Psalms, 'that hast drawn me out of the womb.' Mark that carefully, 'that hast drawn me out of the womb,' since this signifies that he was born without man,

being drawn from the womb and flesh of a virgin; for the manner is different for those born in the ordinary course of marriage" (Cyril of Jerusalem, *Catech.* 12.25 [trans. McCauley and Stephenson, 243]). See the other patristic testimonies mentioned in the previous paragraph.

32. See Bougatsos 1962b, 120.

33. See Gaudemet 1958, 157. Although marriage in this period was still primarily a civil contract, certain prerequisites were required by the Church of those committed to the Christian faith. One of these prerequisites was the blessing of the bishop. As John Meyendorff says, "Every Christian couple desirous of marriage went through the formalities of civil registration, which gave it validity in secular society; and then through their joint participation in the regular Sunday liturgy, in the presence of the entire local Christian community, they received the bishop's blessing. It was then that their civil agreement became also 'sacrament,' with eternal value, transcending their earthly lives because it was also 'inscribed in heaven,' and not only in a secular 'registry'" (Meyendorff 1984, 21-22).

34. Elvira 33: "Bishops, presbyters, and deacons and all other clerics having a position in the ministry are ordered to abstain completely from their wives and not to have children. Whoever, in fact, does this, shall be expelled from the dignity of the clerical state" (trans. Laeuchli, 130).

35. Cf. Vacandard 1905-1923, 1:92-93.

36. See Hefele 1907-1952, 1:431ff.

37. The consistent view of the Eastern Church has always been that a person who embraces the celibate life is inspired not by timidity or egoism, but by the ascetic spirit of the New Testament. Cf. Matt 19:10-12; 1 Cor 7:1-7. See Pierre, Évêque de Chersonèse 1970, 30.

38. Chrysostom writes in this spirit in his Second Exhortation to the fallen ascetic, Theodore (*Theod. laps.* 2): "'Marriage is right,' you say; I also assent to this. For 'marriage,' we read, 'is honorable and the bed undefiled; but fornicators and adulterers God will judge'; but it is no longer possible for thee to observe the right conditions of marriage. For if

he who has been attached to a heavenly bridegroom deserts him, and joins himself to a wife the act is adultery, even if you call it marriage ten thousand times over; or rather it is worse than adultery in proportion as God is greater than man. Let no one deceive thee saying: 'God hath not forbidden to marry'; I know this as well as you; He has not forbidden to marry, but He has forbidden to commit adultery, which is what thou art wishing to do; and may you be preserved from ever engaging thyself in marriage! And why dost thou marvel if marriage is judged as if it were adultery, when God is disregarded?" (trans. *NPNF*[1] 9:113). Canon 16 of Chalcedon takes the same view: "It is not permitted for a virgin who has dedicated herself to the Lord God, or similarly for a monk, to contract marriage. If it is discovered that they have done so, let them be made excommunicate" (trans. Tanner 1990, 95). See Pheidas 1972, 40.

39. The principle of time as the basic element in the candidate cleric's decision for the celibate or the married life may also be observed in Canon 16 of Carthage, which requires readers to marry or commit themselves to continence at the end of adolescence. Cf. *Apostolic Canon* 27: "Of those who come into the clergy unmarried, we permit only the readers and singers, if they have a mind, to marry afterward" (trans. *ANF* 7:501). At first sight, this canon seems to contradict the Carthaginian one. But they both allow marriage to readers. The difference lies only in the absence in *Apostolic Canon* 26 of a specified time for deciding between marriage or celibacy. The Carthaginian canon, as we have seen, prescribes the end of adolescence as the time for making the decision. See Pheidas 1972, 39.

40. Following the canons of Ancyra and Neocaesarea on the marriage of the clergy, the *Apostolic Constitutions*—a work widely disseminated as an authentic expression of ancient Church order—consents to the marriage of clerics who have already taken a wife before entering the ranks of the higher clergy. But as for contracting legitimate marriage after ordination, the *Apostolic Constitutions* forbid it not only to presbyters but even to deacons. See *Const. ap.* 6.17 (cf. Funk 1905, 348,

n. 1). Cf. also Achelis 1912, 2:17-19.

41. Cf. Socrates, *Hist. eccl.* 1.11; Pierre, Évêque de Cherso-nèse 1970, 29.

42. Cf. *Const. ap.* 6.17; *Can. ap.* 17; 18; 19. Carthage 16.

43. Cf. Carthage 38; Basil 88. A law of Honorius and Theodosius II of 420 (*Cod. theod.* 16.2.44) forbids clerics to have *mulieres extraneae* in their households under the name of *sorores* (that is, *subintroductae*). The same law only allows mothers, daughters, and sisters to live in the same house with them. But it adds that the pursuit of purity does not preclude living with wives whose virtues have contributed to the worthy appointment of their husbands as priests.

44. For an analysis of the motives of that party opposed to the imposition of celibacy, see Labriolle 1938, 371-372.

45. See p. 254 above.

46. The authenticity of this incident is disputed. See Hefele 1907-1952, 2:431ff. Cf. Kirsch 1930, 486, n. 352.

47. *Ep. Drac.* 9: "Many also of the bishops have not even married, while monks have been fathers of children; just as conversely we know bishops who are fathers of children and monks 'of the completest kind'" (trans. *NPNF*[2] 4:560).

48. For other examples, see Achelis 1912, 2:18.

49. See Stephanidis 1959, 157-159.

50. The Synodal Letter of the Council of Gangra makes it clear that Eustathius's followers abhorred marriage and believed that no married person could be saved. The letter goes on to state that "neither do they tolerate prayers in the houses of married persons, but, on the contrary, despise such prayers when they are made, and often refuse to partake when Oblations are offered in the houses of married persons; condemning married presbyters, and refusing to touch their ministrations" (trans. *NPNF*[2] 14:91). In his *Ecclesiastical History* (2.43), Socrates further comments on Eustathius's heresy: "In short, he forbade prayers to be offered in the houses of married persons: and declared that both the benediction and the communion of a presbyter who continued to live with a wife whom he might have lawfully married, while still a layman, ought to be shunned as an abomination" (trans.

*NPNF*² 2:72).

51. See Stephanidis 1959, 157ff.

52. Cf. also Canons 1 and 9, which are severe on those who condemn marriage, maintaining that they cannot attain salvation.

53. See pp. 73-74 above.

54. It is worth noting that the above is in full agreement with Socrates' testimony to the firm practice of the Eastern Church on the marriage of the clergy, in contrast to the anomalous practice he had heard about in Thessaly: "I myself, also, learned of another custom in Thessaly. If a clergyman in that country, after taking orders, should sleep with his wife, whom he had legally married before his ordination, he would be degraded. In the East, indeed, all clergymen, and even the bishops themselves, abstain from their wives: but this they do of their own accord, and not by the necessity of any law; for there have been among them many bishops, who have had children by their lawful wives, during their episcopate" (*Hist. eccl.* 5.22 [trans. *NPNF*² 2:132]).

55. See Vacandard 1905-1923, 1:94.

56. We can easily accept the whole account in view of St. Isidore of Pelusium's strictures in the same period (*Ep.* 3.75). He complains about lack of respect for the Church's ordinanaces on the maintenance of chastity by clerics.

57. In the Church of Armenia, the higher clergy were for the most part married. Celibates were the exception. But the Council of Astisat (365) put an end to this custom. By contrast, the Church of Persia, after it went into schism, opposed the institution of celibacy. At the Council of Beit Edrai (486) it manifested an exemplary leniency, permitting marriage to deacons and presbyters even when they were widowers. See Achelis 1912, 2:19, n. 6.

Prerequisites for Entry into the
Clergy in the First Five Centuries
on the Basis of the Sources Reviewed

Canonists divide the prerequisites for entry into the clergy into two classes.[1] The first includes the two fundamental conditions without which any ordination is invalid: male gender and baptism. That these requirements were taken for granted and did not call for any legislative support is apparent from the Church's unvarying practice. The second class includes all the remaining conditions relating to the canonicity of ordination. These conditions are both physical and spiritual. In what follows I shall discuss them on the basis of the ecclesiastical legislation already reviewed. But whereas before I used a historical method, in this chapter I shall examine the main provisions systematically, without regard to chronology.

Physical Criteria

Age qualifications[2]

A candidate seeking to enter the clergy must have attained a minimum age so as to be mature enough to make his decision with the required seriousness and in full awareness of the weighty responsibilities attaching to the priestly office. In the first five centuries there was a noticeable endeavor to define the canonical rules relating to entry into the clergy. But the formulation of these rules in no way implies a comprehensive regulation of the matter in this period. The extant canons deal with entry into the clergy in general terms only. We shall be disappointed if we try to discover precisely defined age requirements for each of the grades of the clergy, obligatory for the whole Church. Usually the Church only addressed the matter in response to particular circumstances. Moreover, many examples show that the canonical age requirements for candidates were not always observed in practice. Indeed, there was a decided lack of unanimity in applying such legislation. The fear of some bishops that they would be unable to find a sufficient number of virtuous candidates often led them to ordain men who had not yet reached the canonically prescribed age. Pressure to bend the rules also came from the people, who often exercised a decisive influence by enthusiastically indicating their preference in the election of their future shepherd.[3]

Before the fourth century there is no document that lays down the minimum age of clerics. The first piece of legislation in the East is Canon 11 of Neocaesarea (315). On the basis of the age at which the Lord began his public ministry, this canon requires candidates for the presbyterate to have attained their thirtieth year.[4] A synod convened a century later at Seleucia (410) repeated the same age requirement for presbyters (Seleucia 16). The *Ecclesiastical Canons* (late third-early fourth century) are vague, simply saying that presbyters must "have attained experience in the world" (*Can. eccl.* 17). In practice, the application of legislation on canonical age followed this approach. But although the East was flexible about the age requirement for presbyters, it was firm where bishops were concerned. Under the influence of the *Teaching of the Apostles* (first half of the third century), the *Apostolic Constitutions* (late fourth–early fifth century) determined the age of fifty as the lower limit for entry into the highest grade of priesthood (*Didasc. ap.* 2.1.1; *Const. ap.* 2.1.1).

In the West the earliest legislative texts on the canonical age of clerics come from local African synods held at the end of the fourth century. The first of these was the Council of Hippo (393), which laid down the age of twenty-five for *clerici* (Canon 1). Subsequently, at the Council of Carthage (397) it was clarified which clergy were intended by the ruling that "no deacon shall be ordained under twenty-five years old" (Canon 4). The African Code of the Carthaginian Council of 419 agrees with this age for deacons (Canon 16). The absence of conciliar rulings in the fifth century on the age for the remaining grades of the clergy was made good by papal decrees. The conditions of the times, when it was difficult to find suitable candidates, made special care necessary. To satisfy local needs, rulings were given by popes Siricius (385) and Zosimus (418). Those of Siricius covered all the grades of the clergy,[5] those of Zosimus only as far as the subdiaconate.[6] Both rulings distinguish between those baptized in their youth and those baptized in adulthood. But while Siricius sets age limits for the different grades of the clergy, Zosimus specifies how long the ministry in each grade should last.

As far as the implementation of this legislation on

the canonical age of clerics is concerned, the examples known to us prove the contrary. Although most of these examples are of well-known figures, whose memory was therefore more likely to be preserved in the historical records, their frequency cannot be coincidental. Most cases concerned laymen who were promoted to episcopal office in response to the enthusiastic demands of the populace without the scrupulous observance of the Church's rules on canonical age and the required period in the various grades. Western cases included: Hosius, who was just forty; Ambrose, ordained at twenty-four, only eight days after his baptism; Augustine, bishop at forty-one, although he had been baptized at thirty-three and was ordained presbyter at Hippo four years later; and Hilary, ordained bishop of Arles at the age of thirty.[7]

In the East, where the canonical situation was much less clear, the picture is no different. There were many promotions to the various grades of the clergy without regard to the relevant ecclesiastical legislation on age. But what does emerge is a faithful adherence to the general principle that the cleric must be of mature years.[8] There are many cases of famous Church fathers who attained ecclesiastical office on account of their exceptional abilities, regardless of their age qualification. Nevertheless, the principle of general maturity in candidates was always observed.

The best known of these fathers are Athanasius, Gregory of Nyssa, and John Chrysostom, who were baptized and ordained readers at an early age. Athanasius became a deacon at twenty-two. Basil, Gregory of Nazianzus, and John Chrysostom all became presbyters after they were thirty, and bishops after they were forty.[9] In none of these cases can we speak of premature promotion, even though their ages did not always correspond to the canonical requirements. We may conclude that although there was some flexibility in how the rules governing the age of candidates were applied, the principle of maturity was always respected.

The period of probation[10]

Complementary to the ineffectual rules on age was the principle of gradual promotion and a period of probation in each of the grades of the clergy.[11] The purpose was to test the candidate and prepare him in a suitable way for the heavy responsibilities of the higher grades. In the case of those baptized as adults, this principle provided the only means of evaluating the candidate's fitness for office. It thus corresponded to the canonical age rule for those who had been baptized as infants. The principle of gradual ascent and a period of probation in each grade began with minor orders. By passing through these candidates came to be equipped, it was hoped, with all the qualifications for office they needed when they reached the highest grade of bishop. Despite the significance of the minor orders, rising through all of them was not as important as the principle of having spent a period of probation in some. From the not infrequent incidence of ascent to episcopal office without having passed through all the intermediate grades,[12] we may infer that this was not indispensable. Moreover, in the early centuries not all the minor orders had been established at the same time throughout the Church.[13] What was important was simply the fact of having spent a period of probation in the minor orders. Only a long period of testing qualified the candidate for rising to the highest grades of the clergy. The principle of rising through all the lower grades was thus dependent on the principle of a period of probation.

It was on the basis of Paul's exhortation: "do not be hasty in the laying on of hands" (1 Tim 5:22), which was also the authority for ecclesiastical legislation on the canonical age, that the rule on a period of proba- tion was established. This rule first found expression at the Council of Nicaea (Canon 2). Without defining the way promotions were to be made, this council, through Canon 2 and the expression "ecclesiastical canon," hints at an unwritten tradition that regulated it. The principle of advancing through intermediate grades before arriv- ing at the highest office was introduced by the Council of Sardica (Canon 10). These intermediate grades are those of reader, deacon and presbyter. What is missing is how long the cleric should remain in each grade. In the West, where from the beginning there was a greater tendency toward legal precision, this lack was made good by the decrees of Popes Siricius and Zosimus. Legislating for those baptized in adulthood and then entering the clergy, Siricius allows them to be ordained readers and exorcists at the same time as their baptism. After a period of two years they become acceptable as acolytes or subdeacons. Five more years are needed in each of these grades before ordination to the diacon- ate. For promotion to the higher grades of presbyter and bishop, another period of probation is laid down without specifying how long it should be (Siricius, *Ep.* 1). Zosimus, more austerely, demands from people baptized as adults five years of probation in the grades of reader or exorcist, and then four years as acolytes or subdeacons, and five years as deacons (*Ep.* 9).

To judge from references in the sources to ordinations carried out without the prescribed probationary period, we are probably entitled to assume that such ordinations were just as common as those carried out before the canonical age. Cyprian's biographer, Pontius, tells us that Cyprian received the two grades of presbyter and bishop one immediately after the other (*Vit. Cypr.* 3). Another example is given by Gregory of Nazianzus, who mentions the case of Basil's predecessor as bishop of Caesarea, Eusebius IV (362-70). In response to popular pressure he was ordained bishop, although he had been baptized only a short time before (Gregory of Nazianzus, *Or.* 19.33-34). Perhaps better known is the case of Ambrose. He was ordained bishop only eight days after his baptism (*Off.* 1.1.4; *Vit. Ambr.* 6). Instances of ordinations to the different grades in rapid succession are provided by Augustine (*Ep.* 21.1-3; 126.7) and Gregory of Nazianzus, who were laymen when they were raised to the priesthood.[14] The other Gregory was a reader when he was appointed bishop of Nyssa (in 372) by his brother, Basil. But meanwhile he had abandoned the duties attached to the office of reader to devote himself fully to a career as a rhetorician. But we have no further information on his restoration to the clergy.[15]

The examples of rapid promotion given so far are

all of distinguished ecclesiastical personages who have
therefore left a record in the historical sources. Insofar
as this reflects the Church's "economy" in dealing with
persons gifted with outstanding virtues, it is easily ex-
plainable. For such persons, even if promoted rapidly,
had much to offer the Church in terms of improving
the quality of the clergy and furthering her pastoral
work. But the same cannot be said for the great number
of clerics, motivated simply by ambition, who were
promoted to the higher grades without the necessary
probationary period, or the qualifications required.
Complaining of this situation, Gregory of Nazianzus
expresses a keen regret that the Church does not have
a system of promotion for clerics analogous to that of
the navy or the army. He thought it desirable that clerics
should work through all the grades of the clergy before
attaining episcopal office, exactly like those promoted to
the highest ranks of the armed forces (*Or. Bas.* 25-28).[16]
Pope Leo I likewise protests at rapid promotions in the
West, recalling the obligation to observe the canonical rules on age and probationary period, but without
prescribing how much time is to be spent in each grade
(*Ep.* 12.2 and 4; 19.1).

From our discussion so far, it appears that in defiance
of Paul's words hands were laid "hastily" and often on
laymen and clerics in the Church of the first five centuries. This indeed happened more frequently once the
Church received official recognition by the state and
became attractive to large numbers of proselytes. New
Christians were promoted to the episcopate immediately after their conversion.[17] Inexperienced laymen

entered the clergy and assumed the heavy responsibilities of ministering to God and exercising pastoral care
over their local churches. Clerics bereft of the necessary
preparation advanced quickly to the higher grades of
the clergy. Often these irregularities were the result of
the ambition of the candidates, the unthinking enthusiasm of the populace, and the weakness of the ordaining
bishop in the face of pressure from below.

On the other hand, the Church showed a certain flexibility about the qualities required in candidates when
circumstances demanded this. Such circumstances were
the following: (i) the persecutions, which deprived the
Church of many of her most capable clerics.[18] Consequently, a void was created that needed to be filled. (ii)
the struggle against heresy, which required the mobili-
zation of the best persons able to defend the orthodox
faith against heresy. Because such persons were rare,
they could not be ignored when they were found.[19] (iii)
the barbarian invasions, which convulsed the Church
and tore gaps in the clergy. Where a person's rapid
promotion to the higher ranks of the clergy cannot be
attributed to human motives, we should perhaps attribute it to the operation of the Holy Spirit in accordance
with God's unsearchable will.[20] It is to the operation
of the Holy Spirit that Eusebius of Caesarea attributes
the election of Pope Fabian in 236 (*Hist. eccl.* 6.29). And
Cyprian's biographer recognizes God's will in the election of Cyprian as bishop of Carthage by the people
(*Vit. Cypr. 5*). The same can be said of Ambrose's election (*Vit. Ambr.* 9). Finally, the intervention of the Holy
Spirit in the rapid promotion of certain people is even

acknowledged by Canon 80 of the *Apostolic Canons*: "for it is not right that a person who is not yet experienced should be a teacher of others; unless indeed this happens through divine grace."

As we have seen, there are situations in which the Church does not cleave to the letter by strictly applying the canonical regulations on the probationary period to be spent in the various grades of the clergy. But in keeping with the tenor of this canonical legislation, she felt the need to insist on an obligation to follow the prescribed step-by-step promotion of the clergy from the lower to the higher grades of priesthood.

Soundness of body and mind[21]

In the beginning, the Church's legislation regulating the question of the physical integrity of candidates was concerned only with those physical disabilities that inhibited the cleric's work. With regard to physical disabilities that did not interfere with his work, Canon 77 of the *Apostolic Canons* ruled: "If anyone has lost an eye or is lame in a leg but is worthy of the episcopate, let him be ordained; for it is not a bodily defect that defiles him but a pollution of the soul." This declaration reveals a disposition, at least in the East, to refrain from making canonical rules on physical integrity in the manner of the Mosaic law (Lev 21:16), and to be content with legislation dealing simply with the practical side of the matter. Thus in Canon 78 of the *Apostolic Canons* the loss of sight or hearing does constitute a reason for exclusion from the clergy: "not because he is thereby defiled, but that the affairs of the Church may not be hindered."

The Council of Nicaea laid down the basis of the law regulating the defect of eunuchism. According to Canon 1 it is decreed that a man castrated by doctors for medical reasons, or by barbarians by force, or by his master if a slave, is not barred from entering the clergy. Only self-inflicted mutilation is an impediment to ordination (Nicaea 1). The *Apostolic Canons* repeat this provision (*Can. ap.* 21-23). Canon 21 declares explicitly that those who are not held responsible for their defect, with the result that they are barred from entering the clergy, are those who are eunuchs by nature or have been mutilated by force. A harsher opinion is expressed by St. Jerome, who regards eunuchism as such as a reason for exclusion from the clergy.[22] Innocent I applies the principle established by Nicaea in a ruling on the loss of a finger. Only a voluntary amputation is regarded by him as a reason for exclusion from the clergy (*Ep.* 37.1.3). As for people possessed by evil spirits, by which we should understand the mentally ill, these are also excluded from the clergy. This is the ruling of Canon 79 of the *Apostolic Canons*. In the West in this period these matters were covered by Canon 29 of Elvira (ca. 306) and Canon 16 of Orange (441).

Spiritual Criteria

Faith[23]

Baptism is a fundamental condition of ordination. That there is no explicit testimony according to which the candidate's baptism is an absolutely necessary condition is because it was considered self-evident. An ordination performed in its absence is regarded as having no subsistence. This is inferred from ancient ecclesiastical practice dating from before the period of Nicaea.[24] According to the Council's nineteenth canon, followers of the heresiarch Paul of Samosata, called Paulianists, who wished to enter the ranks of the orthodox clergy were obliged to be rebaptized before their ordination. And clerics who left them and wanted to join the orthodox had also to be reordained. Another question which occupied the council of Neocaesarea was "clinical" baptism.[25] Baptism constitutes the seal of the faith dwelling in a person. There was concern that the baptism of a person baptized during an illness or in danger of death did not reflect a living active faith. But in the absence of any suspicion that his baptism was evidence of a defective faith, the candidate could be ordained (Neocaesarea 12). The fear that the faith of a recent Christian might not be well-rooted, following the precept laid down by Paul (1 Tim 3:6), was the motive for the framing of Canon 2 of Nicaea. This canon requires a probationary period for a neophyte, though without specifying its duration, so that he can demonstrate the stability of his faith.[26] As we have already seen,[27] the Church was not infrequently flexible on this point too, that is, the exclusion of neophytes without a probationary period, when circumstances demanded.

A more inquiring approach to the candidate's faith is a notable feature of the legislation emanating from the Church of Africa. Two canons, the seventeenth of Hippo (393) and the thirty-sixth of the African Code (Carthage 36), do not confine themselves simply to the candidate's faith. They require the conversion of the candidate's entire household before his ordination, if all its members are not already of the orthodox faith. Despite this, the legislation on the candidate's faith was not applied any more strictly than that on age qualifications and probationary periods. We have already noted some of the more familiar examples of neophytes who were ordained, such as St. Cyprian, Eusebius IV of Caesarea, St. Ambrose, etc.[28] We have also glanced at a few of the pretexts for rapid ordination, some condonable, others not (worldly interests, ambition, ignorance in a number of candidates, enthusiasm of the populace, complicity of the ordaining bishop), as well as circumstances favoring the flexible application of the canonical rule, such as the manifestation of the divine will.[29] Such examples may be replicated with regard to the candidate's faith.

On the matter of the lapsed,[30] Canon 10 of Nicaea lays down that "those who have already been ordained... through the ignorance or even with the previous knowledge of the ordainers...shall be deposed." This approach to the question agrees with the earlier one laid down by Cyprian.[31] It shows that the problem of unworthy and undesirable candidates entering the priesthood was an enduring one. Heretics also continued to be a source of concern to the Church in this period. The Council of Elvira forbade the ordination of heretics and demanded the deposition of those already ordained (Elvira 51). A milder position was taken by the First Ecumenical Council on clerics of the Novatianist schism who wished to return to orthodoxy. It permitted such clerics to remain in the clergy (Nicaea 8), although it required Paulianist clergy, as we have seen above, to be rebaptized and then reordained (Nicaea 19). The reason for this difference, of course, is that the Novatianists were schismatics, not heretics.[32]

In this connection we should not ignore the contents of the letter addressed by the First Ecumenical Council to the Church of Egypt on how clergy from the Melitian schism were to be restored to the catholic Church. The Council decided by letter which of the Melitian clergy were to be received back and how and when this was to be done. These clerics were recognized "by economy," without according them any authority or jurisdiction, and only if any of the canonical bishops happened to die could they be invited to succeed them, "only if they should appear worthy, and that the people choose them, and that the bishop of Alexandria concurs in the election and ratifies it" (Socrates, *Hist. eccl.* 1.9).[33] The Melitians tried to exploit this concession in the period between the death of Alexander of Alexandria and the election of the new bishop. They also attempted to enter into conversations with the orthodox in order to increase the rights accorded to them in an underhand way. But in the end, the election of Athanasius thwarted their plans. They refused to recognize him, so he then took severe measures against them.[34]

The Church of Africa was mobilized by this conciliar legislation to oppose the Donatist schism. As already mentioned, the African Church tradition tended to take a severe line on questions of this kind. Thus it permitted the return of schismatic Donatist clergy to orthodoxy, but only as laymen. The difficulties resulting from such a policy are underlined by the Council of Hippo held in 393 on account of a serious shortage of manpower in the clergy (Canon 37). To fill the gap the synod decided to suspend the old tradition and to recognize Donatists returning to orthodoxy under three conditions: (i) so long as they have not been rebaptized; (ii) so long as they have returned to orthodoxy with their shepherd; and (iii) so long as they were baptized by Donatists as infants. The Carthaginian Council of 397 addressed the same issue, at least so far as it related to those baptized by Donatists in infancy (Canon 48). As in the synods also held in Carthage in 401,[35] it supported the measures of the Council of Hippo, because of the difficult situation caused by a lack of clergy. This motive caused the Carthaginian Synod of September 401 to adopt a position of still greater toleration. The restrictions were removed, leaving the bishop free to receive returning Donatists according to his own discretion. The mention of an "experimental synod,"[36] whose judgments on this matter differed from the one adopted in 401, reveals the existence of conflicting views. But this is readily understandable if we bear in mind that the decisions taken were in response to specific situations and particular heresies, according to the time and place in which they appeared. It was to reconcile these different judgments that the Carthaginian synod of 401 imposed a more lenient order, promoting peace and unity.[37] Consequently, despite the apparent contradiction between certain regulations governing the reception into the clergy of returning heretics, what was to be aimed at in each specific situation was the best interests of the Church.

The differences in approaching the problem should be interpreted in this light, not as evidence for any disagreement about its essential nature. Early Church practice demonstrates that on the issue of receiving heretics and schismatics there was no unified approach. Oscillating between strictness and "economy," according to the circumstances of the case she was dealing with, whether schism partaking of heresy or schism simply as a result of local or temporal circumstances, the Church sometimes applied the canons severely and sometimes made use of "economy."[38]

Education[39]

The cleric's duty to teach and lead the faithful presupposes an appropriate preparation to enable him to perform his spiritual work fruitfully. First, as we have seen, St. Paul mentions in his list of a bishop's qualifications in 1 Timothy that the bishop must be an apt teacher (1 Tim 3:2). Interpreting this passage, St. John Chrysostom emphasizes that this is not required of the simple believer, but is demanded especially of the bishop (*Hom. 1 Tim*. 10.3). In a comment on the passage "he must hold firm to the sure word as taught" in the Epistle to Titus (Titus 1:9), he stresses that the work and care of a bishop is the possession of the sure (that is, true) word handed down by faith "without any need for syllogistic argument or debate" (*Hom. Tit*. 13.1). Then, continuing, he says: "there is no need for flamboyant eloquence, but for intelligence, and experience of the Scriptures, and power of understanding" (*Hom. Tit*. 13.1). As an example, Chrysostom gives the Apostle Paul, "who refuted the whole world and proved stronger than Plato and all the rest" (*Hom. Tit.* 13.1). In his exegesis of 1 Timothy, Theodoret of Cyrus understands by "apt teacher" "not a person endowed with eloquence, but one trained in divine things and able to recommend what is fitting" (*Comm. 1 Tim.* 3).

It was not enough for a candidate for the clergy to possess only the natural abilities fitting him for one of the orders of priesthood. He must also possess, beyond a general education, special knowledge enabling him to exercise more effectively the office he has undertaken. He must therefore have the kind of knowledge that is acquired through study. Of course, the knowledge pertaining to each grade of the clergy is peculiar to it. Moreover, what was demanded educationally of the clergy differed in each period of the Church's development.[40]

It is clear that the aspiring cleric had to know the liturgical functions and general duties and responsibilities pertaining to the order to which he was to be ordained. Through his ordination he received an authority which he had to exercise in a fitting way, and this required a full knowledge of the rights and duties deriving from this authority. He also had to know the Church's canons, and above all, as the Church's representative, he had to be able to give a reliable account of her teaching. Knowledge of the Church's teaching was essential.

To achieve her aim and support her members, and also to repel her enemies both without and within, the Church does not wield a sword or a stick but uses reason and its fruit, persuasion, as her weapons.[41] This is also why, in his Epistle to Titus, Paul emphasizes that the shepherd "must hold firm to the sure word as taught, so that he may be able to give instruction in sound doctrine and also to confute those who contradict it. For there are many insubordinate men, empty talkers and deceivers....They must be silenced" (Titus 1:9-11). On the basis of these words of the Apostle, from the beginning the fathers demanded from the Church's future shepherds that they should above all have a full and precise knowledge of the ecclesiastical teaching handed down by faith. This was so that the shepherds would be able to exhort and teach their flocks, respond to any kind of question or doubt put to them, and, being themselves well-informed about the heresies and other religions, refute these and resist their attacks on the Christian faith.

Besides this, there were some in the early Church who maintained that virtuous conduct and piety were sufficient in a candidate for the clergy. They have as an example the apostles, who from simple fishermen became teachers of the world. But this anti-intellectualism was quickly and successfully opposed by the more distinguished Church fathers, who argued, on the one hand, that virtuous conduct alone did not suffice for the perfect exercise of the shepherd's apostolate, and, on the other hand, that the apostles themselves were not the simple men they liked to portray.

Many fathers emphasized the desirability that candidates should have had an education. St. Jerome's preference was for biblical studies, since he regarded a secular education as somewhat dangerous (*Ep.* 21.13).

This preference is discernible in his recommendation to Nepotianus that he should read the Scriptures (*Ep.* 52, *Ad Nepotianum* 7). By contrast, St. Ambrose considered a secular education necessary if one was to be safeguarded from what was not permitted (*Exp. Luc.*, Prol. 1). St. Basil in general encouraged the pursuit of a classical Greek education.[42] Together with St. Gregory of Nazianzus he had studied philosophy at pagan schools.[43] There is no question that the fourth and fifth centuries provide us with the Church's most brilliant achievements in the field of learning and ecclesiastical literature. A series of famous fathers contributed not only to the shaping of the Church's teaching but also to literature generally.[44] In this connection it is not surprising that this great patristic contribution appeared when late antique education and culture placed such an emphasis on the study of literature, rhetoric, and public speaking.[45] In fact, the late antique rhetorical schools and traditions contributed much to patristic eloquence.[46]

At the beginning clerics were either self-taught or had acquired an education outside the Church. Then, private instruction (*didaskaleia*), such as that offered by Clement or Origen, was important. But from the end of the third century clerics were able to use the catechetical and theological schools that began to develop in Alexandria, Caesarea in Palestine, Antioch, Edessa, and Nisibis.[47] These functioned under the direction of the bishop. They taught Church doctrine, interpreted the Scriptures, and at the same time educated candidates for the clergy. But they could not do enough. For candidates for the higher ecclesiastical offices in particular, the education they offered was not considered adequate. There were therefore many clerics who were self-taught, as already mentioned, or acquired an education from other learned clerics privately, especially in the monasteries, or after hearing lectures in the catechetical schools would continue attending classes with philosophers, teachers of rhetoric, and sophists. Still others first acquired a general education at pagan schools, such as those of Athens, Alexandria, Antioch, or other cities, and only afterwards occupied themselves with the study of sacred Scripture and ecclesiastical authors. There were also many philosophers and people of broad culture who turned from paganism to Christianity and were then catechized by the Church, studying holy Scripture and sacred tradition, and finally becoming clerics and rendering important services to the Church.[48] It is worth noting here the Emperor Julian's ban on Christians teaching in the philosophical schools then functioning, and also other decrees prohibiting the children of Christians from studying at them. By forbidding teachers who did not believe in the pagan myths to teach them, Julian effectively excluded Christians from the more established forms of education, because they were excluded from teaching pagan literature, the basis of education for Christians and pagans alike.[49] By such means Julian, in the words of ecclesiastical writers, sought "by law to exclude Christians from education" and "forbade Christians to study Greek literature" (Socrates, *Hist. eccl.* 3.12.16).[50] This suggests that Christians were willing students at philosophical schools, recognizing the value of Greek culture and perceiving a relationship between

Christian truth and Greek education. Perhaps in reaction to Julian's severe measures, some fathers and ecclesiastical writers conceived the plan of creating a Christian literature to match that of classical antiquity in its forms and language.[51] Another reason for this enterprise may have been to draw Christians away from pagan myths and conceptions.[52]

Finally we can say that since monasticism had already spread widely and was influencing every aspect of Christian life, the monasteries exerted a palpable influence on the formation of future clerics. The fathers and shepherds of the Church were expected to exhibit the best characteristics of secular education and sacred study and thus spent time in the monasteries[53] to become worthy of their apostolate and bring it to successful fruition.[54] In Africa in the fifth century St. Augustine introduced a system of common life for clerics analogous to that of the monasteries, and arranged for the studies of candidate clerics to be undertaken in accordance with this.[55]

It is nevertheless noteworthy that the Church's legislation on the education required for entry into the clergy remained very limited. Canon law was still developing, dealing principally with matters that required urgent attention for the avoidance of abuses. The topic of the education of the clergy was not initially of serious concern to the Church,[56] since the candidate's possession of an elementary education was taken for granted.

The decrees on education in the extant body of legislation are very few and not at all clear. The Council of Hippo (393) required that children destined for the clergy should be taught the Scriptures. It also wanted clerics before their ordination to become acquainted with the synodical rulings which they would be called on to apply (Canons 1 and 2). This second requirement was repeated by the Carthaginian councils of 397 (Canon 3) and 419 (Canon 18 of the African Code). Finally, the Council of Seleucia (410) decreed that the Psalms of David should be learned by heart before entry into the clergy (Canon 16). The catechetical schools in the East also contributed to the education of clerics, though this was not their primary purpose.[57] In Rome from the end of the third century there was the *schola lectorum*.[58] But whether such schools spread in the major provinces is not known. All that can be said with certainty is that in the early centuries clerics either educated themselves or studied privately with other learned clerics. Beyond that general responsibility for supervising the clergy's formation in the Scriptures, doctrine and canon law rested chiefly on the bishop and the educated clergy under him.[59]

The indeterminate character of the education of the clergy is reflected, for example, in the *Ecclesiastical Canons*.[60] There the bishop must have "had some education and be able to interpret the Scriptures; if he is uneducated, let him be gentle and overflowing in love for all" (*Can. eccl.* 16). The only work that contains any details, but then only for bishops, is the *Statuta Ecclesiae Antiqua*, a private collection of the Western Church which was compiled in the second half of the fifth century.[61] The bishop is required to be literate, though it is not specified if it is a secular or a religious education which is meant, and to know the divine law, the Scriptures, and the fundamental teaching of the Church (*Stat. Eccl. Ant.* 1).

Although an admiration of learning and scholarship is one of the more striking marks of the Church in the fourth and fifth centuries, the education of the clergy is very rarely the object of any legislation in the period. But if we take into account that the Church's still developing jurisprudence was occupied with urgent matters needing a speedy resolution, we can well understand why legislation on the education of the clergy did not attract sufficient attention to enable a program of studies for candidates to be established.

As we have seen, the education of clerics in the early Church was undetermined. It presents the following characteristics: on the one hand, its very freedom was the cause of various heresies and controversies arising in the Church; on the other hand, it enabled the Church to acquire able servants capable of defending her with the weapons of the spirit, men admired by all. The same regime also prevailed in the West in the early centuries.

Morality[62]

From her foundation, the Church was eager to find candidates for the clergy endowed with all the virtues to ensure the holiness of the sacred institution of the priesthood. In his pastoral epistles the Apostle Paul gives a sketch of the moral qualities of the ideal cleric. It became common for lists to be drawn up of the prerequisites considered indispensable for entry into the priesthood. The strong influence of Paul's original list is clearly evident in these catalogues.[63] Later writers took words and phrases from him to define the more important qualities. A distinguishing feature of these writers is an emphasis on the moral qualities which an aspiring cleric must possess. The phrase "moral qualities" embraces the whole range, but chief among them was chastity. This is taken for granted by all the decrees aimed at strengthening the esteem in which the clergy were held. From the earliest years chastity was regarded not only as a necessary presupposition but also as an established condition of priests of even the non-Christian religions. Among them the conviction prevailed that a priest must be impeccable and pure if his worship is to be acceptable to the Deity.[64] The Jews especially made every effort to ensure that chastity was preserved by the priests of the Jewish faith, until the lapse of the priesthood after 70 AD. The Law defined in great detail the acts or conditions that rendered a man unfit for priestly office through a lack of the required purity.[65]

In the fathers and ecclesiastical writers of the early centuries, this principle took the form of exalting the priesthood to emphasize the moral integrity that should characterize the aspiring cleric.[66] The same principle was followed by ecclesiastical legislation, as set out in works by anonymous authors, and especially in the canons of local and ecumenical councils. Historically, the promotion of chastity as the shepherd's basic virtue, and ensuring that he observed it throughout his life, was one of the chief concerns of ecclesiastical legislators. Because of the nature of the virtue of chastity, which demands that a person suppress some of his natural instincts, the legislation relating to it has a negative rather than positive character.[67] Factors contributing to this situation were the end of the persecutions and the throngs of new converts coming into the Church. This was at the time of the barbarian invasions and the collapse of the Roman Empire in the West.[68] Each of these factors in its own way contributed to the creation of conditions unfavorable to the safeguarding of the austere moral demands the Church was making on her clergy. Among these conditions were the many recent converts, some of whom were still vulnerable in their new beliefs and lifestyle. The danger of accommodating the new political reality by adjusting hitherto ethical standards necessitated increased vigilance on the part of the Church. As a result, she insisted on the highest possible moral integrity of her clergy.

In the Church's early legislation the chastity of the clergy is treated chiefly in two ways, according to whether the candidates were married or unmarried. Extra-marital relations are classed with carnal sins which destroy the innocence restored by baptism. Those who fall into such sins are to be subjected to public penance, and this fact alone was reckoned to exclude such people from ordination.[69] A candidate for the clergy was under an obligation to keep his purity intact throughout his life. Serious sins against chastity, even if they were committed in the distant past and had in the meantime been forgiven, were a reason for dismissal from the priesthood.[70]

A particular concern for clerical morality was shown by the Council of Elvira. This council not only bars bishops, presbyters, or deacons guilty of fornication from communion (Canon 18), but forbids any circumstances which can lead to misunderstanding. Consequently, a cleric may not have any woman in his household unless she is a sister or daughter, even if she is dedicated to God (Canon 27). A similar attitude is shown by the First Ecumenical Council (Nicaea 3),[71] and the African[72] and Gallic[73] synods of the fifth century. The canons of these Western synods also append penalties in the event of disobedience. Among the African synods, those of Hippo (393 [Canon 24]) and Carthage (397 [Canon 25])[74] forbid clerics even to meet widows or virgins without permission from the bishop and being accompanied by persons of irreproachable character.[75] To reinforce ecclesiastical legislation on these matters, laws were also issued by the state. First, Valentinian threatened severe penalties in 370 against clerics who visited the homes of widows or virgins; in the same decree he forbids clerics to receive a legacy from a woman (*Cod. theod.* 16.2.20). Later, in 420, the emperors Honorius and Theodosius II permit only a cleric's mother, sister, or daughter to live with him. They also forbid the divorce of a wife under the pretext of chastity in accordance with the provisions of Canon 5 of the *Apostolic Canons* (*Cod. theod.* 16.2.44).

The Council of Elvira refers to fornication as a cause of a candidate's exclusion from the order of subdeacon to prevent such offenders from ascending to the higher grades of the clergy (Canon 30). The same spirit informs the Council of Neocaesarea, which threatens a presbyter guilty of adultery or fornication with excommunication (Canon 1). Elsewhere the same synod forbids only the offering of the sacrifice to a priest who confesses to a carnal sin committed before his ordination (Neocaesarea 9). The imposition of this penalty reveals a conviction that it was especially carnal sins that rendered a priest unfit to offer up the bloodless sacrifice. A deacon guilty of the same sin is sentenced to deposition (Neocaesarea 10). The Church of Rome is in agreement with these measures, defining the chastity required in a candidate for the clergy with even greater precision. The council convened by Pope Damasus in about 374 informs us of the Church order prevailing in Rome. This council, as also in its legislation on canonical age, distinguishes between those baptized in infancy and those baptized at a mature age. Ordination is permitted to the former, so long as they have preserved their chastity since childhood. It is also permitted to the latter, provided they have lived a respectable life and have not married more than once.[76] In all cases, the candidate must have maintained the purity acquired through baptism if he were to be considered acceptable for the clergy.

If, against the legislation we have discussed of both Church and state designed to prevent misunderstanding, we set what the fathers have said about the intrusion of unworthy candidates into the clergy, we can justly claim that the decrees about the indispensability of moral probity were not always observed conscientiously. The fathers do not mention what sins were being committed, but refer to a general absence of morality as a cause for anxiety about the prevailing state of affairs. St. Basil, for example, asks for aspiring clerics to be examined because many unworthy candidates were entering the ranks of the clergy (Canon 89). St. Gregory of

Nazianzus (*Or.* 1.8) and St. John Chrysostom (*Sac.* 3.15) also complain about the presence of unworthy clerics in the Church. The aforementioned Roman synod also speaks of the ordination of unworthy clerics.[77] People described as unworthy are laymen excommunicated by their bishop, or clerics censured by him who have nevertheless been ordained or promoted by another bishop. This concerns the ordination of people who have been placed in the ranks of the penitents.[78] They are the object of ecclesiastical legislation particularly from the end of the fourth century.[79] The *Statuta Ecclesiae Antiqua* refer to penitents as unfit for ordination even if they have returned to a moral and virtuous life. A cleric who conceals the fact that he has been subjected to public penance incurs the penalty of deposition. And a bishop who is found to have concurred with the deception is permanently deprived of his right to ordain (*Stat. Eccl. Ant.* 68). This regime against penitents, especially those who had lost their moral integrity, was in force throughout the Church. But this does not mean that the severe treatment of penitents was always regarded as the most effective approach. Apart from anything else, an inflexible austerity would have resulted in difficulty finding suitable candidates for the clergy. This difficulty led the Council of Toledo (400) to adopt a mild policy toward penitents. It consented to admit them under certain conditions to the lower grades of the minor clergy. The grades mentioned are those of doorkeeper and reader. But readers are deprived of the right to read the Gospels or the Pauline Epistles. Should any penitents be already subdeacons, they can retain their office but without the right to touch the sacred vessels (Toledo 2).

As already noted, legislation on the chastity of clerics also covers the marital relations allowed to married candidates. The conduct of a cleric was expected to be irreproachable, but this was difficult if he did not meet the requirements laid down for marriage.[80] On the basis of Paul's injunction, a cleric had to be "the husband of one wife" (1 Tim 3:2; Titus 1:6). This demanded that the candidate should not have been married more than once.[81] A man who had married a second time was not thought to be able to practice a higher morality, and was therefore unfit for the clergy.[82] There was a difference between East and West with regard to the recognition of a marriage contracted before baptism. In the East pre-baptismal marriage was not considered valid,[83] whereas in the West it was.[84] According to the position taken, the same person could be regarded as once or twice married. Exclusion from entry into the clergy even extended to marrying a woman who was not a virgin,[85] including a widow[86] or a woman divorced for adultery.[87] These two requirements of a single marriage and the spouse's virginity were intended, no doubt, to ensure the moral integrity in all things of the ministers of the Most High. On this issue a milder approach is noticeable in the *Apostolic Canons* and the Western synods in comparison with the Church of Rome. Although the former accept a man who has been married twice or has married a widow as a reader or even a subdeacon, the latter normally excludes him even from the lower grades of the clergy.

A Noble Task

Notes

1. See Eutaxias 1872, 39; Milasch 1906, 361.

2. Cf. Lafontaine 1963, 121ff.; Gaudemet 1958, 124ff.; Delmaille 1935; Blokscha 1931.

3. Cases in which the enthusiastic participation of the laity exercised a decisive influence on the election of their shepherd include those of Ambrose (374), Augustine (391), Synesius of Cyrene (410), and Cyril of Alexandria (412).

4. St. Jerome agrees with this age for presbyters. See *Ep.* 82, *Ad Theophilum* 8 and *Comm. Ezech.* 14.47.

5. Siricius allows those baptized in infancy to become readers at a young age and acolytes or subdeacons during adolescence, without defining this age more precisely. For the remaining ranks (of the higher clergy) he lays down the thirtieth year for deacons, with five years of ministry for presbyters and ten years for bishops. See Siricius, *Ep.* 1 (*Ad Himerium episcopum Tarraconensem* 9-10).

6. As the highest age limit for readers baptized in infancy, Zosimus prescribes their twentieth year. Rather than mention any other age, Zosimus lays down the following lengths of time and ministry to be spent in the remaining ranks: four years as acolyte and subdeacon, and five years as deacon. See Zosimus, *Ep.* 9 (*Hesechio episcopo Salonitano* 3.5).

7. See Gaudemet 1958, 127.

8. Pope Leo I also emphasizes this principle in his letter to the bishops of Mauretania (dated to 446). He declares that what is important is the *aetas maturitatis* (*Ep.* 12): "What does 'lay hands hastily' mean except to give the episcopal honor to the untried, to those who have not reached the age of maturity, before the time of examination, before their obedience has been tried, before they have experienced discipline?" (trans. Hunt, 49-50).

9. See Lafontaine 1963, 150ff.

10. Cf. Lafontaine 1963, 235ff.; Gaudemet 1958, 150ff.

11. On the influence of civil legislation on the application of this principle to the Church, see Le Bras 1949, 380.

12. For examples, see Achelis 1912, 2:33 and 419-420; Gaudemet 1958, 336.

13. See Wieland 1897, 42ff., 52ff., 106ff., 125ff.; Gaudemet 1962, 194; 1958, 104.

14. On Augustine, see *Ep.* 21.1-3 and 126.7. On Gregory of Nazianzus, see *Vit.*; *Or.* 1 and 3; Basil, *Ep.* 225.

15. In addition, Gregory was married when he was elected bishop of Nyssa. The married state, however, was not yet an impediment to promotion to episcopal rank. See Daniélou 1956.

16. See also p. 121 above.

17. As mentioned above (p. 194), there were also cases in which people postponed baptism in the pursuit of greater preparation. They lived a virtuous Christian life even though they had not yet been baptized. Among these there were doubtless also those who were put forward for ordination. See Stephanidis 1959, 107.

18. Cf. Zeiller 1938b.

19. Such a person was St. Ambrose, whose election as bishop of Milan gave to the orthodox a rare shepherd who was able to oppose the Arians successfully. See Ambrose, *Paen.* 2.8.72; *Off.* 1.1.4; Paulinus, *Vit. Ambr.* 6. There are also other cases of persons of rare ability promoted to the episcopacy to the Church's advantage, especially in the post-Constantinian period, when the influence of the bishops extended beyond the spiritual sphere into secular matters. See also Lafontaine 1963, 260-263.

20. See Lafontaine 1963, 263ff.

21. Cf. Gaudemet 1958, 127-128; Eutaxias 1872, 58ff.

22. "[L]et a man be deprived of his priesthood, however honest he be, if he is scarred or disfigured in any way" (*Ep.* 52, *Ad Nepotianum* 10; trans. Wright, 217).

23. Cf. Gaudemet 1958, 129ff.; Eutaxias 1872, 120ff.

24. See Eutaxias 1872, 39-40.

25. See Richert 1901, 58-63.

26. Cf. Laodicea 3 and Sardica 10.

27. See p. 281 above.

28. See pp. 200-203 and 279 above.

29. See pp. 279-282 above.

30. See Richert 1901, 47ff.

31. See pp. 186-187 above.

32. See Hefele 1907-1952, 1:408-409.

33. Cf. Trembelas 1965.

34. See Stephanidis 1959, 84. Cf. Pheidas 1969, 60ff.

35. The legal rulings of these synods are presented as Canons 57 and 68 of the African Code of the Carthaginian Council of 419.

36. Canon 68 of the African Code.

37. Ibid.

38. See Karmiris 1954, 6. Cf. Karmiris 1964, 948; Alivizatos 1949, 73ff.; Kotsonis 1957, 180ff.

39. Cf. Lafontaine 1963, 217ff.; Gaudemet 1958, 135-136.

40. Cf. Eutaxias 1872, 69ff.

41. Ibid.

42. Basil, *Leg. lib. gent.* Cf. *Fid.* 1. Cf. also Tatakis 1960, 90ff.

43. Cf. Koukoules 1948, 38ff.

44. The chief organizers of elementary education in the Church were the Three Hierarchs. Cf. Koukoules 1948, 35.

45. Cf. Marrou 1956 and Kennedy 1983.

46. This is particularly true of some of the most famous Greek fathers of this period, including St. Basil the Great and St. John Chrysostom, since they studied under the famous pagan Greek rhetorician Libanius, whose dedication to and mastery of classical Attic literary conventions were universally recognized. For an excellent introduction to the influence of classical rhetoric on Christian homiletics, see Pelikan 2001. For more comprehensive studies, see Kennedy 1983; Anderson 1993; Bowersock 1969.

47. See Stephanidis 1959, 303.

48. See Eutaxias 1872, 86.

49. For a contextualized study of Julian's thought and anti-Christian policies, see Smith 1995, 179-218.

50. Cf. Phytrakis 1968, 23.

51. Of these, Gregory of Nazianzus created a Christian poetry worthy of comparison with the products of classical

Greek civilization. Cf. Phytrakis 1968, 25ff.

52. Phytrakis 1968, 25ff. Cf. Tatakis 1960, 171ff.

53. By the sixth century this custom was so commonplace that some scholars have written that monasteries became, in effect, seminaries for bishops; cf. Sterk 1998.

54. See Phytrakis 1960, 283.

55. See Eutaxias 1872, 87-88.

56. See Lafontaine 1963, 218ff.

57. See p. 239, n. 105 above.

58. Cf. Allard 1895, 25.

59. See Lafontaine 1963, 223ff.

60. See p. 68 above.

61. Cf. Lafontaine 1963, 227-228.

62. Cf. Lafontaine 1963, 155ff.; Gaudemet 1958, 132ff.

63. Cf. Weidinger 1928; Vögtle 1936.

64. See Marquardt 1881-1885, 3:223 and 237ff.

65. Cf. Vaux 1961, 347-348 and 356; Greenberg 1950, 41.

66. See especially the fourth- and fifth-century ecclesiastical writers discussed in pp. 101-173 above.

67. See Christodoulos 1896, 167.

68. For a comprehensive examination of this period, see part 1 of Brown 2003.

69. See Stephanidis 1959, 107-109.

70. See Canons 30 and 76 of Elvira, and Canons 9 and 10 of Neocaesarea.

71. Cf. Basil 88 where this order is applied.

72. Hippo (393) 16; Carthage (397) 17.

73. Andegavum (453) 4; Arles 2 (ca. 450) 3 and 4.

74. This canon is repeated in Canon 38 of the African Code.

75. We have already noted St. Ambrose's exhortations on the same subject (p. 156 above).

76. Canon 5 of the collection *Ad Gallos Episcopos*.

77. Canon 5 of the collection *Ad Gallos Episcopos*.

78. To the class of penitents belonged those who had committed serious sins. Such people were obliged to confess them publicly. Sins which were subject to public penance included adultery, fornication, heresy, apostasy, murder, etc.

See Stephanidis 1959, 107-109. Cf. Gaudemet 1958.

79. Cf. Toledo (400) 2.

80. Cf. Basil 27.

81. See *Can. ap.* 17. See also Basil 12; Rome (374 under Damasus) 5, of the collection *Ad Gallos Episcopos*; Orange (441) 25; Valentinum (374) 1. Although here it is successive digamy that is at issue, there were patristic authors who maintained that the Apostle Paul had only condemned digamy while the first marriage was still valid. See Theodore of Mopsuestia, *Fr. 1 Tim.* 3.; Theodoret of Cyrus, *Comm. 1 Tim.* 3.

82. Cf. Ambrose, *Off.* 1.50.

83. See *Can. ap.* 17. St. Jerome agrees with this view (*Ep.* 69, *Ad Oceanum*).

84. See Ambrose, *Off.* 1.50; Augustine, *Bon. conj.* 21; Valentinum (374) 1.

85. See *Can. ap.* 17 and 18; Arles (314) 25. This canon belongs to a later council of Arles, but it is referred to among the canons of 314. See Mansi 1901-1927, 2:474.

86. See *Can. ap.* 18; Valentinum (374) 1; Toledo (400) 3; Arles 2 (ca. 450) 45.

87. See Neocaesarea 8.

Epilogue

If a manner of life worthy of their privileged position in God's kingdom on earth—his holy Church—is demanded of the laity, obviously more will be required of the laity's spiritual leaders, the clergy.

But on what basis? When laws are framed, historical factors generally dictate their origin. The same may be said about the legislation regulating presuppositions for entering the clergy. More specifically, this legislation was created in response to certain abuses which threatened to compromise the sanctity of the clerical office. Furthermore, the Church did not correct these abuses, or perhaps prevent them, everywhere in the same way. In the primitive Church, the basic prerequisites for entering the clergy were those mentioned in St. Paul's pastoral epistles. Their importance is shown by the fact that St. Paul's lists of desired qualities were the basis of all later lists of prerequisites for entering the clergy. The apostolic fathers not infrequently used words and phrases lifted directly from the pastoral epistles. Next come anonymous works of codification, which also manifest the strong influence of earlier ecclesiastical writings. In the long period from the age succeeding the post-apostolic to the Fourth Ecumenical Council (Chalcedon) of 451, there appeared a number of pastoral works by Church fathers and also the relevant decrees of local and ecumenical councils. These bring us to the age of the true flowering of ecclesiastical legislation.

With regard to the prerequisites for entering the clergy, although there were local variations, two important historical factors prompted their general imposition: on the one hand, the recognition of the Christian faith by the government, which first granted it toleration and then made it the official religion of the state; on the other hand, the barbarian invasions, which disrupted the life of Christian populations. Under these circumstances the Church was faced with many problems. Many candidates for the clergy appeared so lacking that they could sometimes be described as unworthy. The Church, then, had a sacred duty to preserve the moral integrity of the clergy. Her efforts to achieve this reveal a steadfast determination to receive into the ranks of the clergy only persons considered morally irreproachable.

In pursuit of this aim, important works were produced by leading Church fathers, such as Gregory of Nazianzus and John Chrysostom in the East, and Ambrose of Milan in the West. These fathers exalt the priesthood and exhort those who aspire to it to clothe themselves in all the virtues indispensable to the exercise of their ministry. Other fathers, such as Athanasius, Basil, Cyril of Alexandria, Isidore of Pelusium, and Jerome, addressed letters to individuals who desired to know, among other things, how to deal with certain problems relevant to entering the clergy. Because of the great respect and authority that these authors enjoyed in the Church, the views they expressed on matters of general interest to the clergy acquired great authority. They were eventually acknowledged officially by the

Church as important sources of ecclesiastical law. Thus, taking the form of canons, these patristic opinions were recognized as equally authoritative as the canons issued by the councils.

But before the Church made such use of the views expressed by the fathers in their letters, she had already developed a body of legislation through her principal legal organs. These were the local and ecumenical councils. When the Church first addressed issues relating to entry into the clergy, there existed very few relevant canons from ecumenical councils. The work of defining the conditions for entry into the clergy was undertaken largely by local synods held throughout the Empire. By the middle of the fifth century, the basic presuppositions for entry into the clergy had already been fixed.

Our review of the development of these prerequisites allows us to divide them into two groups. To the first group, concerning the validity of ordination, belong the prerequisites of male gender and baptism. These requirements, however, are regarded as self-evident and are taken for granted in the legislative sources of this period. The Church's practice alone confirms them. To the second group, concerning the legitimacy of ordination, belong a series of criteria designed to secure the admission of candidates worthy of ecclesiastical office. The main prerequisites belonging to this group are six, of which three are physical and three spiritual. The physical prerequisites include canonical age, a period of probation, and soundness of mind and body. The canonical age ensures that the candidate has reached maturity, a period of probation tests his perseverance, and soundness of mind and body renders him capable of performing his work as a cleric. The spiritual prerequisites include faith, education, and morality. Faith guarantees the preservation of orthodox teaching, education supplies the means of preserving it and spreading it, and morality enables it to be put into practice, insofar as the cleric is a model to be imitated in the Christian community.

As we can see, there is a close relationship between the prerequisites of each group. A careful examination of them reveals that the aim of the physical criteria is to ensure that the candidate is capable of exercising his office in an acceptable manner. The aim of the spiritual criteria is to form a religious leader worthy of imitation, whose spiritual qualities promise the responsible exercise of his apostolate. If we take into account the natural sequential order of the two groups, we can see that one cannot exist without the other. Consequently, the spiritual criteria are an extension and completion of the physical ones, while the physical criteria presuppose and prepare for the spiritual ones. Thus of the physical criteria, canonical age and a period of probation are closely linked to two of the spiritual ones. By requiring a relative maturity and the gradual assumption of duties, the Church offers the cleric the means by which his faith and morality are duly tested and strengthened. Of these morality, in the form of chastity, is presented as one of the cleric's most important virtues. This virtue, more than any other, has the greatest influence on the spiritual life of believers when it is practiced out of Christian conviction. It endows a person with a moral stature and strength which makes him a model to be imitated. But to establish and consolidate this virtue requires long practice on the cleric's part. This is achieved by applying the two physical criteria just mentioned. By this method the objective presupposition is subjectivized in a very natural and effective way.

As we have demonstrated, although legislation on the prerequisites for entry into the clergy in the first five centuries arose incidentally from the need to deal with specific problems in the life of the Church, the solutions given served a broader purpose. This purpose was to offer the Church clerics worthy of their apostolate in every way, whose irreproachable example would ensure the success of their holy work. It is a purpose that certainly justifies the ecclesiastical legislation framed to support it.

Bibliography

Abbreviations for Editions of Primary Sources Used
(Other editions may be found in the bibliography.)

CSEL Corpus scriptorum ecclesiasticorum latinorum. Vienna, 1866-.

GCS Die griechischen christlichen Schriftsteller der ersten drei Jahrhunderte. 53 vols. Leipzig: Hinrichs, 1897-1969.

PG Patrologia graeca. Edited by Jacques Paul Migne. 162 vols. Paris, 1857-1886.

PL Patrologia latina. Edited by Jacques Paul Migne. 217 vols. Paris, 1844-1864.

Works by Ancient Authors

AMBROSE
De Cain et Abel (PL 14:333-380) [*Cain*]
De fuga saeculi (PL 14:597-624) [*Fug.*]
De obitu Valentiniani consolatio (PL 16:1417-1444) [*Valent.*]
De officiis ministrorum (PL 16:25-194) [*Off.*]
De paenitentia (PL 16:485-546) [*Paen.*]
De sacramentis (PL 16:435-482) [*Sacr.*]
Enarrationes in XII Psalmos davidicos (PL 14:963-1238) [*Enarrat. Ps.*]
Epistulae (PL 16:913-1342) [*Ep.*]
Exhortatio virginitatis (PL 16:351-380) [*Exh. virginit.*]

Expositio evangelii secundum Lucam (PL 15:1607-1944)
[*Exp. Luc.*]
Paulinus Mediolanus: *Vita Ambrosii Mediolanensis* (PL
14:27-46 and 51-72) [*Vit. Ambr.*]

AMBROSIASTER
Commentarius in XIII epistulas Paulinas (PL 17:47-536)
[*Comm. 1 Tim., Comm. Tit.*]

ATHANASIUS
Apologia ad Constantium (*Defense before Constantius*) (PG
25:596ff.) [*Apol. Const.*]
Fragmenta in Matthaeum (*Fragments on Matthew*) (PG
27:1364-1389) [*Fr. Matt.*]
Historia Arianorum (*History of the Arians*) (PG 25:691-796)
[*H. Ar.*]
Epistula ad Dracontium (*Letter to Dracontius*) (PG 25:523-
534) [*Ep. Drac.*]
Epistula ad Rufinianum (*Letter to Rufinianus*) (PG 26:1179-
1182) [*Ep. Rufin.*]

ATHENAGORAS
Legatio pro Christianis (PG 6:889ff.) [*Leg.*]

AUGUSTINE
Epistulae (PL 33) [*Ep.*]

BASIL THE GREAT
Enarratio in prophetam Isaiam (*Commentary on the Prophet
Isaiah*) (PG 30:117ff.) [*Enarrat. Isa.*]
Sermones ascetici (*Ascetic Sermon* 10) (PG 31:620-625)
[*Ascet.*]

Homilia in illud: Attende tibi ipsi (*Homily on "Attend to Yourself"*) (PG 31:197-217) [*Attend.*]

De fide (PG 31:464-472) [*Fid.*]

De humilitate (*Homily 20: On Humility*) (PG 31:525-540) [*Humil.*]

Epistulae (PG 32:220-1112) [*Ep.*]

Regulae fusius tractatae (*Longer Rules*) (PG 31:889-1052) [*Reg. fus.*]

Moralia (PG 31:700-869) [*Moral.*]

Regulae brevius tractatae (*Shorter Rules*) (PG 31:1080-1305) [*Reg. br.*]

Ad adolescentes de legendis libris gentilium (*To Adolescents*) (PG 31:563-590) [*Leg. lib. gent.*]

CLEMENT OF ALEXANDRIA
Stromata (*Miscellanies*) (PG 8-9) [*Strom.*]

CLEMENT OF ROME
1-2 Clement [*1-2 Clem.*]

CYPRIAN OF CARTHAGE
Epistulae (CSEL 3) [*Ep.*]
Pontius Diaconus: *Vita Cypriani* (CSEL 3) [*Vit. Cypr.*]

CYRIL OF ALEXANDRIA
Commentarius in Joannem (*Commentary on John*) (PG 73-74) [*Comm. Jo.*]

Commentarius in XII prophetas (*Commentary on the Minor Prophets*) (PG 71-72) [*Os.–Mal.*]

De adoratione et cultu in spiritu et veritate (*On Worship in Spirit and in Truth*) (PG 68) [*Ador.*]

CYRIL OF JERUSALEM
Catecheses ad illuminandos 1-18 (Catechetical Lecture)
　　(PG 33:369ff.) [*Catech.*]

EPHRAIM THE SYRIAN
On the Priesthood [*Priesthood*]

EPIPHANIUS OF CYPRUS
Panarion (*Refutation of All Heresies*) (PG 41-42) [*Pan.*]

EUSEBIUS OF CAESAREA
Demonstratio evangelica (*Demonstration of the Gospel*) (PG
　　22:13ff.) [*Dem. ev.*]
Historia ecclesiastica (*Ecclesiastical History*) (PG 20:45-906)
　　[*Hist. eccl.*]

GREGORY OF NAZIANZUS
Apologetica (Orat. 2) (PG 35:408-513) [*Apol.*]
De vita sua (Ode 11) (*On His Own Life*) (PG 37) [*Vit.*]
Oratio in laudem Basilii (Orat. 43) (PG 36) [*Or. Bas.*]
In laudem Athanasii (Orat. 21) (PG 35:1081-1128) [*Athan.*]
Orationes (*Orations*) (PG 35-36) [*Or.*]
Odae (*Poems*) (PG 37-38) [*Od.*]

GREGORY OF NYSSA
De virginitate (*On Virginity*) (PG 46:317ff.) [*Virg.*]
Epistulae (PG 44:999-1108) [*Ep.*]
Epistula canonica ad Letoium (*Letter to Letoius*) (PG 45:221-
　　236) [*Ep. can.*]
In baptismum Christi (PG 46:577ff.) [*Bapt.*]

HERMAS

Shepherd of Hermas [Herm. *Mand.*; Herm. *Sim.*; Herm. *Vis.*]

HIPPOLYTUS

Traditio apostolica (*The Apostolic Tradition*) [*Trad. ap.*]
Commentarium in Danielem (*Commentary on Daniel*) (GCS 1) [*Comm. Dan.*]
Refutatio omnium haeresium (PG 16:3017ff.) [*Haer.*]

IGNATIUS OF ANTIOCH

Letters [*Eph.* = *To the Ephesians*; *Magn.* = *To the Magnesians*; *Phld.* = *To the Philadelphians*; *Pol.* = *To Polycarp*; *Smyrn.* = *To the Smyrnaeans*]

IRENAEUS OF LYONS

Adversus haereses (*Against Heresies*) (PG 7) [*Haer.*]

ISIDORE OF PELUSIUM

Epistulae (PG 78) [*Ep.*]

JEROME

Commentariorum in epistulam ad Titum liber (PG 26) [*Comm. Tit.*]
Epistulae (CSEL 54) [*Ep.*]

JOHN CHRYSOSTOM

Adversus oppugnatores vitae monasticae (*Against Those Who Attack the Monastic Life*) (PG 47:319-386) [*Oppugn.*]
Homiliae in epistulam i ad Timotheum (PG 62:501-600) [*Hom. 1 Tim.*]

Homiliae in epistulam ii ad Timotheum (PG 62:599-662) [*Hom. 2 Tim.*]

Homiliae in epistulam ad Titum (*Homilies on the Epistle to Titus*) (PG 62:663-700) [*Hom. Tit.*]

Non esse ad gratiam concionandum (PG 50:653-662) [*Grat.*]

De sacerdotio (*Priesthood*) (PG 47:623-692) [*Sac.*]

De virginitate (PG 48) [*Virg.*]

Ad Theodorum lapsum (*Exhortation to Theodore after His Fall*) (PG 47) [*Theod. laps.*]

Ad populum Antiochenum de statuis (PG 49:15-222) [*Stat.*]

JUSTIN MARTYR
Apologia i (*First Apology*) (PG 6) [*1 Apol.*]

LEO I
Epistulae (PL 54) [*Ep.*]

ORIGEN
Contra Celsum (*Against Celsus*) (PG 11; GCS 2-3) [*Cels.*]

Commentarium in evangelium Matthaei (*Commentary on Matthew*) (PG 13; GCS 38) [*Comm. Matt.*]

Homiliae in Leviticum (*Homilies on Leviticus*) (PG 12; GCS 29) [*Hom. Lev.*]

POLYCARP OF SMYRNA
To the Philippians [*Phil.*]

SIRICIUS
Epistulae (PL 13) [*Ep.*]

SOCRATES
Historia ecclesiastica (*Ecclesiastical History*) (PG 67:29-872) [*Hist. eccl.*]

SOZOMEN
Historia ecclesiastica (*Ecclesiastical History*) (PG 67:844-1630) [*Hist. eccl.*]

TERTULLIAN
De baptismo (*Baptism*) (PL 1) [*Bapt.*]
De paenitentia (*Repentance*) (PL 1) [*Paen.*]
De praescriptione haereticorum (*Prescription against Heretics*) (PL 2; CSEL 47) [*Praescr.*]
De virginibus velandis (*The Veiling of Virgins*) (PL 2) [*Virg.*]

THEODORE OF MOPSUESTIA
In epistulam i ad Timotheum (*Commentary on 1 Timothy*) (PG 66) [*Fr. 1 Tim.*]

THEODORET OF CYRUS
Interpretatio in xiv epistulas sancti Pauli (*Commentary on the 14 Epistles of St Paul*) (PG 82:35-878) [*Comm. Phil., Comm. Tit., Comm. 1 Tim.*]
Historia ecclesiastica (*Ecclesiastical History*) (PG 82:882-1280) [*Hist. eccl.*]

ZOSIMUS
Epistulae (Mansi 3) [*Ep.*]

ANONYMOUS WORKS

Canones apostolicae (*Apostolic Canons*) [*Can. ap.*]

Canones ecclesiastici (*Ecclesiastical Canons of the Holy Apostles*) [*Can. eccl.*]

Canones Hippolyti (*Canons of Hippolytus*) [*Can. Hippol.*]

Constitutiones apostolicae (*Apostolic Constitutions*) [*Const. ap.*]

Didache [*Did.*].

Testament of Our Lord Jesus Christ [*Test. Dom.*]

CODES OF CIVIL LAW

Codex Theodosianus [*Cod. theod.*]

Justinian's *Novellae* [*Nov.*]

Secondary Literature (together with Editions and Translations of Primary Sources)

Achelis, Hans. 1891. *Die Canones Hippolyti*. Texte und Untersuchungen zur Geschichte der altchristlichen Literatur 6. Leipzig: J. C. Hinrichs.

————. 1902. *Virgines subintroductae: Ein Beitrag zum VII. Kapitel des I. Korintherbriefs*. Leipzig: J. C. Hinrichs.

————. 1912. *Das Christentum in den ersten drei Jahrhunderten*. 2 vols. Leipzig: Quelle & Meyer.

Achelis, Hans, and Johannes Flemming. 1904. *Die syrische Didaskalia*. Texte und Untersuchungen zur Geschichte der altchristlichen Literatur 25. Leipzig: J. C. Hinrichs.

Adam, Alfred. 1957. Die Entstehung des Bischofsamtes. *Wort und Dienst* 5:104-113.

Alivizatos, Amilkas S. 1910. Ê sêmasia tou episkopikou axiômatos kata ton Eirênaion. *Nea Sion* 10:336-355.

———. 1949. *Ê Oikonomia kata to kanonikon dikaion tês Orthodoxou Ekklêsias*. Athens: Astêr.

Allard, P. 1895. Le clergé chrétien. *Revue des questions historiques* 58.

Altaner, Berthold. 1958. *Patrologie: Leben, Schriften und Lehre der Kirchenväter*. 5th ed. Freiburg im Breisgau: Herder. Translated by Hilda C. Graef as *Patrology* (2d ed.; New York: Herder & Herder, 1961).

Ambrose. *Letters*. 1954. Translated by Mary Melchior Beyenka. Fathers of the Church 26. New York: Fathers of the Church.

———. *Theological and Dogmatic Works*. 1963. Translated by Roy J. Deferrari. Fathers of the Church 44. Washington, DC: Catholic University of America Press.

———. *Exposition of the Holy Gospel according to Saint Luke*. 1998. Translated by Theodosia Tomkinson. Etna, CA: Center for Traditionalist Orthodox Studies.

———. *De officiis*. 2001. Edited and translated by Ivor J. Davidson. 2 vols. Oxford Early Christian Studies. Oxford: Oxford University Press.

Anderson, Graham. 1993. *The Second Sophistic: A Cultural Phenomenon in the Roman Empire*. London: Routledge.

Androutsos, Chrêstos. 1907. *Dogmatikê tês Orthodoxou Anatolikês Ekklêsias*. Athens.

Anger, Joseph. 1946. *La doctrine du corps mystique de Jésus-Christ d'après les principes de la théologie de Saint-Thomas*. 8th rev. ed. Paris: Beauchesne. Translated by John J. Burke as *The Doctrine of the Mystical Body of Christ according to the Principles of the Theology of St. Thomas* (New York: Benziger Brothers, 1931).

Ante-Nicene Fathers. 1885-1887. Edited by Alexander Roberts and James Donaldson. 10 vols. Repr. Peabody, MA: Hendrickson, 1994.

The Apostolic Fathers. Edited and translated by Bart D. Ehrman. 2 vols. Loeb Classical Library. Cambridge, MA: Harvard University Press, 2003.

Assemani, J. S. 1732-1746. *Sancti patris nostri Ephraem Syri Opera omnia quae exstant: Graece, Syriace, Latine ad mss. Codices Vaticanos*. 6 vols. Rome: Typographia Vaticana.

Audet, Jean Paul. 1967. *Mariage et célibat dans le service pastoral de l'Église: Histoire et orientations*. Paris: Editions de l'Orante. Translated by Rosemary Sheed as *Structures of Christian Priesthood: A Study of Home, Marriage, and Celibacy in the Pastoral Service of the Church* (New York: Macmillan, 1968).

Aune, David E. 1983. *Prophecy in Early Christianity and the Ancient Mediterranean World*. Grand Rapids, MI: Eerdmans.

Balanos, Dêmêtrios S. 1926. *Oi Treis Ierarchai kai ê epochê tôn*. Athens.

———. 1930. *Patrologia*. Athens.

———. 1961. *Oi Pateres kai syngrapheis tês Archaias Ekklêsias*. 2d ed. Athens.

Bardy, Gustave. 1937a. Aux origines de l'école d'Alexandrie. *Recherches de science religieuse* 27:65-90.

———. 1937b. Canons apostoliques. Pages 1288-1295 in vol. 2 of *Dictionnaire d'archéologie chrétienne et de liturgie*. Edited by Fernand Cabrol. 15 vols. Paris: Letouzey et Ané, 1907-1953.

————. 1937c. Le sacerdoce chrétien d'après les pères apostoliques. *Vie spirituelle* 53:1-28.

————. 1942. Pour l'histoire de l'école d'Alexandrie. *Vivre et penser* 2:80-109.

————. 1949. *La conversion au christianisme durant les premiers siècles*. Théologie 15. Paris: Aubier.

Bareille, G. 1923. II. Baptême d'après les pères grecs et latins. Pages 178-219 in vol. 2.1 of *Dictionnaire de théologie catholique*. 15 vols. Paris, 1903-1950.

Barnes, Timothy D. 1993. *Athanasius and Constantius: Theology and Politics in the Constantinian Empire*. Cambridge, MA: Harvard University Press.

Barnett, James Monroe. 1981. *The Diaconate: A Full and Equal Order*. New York: Seabury.

Bartlett, James Vernon. 1916. The Ordination Prayers in the Ancient Church Order. *Journal of Theological Studies* 17:248-256.

————. 1943. *Church-life and Church-orders during the First Four Centuries, with Special Reference to the Early Eastern Church-orders*. Edited by Cecil John Cadoux. Oxford.

Basil. *Saint Basil: The Letters*. 1926-1934. Translated by Roy J. Deferrari. 4 vols. Loeb Classical Library. Cambridge, MA: Harvard University Press.

————. *St. Basil the Great: Commentary on the Prophet Isaiah*. 2001. Translated by Nikolai A. Lipatov. Texts and Studies in the History of Theology 7. Mandelbachtal/ Cambridge: Edition Cicero.

Batiffol, P. 1911. Les premiers chrétiens et la guerre d'après le 7me canon du concile de Chalcédoine. *Bulletin de la Société nationale des antiquaires de France*.

Bauer, W. 1923. Excurs. Pages 201ff. in *Handbuch zum Neuen Testament: Ergänzungsband: Die apostolischen Väter*. Edited by Hans Lietzmann. Tübingen: Mohr.

Baus, Karl. 1962. *Von der Urgemeinde zur frühchristlichen Grosskirche*. Vol. 1 of *Handbuch der Kirchengeschichte*. Edited by Hubert Jedin. 7 vols. Freiburg: Herder, 1962-1979.

Beaucamp, P. 1949. Un évêque du IIIe siècle aux prises avec les pécheurs: Son activité apostolique. *Bulletin de littérature ecclésiastique* 69:26-47.

Behm, Johannes. 1911. *Die Handauflegung im Urchristentum: Nach Verwendung, Herkunft und Bedeutung in religionsgeschichtlichem Zusammenhang untersucht*. Leipzig: A. Deichert.

Behr-Sigel, Elisabeth. 1991. *The Ministry of Women in the Church*. Translated by Steven Bigham. Redondo Beach, CA: Oakwood Publications.

Behr-Sigel, Elisabeth, and Kallistos Ware. 2000. *The Ordination of Women in the Orthodox Church*. Risk Book Series 92. Geneva: World Council of Churches Publications.

Beyer, Hermann W. 1964. *"Episkeptomai, episkopeô, ktl."* Pages 599-622 in vol. 2 of *Theological Dictionary of the New Testament*. Edited by Gerhard Kittel and Gerhard Friedrich. Translated by Geoffrey W. Bromiley. 10 vols. Grand Rapids, MI: Eerdmans, 1964-1976.

Bickel, E. 1916. Das asketische Ideal bei Ambrosius, Hieronymus und Augustinus: Ein kulturgeschichtliche Studie. *Neue Jahrbücher für das klassische Altertum* 19:437-74.

Bihlmeyer, Karl. 1951-1956. *Kirchengeschichte*. Edited by

Hermann Tüchle. 3 vols. Wissenschaftliche Handbibliothek: Eine Sammlung theologischer Lehrbücher. Paderborn: F. Schöningh.

Blokscha, J. 1931. Die Altersvorschriften für die höhen Weihen im ersten Jahrtausend. *Archiv für katholisches Kirchenrecht* 3:31ff.

Böhmer, Heinrich. 1916. Die Entstehung des Zölibates. In *Geschichtliche Studien Albert Hauck zum 70. Geburtstage dargebracht von Freunden, Schülern, Fachgenossen und dem Mitarbeiterkreise der Realenzyklopädie für protestantische Theologie und Kirche.* Leipzig.

Boissier, Gaston. 1909. *La fin du paganisme: Étude sur les dernières luttes religieuses en Occident au quatrième siècle.* 6th ed. 2 vols. Paris: Hachette.

Bonis, Kônstantinos G. 1953. *Grêgorios o Theologos: Êtoi to genealogikon dendron Grêgoriou tou Nazianzênou kai o pros ton Amphilochion Ikoniou syngenikos autou desmos.* Athens.

———. 1958. O agios Ignatios o Theophoros kai ai peri Ekklêsias antilêpseis autou. *Orthodoxos Skepsis* 1:10-12, 21-22, 39-41.

Botte, B. 1962. The Collegiate Character of the Presbyterate and Episcopate. In *The Sacrament of Holy Orders.* Collegeville, MN: Liturgical Press.

Bougatsos, N. 1962a. Agamia. Pages 116-118 in vol. 1 of *Thrêskeutikê kai êthikê enkyklopaideia.* 12 vols. Athens, 1962-1968.

———. 1962b. Agamia tou Klêrou. Pages 118-124 in vol. 1 of *Thrêskeutikê kai êthikê enkyklopaideia.* 12 vols. Athens, 1962-1968.

Bowersock, G. W. 1969. *Greek Sophists in the Roman Em-*

pire. Oxford: Clarendon Press.

Brakke, David. 1995. *Athanasius and the Politics of Asceticism*. Oxford Early Christian Studies. Oxford: Clarendon Press.

Bratsiotis, P. 1955. *Peri to "vasileion ierateuma."* Offprint from *Gregorios Palamas*. Thessalonica.

Bréhier, Louis. 1937. La vie chrétienne. In vol. 4 of *Histoire de l'Église, depuis les origines jusqu' à nos jours*. Edited by Augustin Fliche and Victor Martin. Paris: Bloud & Gay [1934-].

——. 1941. L'enseignement classique et l'enseignement religieux à Byzance. *Revue d'histoire et de philosophie religieuses* 21.

——. 1946-1950. *Le monde byzantin*. 3 vols. Paris: A. Michel.

Bright, William. 1882. *Notes on the Canons of the First Four General Councils*. Oxford: Clarendon Press.

Broek, Roelof van den. 1995. The Christian 'School' of Alexandria in the Second and Third Centuries. Pages 39-47 in *Centres of Learning: Learning and Location in Pre-modern Europe and the Near East*. Edited by Jan Willem Drijvers and Alasdair A. MacDonald. Brill's Studies in Intellectual History 61. Leiden: Brill.

Brown, Peter. 1988. *The Body and Society: Men, Women, and Sexual Renunciation in Early Christianity*. New York: Columbia University Press.

——. 1989. *The World of Late Antiquity: AD 150-750*. Library of World Civilization. New York: Norton.

——. 2002. *Poverty and Leadership in the Later Roman Empire*. The Menahem Stern Jerusalem Lectures. Hanover, NH: University Press of New England.

————. 2003. *The Rise of Western Christendom: Triumph and Diversity, A.D. 200-1000.* 2d ed. The Making of Europe. Malden, MA: Blackwell.

Burton-Christie, Douglas. 1993. *The Word in the Desert: Scripture and the Quest for Holiness in Early Christian Monasticism.* New York: Oxford University Press.

Campenhausen, Hans Freiherr von. 1953. *Kirchliches Amt und geistliche Vollmacht in den ersten drei Jahrhunderten.* Tübingen: Mohr. Translated by J. A. Baker as *Ecclesiastical Authority and Spiritual Power in the Church of the First Three Centuries* (Stanford, CA: Stanford University Press, 1969).

The Canons of Hippolytus. 1987. Edited by Paul Bradshaw. Translated by Carol Bebawi. Alcuin/GROW Liturgical Study 2. Grove Liturgical Study 50. Bramcote/Nottingham: Grove Books.

Chabot, J. B. 1902. *Synodicon orientale.* Paris.

Chadwick, Henry. 1950. The Silence of Bishops in Ignatius. *Harvard Theological Review* 43:169-172.

Chadwick, Henry, Edward C. Hobbs, and Wilhelm Wuellner, eds. 1980. *The Role of the Christian Bishop in Ancient Society: Protocol of the Thirty-Fifth Colloquy, 25 February 1979.* Colloquy: Center for Hermeneutical Studies in Hellenistic and Modern Culture. Berkeley, CA: The Center.

Chitty, Derwas J. 1966. *The Desert a City: An Introduction to the Study of Egyptian and Palestinian Monasticism under the Christian Empire.* Oxford: Blackwell.

Christodoulos, A. 1896. *Dokimion Ekklêsiastikou Dikaiou.* Constantinople.

Christophilopoulos, Anastasios P. 1954. *Ellênikon Ek-*

klêsiastikon Dikaion ii. Athens.

Christou, P. 1960. *Iôannou tou Chrysostomou, Oi peri ierôsynês logoi*. 2d ed. Thessalonica.

Clark, Elizabeth A. 2004. *History, Theory, Text: Historians and the Linguistic Turn*. Cambridge, MA: Harvard University Press.

Clement of Alexandria. *Stromateis: Books 1-3*. 1991. Translated by John Ferguson. Fathers of the Church 85. Washington, DC: Catholic University of America Press.

Collins, John N. 1990. *Diakonia: Reinterpreting the Ancient Sources*. Oxford: Oxford University Press.

Colson, Jean. 1951. L'évêque dans la Didascalie des Apôtres. *Vie spirituelle* 18:271-290.

———. 1956. *Les fonctions ecclésiales: Aux deux premiers siècles*. Textes et études théologiques. Paris: Desclée de Brouwer.

———. 1960. *La fonction diaconale aux origines de l'église*. Textes et études théologiques. Paris: Desclée de Brouwer.

———. 1963. *L'épiscopat catholique: Collégialité et primauté dans les trois premiers siècles de l'Église*. Unam Sanctam 43. Paris: Éditions du Cerf, 1963.

———. 1964. Der apostolische Dienst in der frühchristlichen Literatur—Apostel und Bischöfe: "Heiligmacher der Völker." In *Das Bischofsamt und die Weltkirche*. Edited by Yves Congar, Käthe Friederike Krause, and Peter Müller. Stuttgart: Schwabenverlag.

Connolly, R. Hugh. 1916a. The Ordination Prayers of Hippolytus. *Journal of Theological Studies* 18:55-58.

———. 1916b. *The So-called Egyptian Church Order and*

Derived Documents. Texts and Studies 8. Cambridge: Cambridge University Press.

———. 1924. New Fragments of the *Didache. Journal of Theological Studies* 25:151-153.

———. 1929. *Didascalia Apostolorum*. Oxford: Clarendon Press.

Cooper, James, and Arthur John Maclean. 1902. *The Testament of Our Lord: Translated into English from the Syriac with Introduction and Notes*. Edinburgh: T & T Clark.

Coppens, Joseph. 1925. *L'imposition des mains et les rites connexes dans le Nouveau Testament et dans l'église ancienne: Étude de théologie positive*. Universitas catholica lovaniensis: Dissertationes ad gradum magistri in Facultate theologica consequendum conscriptae 2.15. Paris: Gabalda.

Croce, Walter. 1948. Die niederen Weihen und ihre hierarchische Wertung: Eine geschichtliche Studie. *Zeitschrift für katholische Theologie* 70:257-314.

Cyprian. *De lapsis; De ecclesiae catholicae unitate*. 1971. Edited and translated by Maurice Bévenot. Oxford Early Christian Texts. Oxford: Clarendon Press.

———. *The Letters of St. Cyprian of Carthage: Letters 1-27*. 1984a. Translated by G. W. Clarke. Ancient Christian Writers 43. New York: Newman Press.

———. *The Letters of St. Cyprian of Carthage: Letters 28-54*. 1984b. Translated by G. W. Clarke. Ancient Christian Writers 44. New York: Newman Press.

———. *The Letters of St. Cyprian of Carthage: Letters 55-66*. 1986. Translated by G. W. Clarke. Ancient Christian Writers 46. New York: Newman Press.

————. *The Letters of St. Cyprian of Carthage: Letters 67-82*. 1989. Translated by G. W. Clarke. Ancient Christian Writers 47. New York: Newman Press.

Cyril of Alexandria. *Letters 51-110*. 1987. Translated by John I. McEnerney. Fathers of the Church 77. Washington, DC: Catholic University of America Press.

Cyril of Jerusalem. *The Works of Saint Cyril of Jerusalem: Volume 1*. 1969. Translated by Leo P. McCauley and Anthony A. Stephenson. Fathers of the Church 61. Washington, DC: Catholic University of America Press.

Daniélou, Jean. 1956. Le mariage de Grégoire de Nysse et la chronologie de sa vie. *Revue des études augustiniennes* 2:71-78.

————. 1958. *Théologie du judéo-christianisme*. Bibliothèque de théologie: Histoire des doctrines chrétiennes avant Nicée 1. Paris: Desclée. Translated and edited by John A. Baker as *The Theology of Jewish Christianity* (London: Darton, Longman & Todd, 1964).

Davies, J. G. 1963. Deacons, Deaconesses and the Minor Orders in the Patristic Period. *Journal of Ecclesiastical History* 14:1-15.

Declareuil, J. 1935. Les curies municipales et le clergé du Bas-Empire. *Revue historique de droit français et étranger* 14:26-53.

Delmaille, J. 1935. Age. Pages 315-348 in vol. 1 of *Dictionnaire d'archéologie chrétienne et de liturgie*. Edited by Fernand Cabrol. 15 vols. Paris: Letouzey et Ané, 1907-1953.

Dentakis, Vasileios L. 1970. *Oion dei einai ton Episkopon kata tous Treis Ierarchas*. Athens.

The Didascalia Apostolorum in Syriac: Chapters I-X. 1979a. Edited and translated by Arthur Vööbus. Corpus scriptorum christianorum orientalium 402: Scriptores Syri 176. Louvain: Secrétariat du CorpusSCO.

The Didascalia Apostolorum in Syriac: Chapters XI-XXVI. 1979b. Edited and translated by Arthur Vööbus. Corpus scriptorum christianorum orientalium 408: Scriptores Syri 180. Louvain: Secrétariat du CorpusSCO.

Dix, Gregory. 1947. The Ministry in the Early Church. Pages 216ff. in *The Apostolic Ministry: Essays on the History and the Doctrine of Episcopacy*. Edited by K. E. Kirk. London: Hodder & Stoughton.

Dölger, F. 1930. Die Taufe des Novatian. *Antike und Christentum* 2:258-267.

Drake, H. A. 2000. *Constantine and the Bishops: The Politics of Intolerance*. Ancient Society and History. Baltimore: Johns Hopkins University Press.

Dumortier, J. 1955. Les idées morales de saint Jean Chrysostome. *Mélanges de science religieuse* 12:27-36.

Dvornik, Francis. 1933. *Les légendes de Constantin et de Méthode vues de Byzance*. Byzantinoslavica: Supplementa 1. Prague: Commissionnaire "Orbis."

Early Christian Biographies. 1952. Translated by Roy J. Deferrari. Fathers of the Church 15. New York: Fathers of the Church.

Echlin, Edward P. 1971. *The Deacon in the Church: Past and Future*. Staten Island, NY: Alba House.

Eichmann, Eduard. 1967. *Lehrbuch des Kirchenrechts auf Grund des Codex Iuris Canonici*. Edited by Klaus Mörsdorf. 12th ed. Wissenschaftliche Handbibliothek. Munich: F. Schöningh.

Epiphanius. *The Panarion of Epiphanius of Salamis: Books 2 and 3 (Sects 47-80,* De Fide). 1994. Translated by Frank Williams. Nag Hammadi and Manichaean Studies 36. Leiden: Brill.

Eutaxias, I. 1872. *Tou Kanonikou Dikaiou tês Orthodoxou Anatolikês Ekklêsias, ta peri ieratikês exousias.* Athens.

Faivre, Alexandre. 1977. *Naissance d'une hiérarchie: Les premières étapes du cursus clérical.* Théologie historique 40. Paris: Éditions Beauchesne.

Falesiedi, Ugo. 1995. *Le diaconie: I servizi assistenziali nella Chiesa antica.* Sussidi patristici 8. Rome: Istituto patristico Augustinianum.

Fascher, Erich. 1927. *Prophetes: Eine sprach- und religions-geschichtliche Untersuchung.* Giessen: A. Töpelmann.

Feine, Hans Erich Alfred. 1955. *Kirchliche Rechtsgeschichte.* 3d ed. Weimar: H. Böhlaus Nachfolger.

Ferguson, E. 1968. Church Order in the Sub-Apostolic Period: A Survey of Interpretations. *Restoration Quarterly* 11:225-248.

Fischer, Joseph A. 1981. *Die Apostolischen Väter.* 8th ed. Schriften des Urchristentums 1. Darmstadt: Wissenschaftliche Buchgesellschaft.

FitzGerald, Kyriaki Karidoyanes. 1998. *Women Deacons in the Orthodox Church: Called to Holiness and Ministry.* Brookline, MA: Holy Cross Orthodox Press.

———. 2002. The Eve–Mary Typology and Women in the Orthodox Church: Reconsidering Rhodes. *Anglican Theological Review* 84:627-644.

FitzGerald, Kyriaki Karidoyanes, ed. 1999. *Orthodox Women Speak: Discerning the "Signs of the Times."* Brookline, MA: Holy Cross Orthodox Press.

Fleury, E. 1930. *Hellénisme et Christianisme: Saint Grégoire de Nazianze et son temps.* Études de Theologie Historique. Paris: Gabriel Beauchesne.

Flint, Peter W., and James C. VanderKam, eds. 1998-1999. *The Dead Sea Scrolls after Fifty Years: A Comprehensive Assessment.* 2 vols. Leiden: Brill.

Foerster, Werner. 1965. "*Klêros, klêroô, ktl.*" Pages 758-785 in vol. 3 of *Theological Dictionary of the New Testament.* Edited by Gerhard Kittel and Gerhard Friedrich. Translated by Geoffrey W. Bromiley. 10 vols. Grand Rapids, MI: Eerdmans, 1964-1976.

Fouyas, Metropolitan M. 1971-1972. Genesis kai anaptyxis tês Christianikês ierôsynês. *Ekklêsiastikos Pharos* 53 (1971):533-549; 54 (1972): 5-34, 133-193, 479-509.

Fransen, Piet. 1962. Ordo, Ordination. Pages 1212-1220 in vol. 7 of *Lexikon für Theologie und Kirche.* Edited by Josef Höfer and Karl Rahner. 10 vols. 2d ed. Freiburg: Herder, 1957-1965.

Frend, W. H. C. 1965. *Martyrdom and Persecution in the Early Church: A Study of a Conflict from the Maccabees to Donatus.* Oxford: Blackwell.

Funk, Franz Xavier. 1891. *Die apostolischen Konstitutionen: Eine litterar-historische Untersuchung.* Rottenburg am Neckar: W. Bader.

———. 1901. *Das Testament unseres Herrn und die verwandten Schriften.* Forschungen zur christlichen Litteratur- und Dogmengeschichte 2. Mainz: F. Kirchheim.

———. 1905. *Didascalia et Constitutiones Apostolorum.* 2 vols. Paderborn: F. Schöningh.

Gallay, Paul. 1943. *La vie de Saint Grégoire de Nazianze.* Lyon: E. Vitte.

Galtier, Paul. 1932. *L'église et la rémission des péchés aux premiers siècles*. Bibliothèque de théologie historique. Paris: Beauchesne.

Gaudemet, Jean. 1958. *L'Église dans l'Empire romain: IVe-Ve siècles*. Histoire du droit et des institutions de l'Église en Occident 3. Paris: Sirey.

—————. 1962. Holy Orders in Early Conciliar Legislation. In *The Sacrament of Holy Orders*. Collegeville, MN: Liturgical Press.

Gedeôn, Manouêl I. 1885. *Patriarchikoi pinakes: Eidêseis historikai viographikai peri tôn patriarchôn Kônstanti-noupoleôs apo Andreou tou Prôtoklêtou mechris Iôakeim G' tou apo Thessalonikês, 36-1884*. Constantinople.

Gennadios, Mêtropolitês Êlioupoleôs kai Theirôn. 1953. *Istoria tou Oikoumenikou Patriarcheiou*. Athens.

Gewiess, Josef. 1958. Bischof: I. Biblisch. Pages 491-492 in vol. 2 of *Lexikon für Theologie und Kirche*. Edited by Josef Höfer and Karl Rahner. 10 vols. 2d ed. Freiburg: Herder, 1957-1965.

Giet, Stanislas. 1941. *Les idées et l'action sociales de Saint Basile*. Paris: J. Gabalda.

Gillmann, Franz. 1903. *Das Institut der Chorbischöfe im Orient*. Munich: Lentner'schen.

Goguel, Maurice. 1947. *L'Église primitive*. Bibliothèque historique. Paris: Payot. Translated by H. C. Snape as *The Primitive Church* (London: Allen & Unwin, 1964).

Gould, Graham. 1993a. *The Desert Fathers on Monastic Community*. Oxford Early Christian Studies. Oxford: Clarendon Press.

—————. 1993b. Lay Christians, Bishops and Clergy in the

Apophthegmata Patrum. Studia patristica 25:396-404.

Granfield, Patrick. 1976. Episcopal Elections in Cyprian: Clerical and Lay Participation. *Theological Studies* 37:41-52.

Grant, Robert M., ed. 1964-. *The Apostolic Fathers: A New Translation and Commentary.* 6 vols. New York: T. Nelson.

Greenberg, M. 1950. A New Approach to the History of the Israelite Priesthood. *Journal of the American Oriental Society* 70:41ff.

Gryson, Roger. 1968. *Le prêtre selon Saint Ambroise.* Universitas Catholica Lovaniensis: Dissertationes ad gradum magistri in Facultate Theologica vel in Facultate Juris Canonici consequendem conscriptae 3.11. Louvain: Édition orientaliste.

———. 1970. *Les origines du célibat ecclésiastique du premier au septième siècle.* Recherches et synthèses: Section d'histoire 2. Gembloux: J. Duculot.

Guillet, H. 1948. *La perfection sacerdotale: D'après le Dialogue sur le sacerdoce de saint Jean Chrysostome.* Rennes: Oberthur.

Gy, P. M. 1962. Notes on the Early Terminology of Christian Priesthood. Pages 98-115 in *The Sacrament of Holy Orders.* Collegeville, MN: Liturgical Press.

Hardy, E. R. 1968. Deacons in History and Practice. In *The Diaconate Now.* Edited by Richard T. Nolan and Edmond La Beaume Cherbonnier. Washington: Corpus Books.

Harnack, Adolf von. 1884. *Die Lehre der zwölf Apostel: Nebst Untersuchungen zur ältesten Geschichte der Kirchenverfassung und des Kirchenrechts.* Texte und

Untersuchungen zur Geschichte der altchristlichen Literatur 2/1-2. Leipzig: J. C. Hinrichs.

————. 1886. *Die Quellen der sogenannten apostolischen Kirchenordnung: Nebst einer Untersuchung über den Ursprung des Lectorats und der anderen niederen Weihen.* Texte und Untersuchungen zur Geschichte der alt– christlichen Literatur 2/5. Leipzig: J. C. Hinrichs. Translated by Leonard A. Wheatley as *Sources of the Apostolic Canons, with a Treatise on the Origin of the Readership and Other Lower Orders* (London: Norgate, 1895).

————. 1924. *Die Mission und Ausbreitung des Christen- tums in den ersten drei Jahrhunderten.* 2 vols. 4th ed. Leipzig: J. C. Hinrichs. Translated by James Moffatt as *The Mission and Expansion of Christianity in the First Three Centuries* (New York: Harper, 1962).

Hastoupis, A. 1958. To en tois cheirographois tês Nekras Thalassês Encheiridion Peitharchias. In *Eucharistêrion: Timêtikos tomos epi tê 45etêridi tês epistêmonikês draseôs kai tê 35etêridi taktikês kathêgesias Amilka S. Alivizatou.* Athens.

Hatch, Edwin. 1881. *The Organization of the Early Chris- tian Churches.* The Bampton Lectures: 1880. London: Rivington's.

Hauler, Edmund. 1900. *Didascaliae apostolorum fragmenta ueronensia Latina: Accedunt canonum qui dicuntur apos- tolorum et Aegyptiorum reliquies.* Leipzig: Teubner.

Hefele, Karl Joseph. 1907-1952. *Histoire des conciles d'après les documents originaux.* 11 vols. Paris: Letouzey et Ané.

Heiss, R. 1928. Mönchtum, Seelsorge und Mission nach

dem hl. Johannes Chrysostomus. Pages 1-23 in *Lumen Caecis*. Oberbayern: Missionsverlag St. Ottilien.

Hennesy, L. R. 1986. Diakonia and Diakonoi in the Pre-Nicene Church. Pages 60-86 in *Diakonia: Studies in Honor of Robert T. Meyer*. Edited by Thomas Halton and Joseph P. Williman. Washington, DC: Catholic University of America Press.

Hess, Hamilton. 1958. *The Canons of the Council of Sardica, A.D. 343: A Landmark in the Early Development of Canon Law*. Oxford Theological Monographs 1. Oxford: Clarendon Press.

Heubach, Joachim. 1956. *Die Ordination zum Amt der Kirche*. Arbeiten zur Geschichte und Theologie des Luthertums 2. Berlin: Lutherisches Verlagshaus.

Hoek, Annewies van den. 1997. The "Catechetical" School of Early Christian Alexandria and its Philonic Heritage. *Harvard Theological Review* 90:59-87.

Holl, Karl. 1898. *Enthusiasmus und Bussgewalt beim griechischen Mönchtum: Eine Studie zu Symeon dem neuen Theologen*. Leipzig: J. C. Hinrichs.

———. 1904. *Amphilochius von Ikonium in seinem Verhältnis zu den grossen Kappadoziern*. Tübingen: J. C. B. Mohr.

Hopko, Thomas, ed. 1999. *Women and the Priesthood*. Rev. ed. Crestwood, NY: St. Vladimir's Seminary Press.

Horner, G. 1904. *The Statutes of the Apostles*. London: Williams and Norgate.

Javierre, A. M. 1957a. Es "apostolica" la primera "diadoche" de la Patristica (I Klemens 44, 2)? *Salesianum* 19:83-113.

———. 1957b. Los "ellogimoi andres" de la Clementis

y la sucesión apostólica. *Salesianum* 19.

————. 1964. Das Thema von der Nachfolge der Apostel in der christlichen Literatur der Urkirche. In *Das Bischofsamt und die Weltkirche*. Edited by Yves Congar, Käthe Friederike Krause, and Peter Müller. Stuttgart: Schwabenverlag.

Jay, Eric George. 1981. From Presbyter-Bishops to Bishops and Presbyters: Christian Ministry in the Second Century: A Survey. *Second Century* 1:125-162.

Jefford, Clayton N. 1989. Presbyters in the Community of the *Didache*. *Studia patristica* 21:122-128.

Jerome. *Select Letters of St. Jerome*. 1933. Translated by F. A. Wright. Loeb Classical Library. Cambridge, MA: Harvard University Press.

Jonkers, E. J. 1942. Das Verhalten der alten Kirche hinsichtlich der Ernennung zum Priester von Sklaven, Freigelassenen und Curiales. *Mnemosyne* 10:286-302.

Jouassard, G. 1959. Pour une étude du sacerdoce au temps des pères. In *La tradition sacerdotale: Études sur le sacerdoce*. Edited by René Fourrey et al. Bibliothèque de la Faculté catholique de théologie de Lyon 7. Le Puy: Mappus.

Justin Martyr. *St. Justin Martyr: The First and Second Apologies*. 1997. Translated by Leslie William Barnard. Ancient Christian Writers 56. New York: Paulist Press.

Kalogiros, I. 1965. Klêros: To mystêrion tês ierôsynês. Pages 656-679 in vol. 7 of *Thrêskeutikê kai êthikê enkyklopaideia*. 12 vols. Athens, 1962-1968.

Karmiris, Iôannês. 1954. *Pôs dei dechesthai tous prosiontas tê Orthodoxia eterodoxous*. Athens. Offprint from

Theologia 25 (1954).

———. 1964. Eterodoxôn, eisdochê. Pages 948-952 in vol. 5 of *Thrêskeutikê kai êthikê enkyklopaideia.* 12 vols. Athens, 1962-1968.

———. 1960-1968. *Ta dogmatika kai symbolika mnêmeia tês Orthodoxou Katholikês Ekklêsias.* 2 vols. 2d ed. Athens.

———. 1970. Orthodoxos Ekklêsiologia. *Theologia* 41:21-22.

———. 1973. *Plêrestera symmetochê tou laikou stoicheiou en tê latreutikê kai tê allê zôê tês ekklêsias.* Athens. Translated by Evie Marie Zachariades-Holmberg as *The Status and Ministry of the Laity in the Orthodox Church* (Brookline, MA: Holy Cross Orthodox Press, 1994).

Kennedy, George A. 1983. *Greek Rhetoric under Christian Emperors.* A History of Rhetoric 3. Princeton, NJ: Princeton University Press.

Kirsch, Johann Peter. 1930. *Die Kirche in der antiken griechisch-römischen Kulturwelt.* Kirchengeschichte 1. Freiburg im Breisgau: Herder.

Kollontai, Pauline. 2000. Contemporary Thinking on the Role and Ministry of Women in the Orthodox Church. *Journal of Contemporary Religion* 15:165-179.

Konidaris, Gerasimos I. 1959a. *Peri tês pheromenês diaphoras morphôn en tô politeumati tou archikou Christianismou (34-156 m. Ch.).* 2d ed. Athens.

———. 1959b. *Neai ereunai pros lysin tôn provlêmatôn tôn pêgôn tou ekklêsiastikou politeumatos tou archikou Christianismou (34-156 m. Ch.).* Athens.

Koukoules, Ph. 1948. *Vyzantinôn vios kai politismos.* A' 1. Athens.

Kotsonis, I. 1952. *To enthousiastikon stoicheion eis tên Ek-*

klêsian tôn martyrôn. Athens.

————. 1957. *Provlêmata tês "ekklêsiastikês oikonomias."* Athens.

————. 1965. Ierateuma, vasileion. Pages 770-772 in vol. 6 of *Thrêskeutikê kai êthikê enkyklopaideia*. 12 vols. Athens, 1962-1968.

Kourilas, Eulogios. 1929. *Istoria tou askêtismou: Athônitai*. Thessalonica: Akouarônê.

Krueger, Derek. 1993. Diogenes the Cynic among the Fourth Century Fathers. *Vigiliae christianae* 47:29-49.

Labriolle, P. de. 1921. Le mariage spirituel dans l'antiquité chrétienne. *Revue d'histoire ecclésiastique* 17:205-255.

————. 1938. Morale et spiritualité. In vol. 3 of *Histoire de l'Église, depuis les origines jusqu' à nos jours*. Edited by Augustin Fliche and Victor Martin. Paris: Bloud & Gay [1934-].

Laeuchli, Samuel. 1972. *Power and Sexuality: The Emergence of Canon Law at the Synod of Elvira*. Philadelphia: Temple University Press.

Lafontaine, Paul Henri. 1963. *Les conditions positives de l'accession aux ordres dans la première législation ecclésiastique (300-492)*. Les Publications sériées de l'Université d'Ottawa 71. Ottawa: Éditions de l'Université d'Ottawa.

Lagarde, Paul de. 1883. *Aegyptiaca*. Göttingen: A. Hoyer.

Lane Fox, Robin. 1987. *Pagans and Christians*. New York: Knopf.

Lea, Henry C. 1884. *An Historical Sketch of Sacerdotal Celibacy in the Christian Church*. 2d ed. Boston: Houghton, Mifflin & Co.

Le Bras, G. 1949. Le droit romain au service de la domination pontificale. *Revue historique de droit français et étranger* 27.

Lebreton, Jules, and Jacques Zeiller. 1942-1949. *The History of the Primitive Church*. Translated by Ernest C. Messenger. 4 vols. London: Burns, Oates & Washbourne.

Leclercq, Henri. 1914a. Chorévêques. Pages 1423-1452 in vol. 3 of *Dictionnaire d'archéologie chrétienne et de liturgie*. Edited by Fernand Cabrol. 15 vols. Paris: Letouzey et Ané, 1907-1953.

————. 1914b. Cliniques. Pages 1942-1944 in vol. 3 of *Dictionnaire d'archéologie chrétienne et de liturgie*. Edited by Fernand Cabrol. 15 vols. Paris: Letouzey et Ané, 1907-1953.

————. 1928. Laïques. Pages 1053-1064 in vol. 8 of *Dictionnaire d'archéologie chrétienne et de liturgie*. Edited by Fernand Cabrol. 15 vols. Paris: Letouzey et Ané, 1907-1953.

Leder, Paul August. 1905. *Die Diakonen der Bischöfe und Presbyter und ihre urchristlichen Vorläufer: Untersuchungen über die Vorgeschichte und die Anfänge des Archidiakonats*. Kirchenrechtliche Abhandlungen 23-24. Stuttgart: F. Enke.

Lemaire, André. 1971. *Les ministères aux origines de l'église: Naissance de la triple hiérarchie: évêques, presbytres, diacres*. Lectio divina 68. Paris: Éditions du Cerf.

Leo I. *Letters*. 1957. Translated by Edmunt Hunt. Fathers of the Church 34. New York: Fathers of the Church.

Liebeschuetz, J. H. W. G. 1986. Why did Synesius become bishop of Ptolemais? *Byzantion* 56:180-195.

Lienhard, J. T. 1984. *Ministry*. Wilmington: Glazier.

Lietzmann, Hans. 1914. Zur altchristlichen Verfassungs-geschichte. *Zeitschrift für wissenschaftliche Theologie* 55:97ff.

———. 1932-1944. *Geschichte der alten Kirche*. 4 vols. Berlin and Leipzig: De Gruyter. Translated by B. H. Woolf as *A History of the Early Church* (Cambridge: Clarke, 1993).

Limouris, Gennadios, ed. 1992. *The Place of the Woman in the Orthodox Church and the Question of the Ordination of Women*. Katerini: Tertios.

Lohse, Eduard. 1951. *Die Ordination im Spätjudentum und im Neuen Testament*. Göttingen: Vandenhoeck & Ruprecht.

———. 1953. Ursprung und Prägung des christlichen Apostolates. *Theologische Zeitschrift* 9:259-275.

Long, A. A. 2002. *Epictetus: A Stoic and Socratic Guide to Life*. Oxford: Oxford University Press.

Luttenberger, Gerard H. 1981. The Decline of Presbyteral Collegiality and the Growth of the Individualization of the Priesthood (4th-5th Centuries). *Recherches de théologie ancienne et médiévale* 48:14-58.

Madigan, Kevin, and Carolyn Osiek, eds. 2005. *Ordained Women in the Early Church: A Documentary History*. Baltimore: Johns Hopkins University Press.

McGuckin, John A. 2001. *St. Gregory of Nazianzus: An Intellectual Biography*. Crestwood, NY: St. Vladimir's Seminary Press.

Maier, Harry O. 1991. *The Social Setting of the Ministry as Reflected in the Writings of Hermas, Clement, and Ignatius*. Dissertations SR 1. Waterloo: Wilfrid Laurier

University Press.

———. 1994. Clement of Alexandria and the Care of the Self. *Journal of the American Academy of Religion* 62:719-745.

Mansi, J. D. 1901-1927. *Sacrorum conciliorum nova et amplissima collectio.* 54 vols. Paris.

Marquardt, Joachim. 1881-1885. *Römische Staatsverwaltung.* 3 vols. 2d ed. Handbuch der römischen Alterthümer 4-6. Leipzig: S. Hirzel.

Marrou, Henri Irénée. 1956. *A History of Education in Antiquity.* Translated by George Lamb. New York: Sheed and Ward.

Matesis, Antônios S. 1898. *Nearai Ioustinianou: Meta parapompôn eis ta schetika chôria tôn vasilikôn kai tês hexavivlou tou Harmenopoulou.* Athens.

Menn, D. 1904. Zur Pastoraltheologie Gregors von Nazianz. *Revue internationale de théologie* 47:427-440.

———. 1905. Zur Lehre des hl. Johannes Chrysostomos über das geistliche Amt. *Revue internationale de théologie* 49:87ff. and 50:308-321.

Meyendorff, John. 1984. *Marriage: An Orthodox Perspective.* Crestwood, NY: St. Vladimir's Seminary Press.

Michel, Anton. 1932. Ordre, Ordination. Pages 1193-1405 in vol. 11.2 of *Dictionnaire de théologie catholique.* 15 vols. Paris, 1903-1950.

———. 1936. Prêtre. Pages 138-161 in vol. 13.1 of *Dictionnaire de théologie catholique.* 15 vols. Paris, 1903-1950.

———. 1959. *Die Kaisermacht in der Ostkirche: 843-1204.* Darmstadt: Wissenschaftliche Buchgesellschaft.

Milasch, N. 1906. *To Ekklêsiastikon Dikaion tês Orthodoxou Anatolikês Ekklêsias.* Translated by M. Apostolopoulos.

Athens.

Mitsopoulos, Nikolaos E. 1972a. *Ê en Christô Iêsou doxa tou anthrôpou.* Athens.

———. 1972b. *Tria theia idiômata kai to trisson tou Christou kai en Christô axiôma.* Athens: Parisianos.

Mommsen, T., and P. M. Meyer. 1954. *Theodosiani libri xvi cum constitutionibus Sirmondianis et leges novellae ad Theodosianum pertinentes.* 2d ed. Berlin.

Mouratidis, Kônstantinos D. 1956. *Ê Monachikê ypakoê en tê archaia Ekklêsia: Symvolê eis tên istorian tou kanonikou dikaiou tês orthodoxou katholikês ekklêsias.* Athens.

———. 1958. *Ê Ousia kai to politeuma tês Ekklêsias: Kata tê didaskalia Iôannou tou Chrysostomou.* Athens.

———. 1962. *Christokentrikê poimantikê en tois askêtikois tou Megalou Vasileiou.* Athens.

Müller, Karl. 1929. Kleine Beiträge zur alten Kirchengeschichte: 16. Die älteste Bischofswahl und -weihe in Rom und Alexandrien. *Zeitschrift für die neutestamentliche Wissenschaft und die Kunde der älteren Kirche* 28:274-296.

Nairne, Alexander. 1916. The Prayer for the Consecration of a Bishop in the Church Order of Hippolytus. *Journal of Theological Studies* 17:398-399.

Nelz, Hermann Robert. 1916. *Die theologischen Schulen der morgenländischen Kirchen während der sieben ersten christlichen Jahrhunderte in ihrer Bedeutung für die Ausbildung des Klerus.* Bonn: Rhenania.

Neymeyr, Ulrich. 1989. *Die christlichen Lehrer im zweiten Jahrhundert: Ihre Lehrtätigkeit, ihr Selbstverständnis und ihre Geschichte.* Supplements to Vigiliae Christianae 4. Leiden: Brill.

Nicene and Post-Nicene Fathers, Series 1. 1886-1889. Edited by Philip Schaff. 14 vols. Repr. Peabody, MA: Hendrickson, 1994.

Nicene and Post-Nicene Fathers, Series 2. 1890-1900. Edited by Philip Schaff and Henry Wace. 14 vols. Repr. Peabody, MA: Hendrickson, 1994.

Noll, Ray Robert. 1975. The Search for a Christian Ministerial Priesthood in 1 Clement. *Studia patristica* 13:250-254.

Origen. *Contra Celsum*. 1953. Translated by Henry Chadwick. Cambridge: Cambridge University Press.

———. *Homilies on Leviticus 1-16*. 1990. Translated by Gary Wayne Barkley. Fathers of the Church 83. Washington, DC: Catholic University of America Press.

Otterbein, Adam. 1945. *The Diaconate according to the Apostolic Tradition of Hippolytus and Derived Documents*. Washington: Catholic University of America Press.

Palanque, Jean-Rémy. 1933. *Saint Ambroise et l'Empire romain: Contribution à l'histoire des rapports de l'église et de l'état à la fin du quatrième siècle*. Paris: E. de Boccard.

Palmer, E. J. 1937. A New Approach to an Old Problem: The Development of the Christian Ministry. In *The Ministry and the Sacraments*. Edited by Arthur C. Headlam and Roderic Dunkerley. London: Student Christian Movement Press.

Panagiotakos, Panagiotes I. 1951. *Ê ierôsynê kai ai ex autês nomokanonikai synepeiai: Kata to dikaion tês Anatolikês Orthodoxou Ekklêsias kai ta en Elladi kratounta*. Athens: Ekdotikos Oikos "Astêr."

Papadopoulos, Ch. 1912. *Peri ierôsynês*. Athens.

Papaevangelos, P. 1967. Phylaktêrion. Pages 1227-1228 in vol. 11 of *Thrêskeutikê kai êthikê enkyklopaideia*. 12 vols. Athens, 1962-1968.

Patsavos, Lewis J. 1976. The Image of the Priest according to the Three Hierarchs. *Greek Orthodox Theological Review* 21:55-70.

Pelikan, Jaroslav. 2001. *Divine Rhetoric: The Sermon on the Mount as Message and as Model in Augustine, Chrysostom, and Luther*. Crestwood, NY: St. Vladimir's Seminary Press.

Perini, Celso. 1963. Il celibato ecclesiastico nel pensiero di S. Ambrogio. *Divus Thomas* 66:432-450.

Perler, O. 1962. L'évêque, représentant du Christ selon les documents des premiers siècles. In *L'épiscopat et l'église universelle*. Edited by Yves Congar and Bernard Dominique Dupuy. Unam sanctam 39. Paris: Du Cerf.

Peterson, Erik. 1949. La *Leitourgia* des prophètes et des didascales à Antioche. *Recherches de science religieuse* 36:577-579.

Pheidas, V. 1969. *Proypotheseis diamorphôseôs tou thesmou tês pentarchias tôn patriarchôn*. Athens.

———. 1972. *Istorikokanonikai kai ekklêsiologikai proypotheseis ermêneias tôn ierôn kanonôn*. Athens.

Philippidis, L. 1958. *Istoria tês epochês tês Kainês Diathêkês*. Athens.

Phytrakis, A. 1936. *Oi politikoi kai ekklêsiastikoi archontes kata Isidôron ton Pêlousiôtên*. Mytilene.

———. 1945. *Ta ideôdê tou monachikou viou kata ton 4 m. Ch. aiôna epi tê vasei agiologikôn pêgôn*. Athens.

———. 1950. *Oi monachoi ôs koinônikoi didaskaloi kai ergatai en tê archaia Anatolikê Ekklêsia*. Athens.

————. 1960. *O monachikos vios en tê Orthodoxô Ekklêsia.* Offprint from *Agios Grêgorios Palamas 1359-1959.* Thessalonica.

————. 1968. *To poiêtikon ergon Grêgoriou tou Nazianzênou.* Athens.

Pierre, Évêque de Chersonèse. 1970. Le célibat ecclési-astique. *Messager de l'exarchat du patriarche russe en Europe occidentale* 69:27-37.

Piganiol, André. 1947. *L'empire chrétien (325-395).* Histoire générale: Histoire romaine 4.2. Paris: Presses universitaires de France.

Pontius. *Life of St. Cyprian.* 1952. Translated by Mary Magdeleine Müller and Roy J. Deferrari. Pages 3-24 in *Early Christian Biographies.* Edited by Roy J. Deferrari. Fathers of the Church 15. New York: Fathers of the Church.

Poschmann, Bernhard. 1940. *Paenitentia secunda: Die kirchliche Busse im ältesten Christentum bis Cyprian und Origenes: Eine dogmengeschichtliche Untersuchung.* Theophaneia: Beiträge zur Religions- und Kirchenge-schichte des Altertums 1. Bonn: P. Hanstein.

Poulitsas, Panagiôtis. 1946. *Schesis politeias kai ekklêsias: Idia epi eklogês episkopôn, eisêgêtikê ekthesis pros to Symvoulion tês Epikrateias.* Athens.

Preuschen, Erwin, and Gustav Krüger. 1923. *Das Altertum.* 2d ed. Handbuch der Kirchengeschichte für Studierende 1. Tübingen: J. C. B. Mohr (Paul Siebeck).

Price, Richard and Gaddis, Michael. 2005. *The Acts of the Council of Chalcedon.* Translated Texts for Historians 45. 3 vols. Liverpool: Liverpool University Press.

Probst, Ferdinand. 1873. *Kirchliche Disciplin: In den drei er-*

sten christlichen Jahrhunderten. Tübingen: H. Laupp.

Quasten, Johannes. 1940. "Vetus Superstitio et Nova Religio": The Problem of *Refrigerium* in the Ancient Church of North Africa. *Harvard Theological Review* 33:253-266.

———. 1950-1986. *Patrology*. 4 vols. Westminster, MD: Newman Press.

Rahmani, I. 1899. *Testamentum domini nostri Jesu Christi*. Mainz.

Rahner, Karl. 1950. Busslehre und Busspraxis der Didascalia Apostolorum. *Zeitschrift für katholische Theologie* 72:257ff.

Rapp, Claudia. 2005. *Holy Bishops in Late Antiquity: The Nature of Christian Leadership in an Age of Transition*. Transformation of the Classical Heritage 37. Berkeley, CA: University of California Press.

Rhallês, G. A., and M. Potlês. 1852-1859. *Syntagma tôn theiôn kai ierôn kanonôn tôn te agiôn kai paneuphêmôn apostolôn, kai tôn ierôn oikoumenikôn kai topikôn synodôn, kai tôn kata meros agiôn paterôn*. 6 vols. Athens.

Richert, Camill. 1901. *Die Anfänge der Irregularitäten bis zum ersten allgemeinen Konzil von Nicäa: Eine kirchenrechtliche Untersuchung*. Strassburger theologische Studien 4. Freiburg im Breisgau: Herder.

Roberti, A. 1940. S. Ambrogio e il monachismo. *Scuola cattolica* 68:140-159.

Rousseau, Philip. 1999. *Pachomius: The Making of a Community in Fourth-Century Egypt*. 2d ed. Transformation of the Classical Heritage 6. Berkeley: University of California Press.

Rowland, Christopher. 2002. *Christian Origins: An Account of the Setting and Character of the Most Important*

Messianic Sect of Judaism. 2d ed. London: SPCK.

Rubenson, Samuel. 1990. *The Letters of St. Antony: Ori-genist Theology, Monastic Tradition and the Making of a Saint.* Bibliotheca historico-ecclesiastica Lundensis 24. Lund: Lund University Press.

Russell, Norman. 2003. Bishops and Charismatics in Early Christian Egypt. Pages 99-110 in *Abba: The Tradition of Orthodoxy in the West: Festschrift for Bishop Kallistos (Ware) of Diokleia.* Edited by John Behr, Andrew Louth, and Dimitri Conomos. Crestwood, NY: St. Vladimir's Seminary Press.

———. 2007. *Theophilus of Alexandria.* Early Church Fathers. London/New York: Routledge.

Ryan, L. 1962. Patristic Teaching on the Priesthood of the Faithful. *International Theological Quarterly* 19:25-51.

Schermann, Theodor. 1914-1916. *Die allgemeine Kirchenordnung: Frühchristliche Liturgien und kirchliche Überlieferung.* 3 vols. Paderborn: F. Schöningh.

Schillebeeckx, Edward. 1985. *The Church with a Human Face: A New and Expanded Theology of Ministry.* Translated by John Bowden. London: SCM.

Schmaus, Michael. 1958. Bischof. II. Theologisch. Pages 492-497 in vol. 2 of *Lexikon für Theologie und Kirche.* Edited by Josef Höfer and Karl Rahner. 10 vols. 2d ed. Freiburg: Herder, 1957-1965.

Schmidt, K. L. 1937. Le ministère et les ministères dans l'église du N.T. *Revue d'histoire et de philosophie religieuses* 17:314ff.

Schmitt, J. 1962. Jewish Priesthood and Christian Hierarchy in the Early Palestinian Communities. In *The Sacrament of Holy Orders.* Collegeville, MN: Liturgical Press.

Schnackenburg, R. 1949. Episkopos und Hirtenamt. Pages 66-88 in *Episcopus, Studien über das Bischofsamt: Seiner Eminenz Michael Kardinal von Faulhaber, Erzbischof von München-Freising zum 80. Geburtstag*. Regensburg: Gregorius-Verlag vorm. Friedrich Pustet.

Scholten, Clemens. 1992. Der Chorbischof bei Basilius. *Zeitschrift für Kirchengeschichte* 103:149-173.

Schroeder, David. 1959. *Die Haustafeln des Neuen Testaments: Ihre Herkunft und ihr theologischer Sinn*. Hamburg.

Schwartz, Eduard. 1910. Die Konzilien des 4. und 5. Jahrhunderts. *Historische Zeitschrift* 104:1-37.

———. 1911. *Bussstufen und Katechumenatsklassen*. Schriften der Wissenschaftlichen Gesellschaft in Strassburg 7. Strassburg: Trübner.

The Scriptores Historiae Augustae. 1922-1932. Translated by David Magie. 3 vols. Loeb Classical Library. London: Heinemann.

Sellars, John. 2006. *Stoicism*. Berkeley: University of California Press.

Simonin, H. D. 1939. La prière de la consécration épiscopal dans la Tradition apostolique d'Hippolyte de Rome. *Vie spirituelle* 60:65-86.

Siotis, Markos Antonios. 1951. *Die klassische und christliche Cheirotonie in ihrem Verhältnis*. Athens.

Smith, Rowland. 1995. *Julian's Gods: Religion and Philosophy in the Thought and Action of Julian the Apostate*. London: Routledge.

Sohm, Rudolf. 1949. *Institutionen: Geschichte und System des römischen Privatrechts*. 17th ed. Berlin: Duncker & Humblot. Translated by James Crawford Ledlie as *The Institutes of Roman Law* (Oxford: Clarendon

Press, 1892).

Spicq, Ceslas. 1946. L'origine évangélique des vertus épiscopales selon saint Paul. *Revue biblique* 53:36-46.

———. 1947. *Saint Paul: Les épitres pastorales*. Etudes bibliques. Paris: Librairie Lecoffre.

Stander, H. F. 1984-1985. Prophets in the Early Christian Church. *Ekklêsiastikos Pharos* 66 (1984):66-67; 67 (1985):113-122.

The Statutes of the Apostles or Canones Ecclesiastici. 1904. Edited and translated by G. Horner. London: Williams & Norgate.

Stephanidis, V. 1959. *Ekklêsiastikê Istoria*. 2d ed. Athens.

Sterk, Andrea. 1998. On Basil, Moses, and the Model Bishop: The Cappadocian Legacy of Leadership. *Church History* 67:227-253.

———. 2004. *Renouncing the World Yet Leading the Church: The Monk-Bishop in Late Antiquity*. Cambridge, MA: Harvard University Press.

Stiglmayr, J. 1929. Zur Aszese des hl. Chrysostomus. *Zeitschrift für Aszese und Mystik* 4:29-49.

Tanner, Norman P., ed. 1990. *Decrees of the Ecumenical Councils*. 2 vols. London: Sheed & Ward.

Tatakis, V. 1960. *Ê symvolê tês Kappadokias stê christianikê skepsê*. Athens.

Teeter, Timothy M. 1994. Review of T. D. Barnes, *Athanasius and Constantius*. *Vigiliae christianae* 48:398-401.

Telfer, William. 1962. *The Office of a Bishop*. London: Darton, Longman & Todd.

Tertullian. *Tertullian*. 2004. Translated by Geoffrey D. Dunn. Early Church Fathers. London: Routledge.

Thamin, Raymond. 1895. *Saint Ambroise et la morale chrétienne au IVe siècle: Étude comparée des traités "Des devoirs" de Cicéron et de saint Ambroise.* Annales de l'Université de Lyon 8. Paris: G. Masson.

Theodôrou, E. 1954. *Ê "cheirotonia" ê "cheirothesia" tôn diakonissôn.* Athens.

————. 1992. The Institution of Deaconesses in the Orthodox Church and the Possibility of its Restoration. In *The Place of the Woman in the Orthodox Church and the Question of the Ordination of Women.* Edited by Gennadios Limouris. Katerini: Tertios.

The Theodosian Code and Novels and the Sirmondian Constitutions. 1952. Translated by Clyde Pharr. Corpus of Roman Law 1. Princeton: Princeton University Press.

Tixeront, Joseph. 1925. *L'ordre et les ordinations: Étude de théologie historique.* Paris: V. Lecoffre.

Trembelas, Panagiôtês. 1926. *O gamos tôn klêrikôn.* Athens.

————. 1931. Oi laikoi en tê Orthodoxô Ekklêsia. *Ekklêsia* 9:20-22, 25-27, 33-36, 49-50.

————. 1955. *Ê symmetochê tou laou en tê eklogê tôn episkopôn.* Athens.

————. 1957. *Oi laikoi en tê ekklêsia: To "vasileion ierateuma."* Athens.

————. 1959-1961. *Dogmatikê tês Orthodoxou Katholikês Ekklêsias.* 3 vols. Athens.

————. 1965. Klêros: Ê eklogê tôn poimenôn. Pages 679-687 in vol. 7 of *Thrêskeutikê kai êthikê enkyklopaideia.* 12 vols. Athens, 1962-1968.

Turner, C. H. 1915. The Ordination Prayer for a Presbyter in the Church Order of Hippolytus. *Journal of Theological Studies* 16:542-547.

Ülhof, Wilhelm. 1962. *Die Zuständigkeit zur Weihespendung mit besonderer Berücksichtigung des Zusammenhangs mit dem Weihetitel und der Inkardination*. Münchener theologische Studien 3: Kanonistische Abteilung 15. Munich: Hueber.

Vacandard, Elphège. 1905-1923. *Études de critique et d'histoire religieuse*. 4 vols. Paris: V. Lecoffre.

Vapheidis, Philaretos I. 1884. *Ekklêsiastikê Istoria: Apo tou Kyriou hêmôn Iêsou Christou mechri tôn kath' hêmas chronôn*. Constantinople: S. I. Voutyra.

Vaux, Roland de. 1961. *Ancient Israel: Its Life and Institutions*. Translated by John McHugh. New York: McGraw-Hill.

Vögtle, Anton. 1936. *Die Tugend- und Lasterkataloge im Neuen Testament: Exegetisch, religions- und formgeschichtlich Untersucht*. Neutestamentliche Abhandlungen 16.4-5. Münster: Aschendorff.

Volk, J. 1895. Die Schutzrede des Gregor von Nazianz und die Schrift über das Priestertum von Johannes Chrysostomus. *Zeitschrift für praktische Theologie* 17:56-63.

Weidinger, Karl. 1928. *Die Haustafeln: Ein Stück urchristlicher Paränese*. Untersuchungen zum Neuen Testament 14. Leipzig: J. C. Hinrichs.

Weiss, Bernhard. 1902. *Die Briefe Pauli an Timotheus und Titus*. 7th ed. Kritisch-exegetischer Kommentar über das Neue Testament 11. Göttingen: Vandenhoeck & Ruprecht.

Wieland, Franz. 1897. *Die genetische Entwicklung der*

sogenannten Ordines Minores in den drei ersten Jahr-hunderten. Römische Quartalschrift für christliche Altertumskunde und Kirchengeschichte: Supplementheft 7. Rome: In commission der Herder'schen Verlagshandlung zu Freiburg im Breisgau und der Buchhandlung Spithöver zu Rom.

Wilken, Robert Louis. 1984. Alexandria: A School for Training in Virtue. Pages 15-18 in *Schools of Thought in the Christian Tradition.* Edited by Patrick Henry. Philadelphia: Fortress.

Wordsworth, John. 1901. *The Ministry of Grace: Studies in Early Church History with reference to Present Problems.* London: Longmans, Green.

Young, Frances M. 1994. On *Episkopos* and *Presbuteros. Journal of Theological Studies* 45:142-148.

Ysebaert, Joseph. 1991. The Deaconnesses in the Western Church of Late Antiquity and Their Origin. Pages 421-436 in *Eulogia: Mélanges offerts à Antoon A. R. Bastiaensen à l'occasion de son soixante-cinquième anniversaire.* Edited by G. J. M. Bartelink, A. Hilhorst, and C. H. Kneepkens. Instrumenta patristica 24. The Hague: Nijhoff.

————. 1994. *Die Amtsterminologie im Neuen Testament und in der alten Kirche: Eine lexikographische Untersuchung.* Breda: Eureia.

Zeiller, J. 1938a. Les chrétiens et la vie civique. Pages 429ff. in vol. 2 of *Histoire de l'Église, depuis les origines jusqu'à nos jours.* Edited by Augustin Fliche and Victor Martin. Paris: Bloud & Gay [1934-].

————. 1938b. La dernière persécution. Pages 457-479 in vol. 2 of *Histoire de l'Église, depuis les origines jusqu' à nos jours*. Edited by Augustin Fliche and Victor Martin. Paris: Bloud & Gay [1934-].

Zhishman, J. 1913. *To dikaion tou gamou*. Translated by M. Apostopoulos. 2 vols. Athens.

Zimmermann, Otto. 1933. *Grundriss der Aszetik: Nach dem Lehrbuch*. Edited by Carl Haggeney. Freiburg i. B: Herder.

Zizioulas, John D. 1965. *Ê enotês tês Ekklêsias en tê theia eucharistia kai tô episkopô kata tous treis prôtous aiônas*. Athens. Translated by Elizabeth Theokritoff as *Eucharist, Bishop, Church: The Unity of the Church in the Divine Eucharist and the Bishop during the First Three Centuries* (Brookline, MA: Holy Cross Orthodox Press, 2001).

———. 1985. *Being as Communion: Studies in Personhood and the Church*. Contemporary Greek Theologians 4. Crestwood, NY: St. Vladimir's Seminary Press.

Index

didaskaleia 220, 239, 291
Dionysius of Rome 49
Dix, G. 237
Donatists 286-287
Dorotheus, presbyter 197
Dracontius, Egyptian
  ascetic 110, 260, 268
drunkenness 79-80, 84-85, 97

*Ecclesiastical Canons of the
  Holy Apostles* 67-73, 192,
  235, 240, 267, 274, 294
Ecclesiastical History of
  Eusebius of Caesarea 48-51
Edessa 291
education 219-221, 288-295
Egypt 67
Eleazar, priest 104
Eleutherus, pope 237
Elijah, prophet 110
Elisha, prophet 110
Elvira, Council of (ca. 306)
  236, 237, 241, 255-256,
  269, 283, 285, 297-298
encratites 252
Ephraim the Syrian
  102-104, 173
Epictetus, philosopher 249
Epiphanius of Salamis 57,
  197, 240, 241, 253, 268
Epitome 75, 93, 95
Eulalius of Caesarea 261
eunuchism 87, 97, 196-
  198, 245, 283
Eusebius of Caesarea in
  Cappadocia 175, 279, 285
Eusebius of Caesarea
  in Palestine 43, 48-51,
  94, 238-239, 254, 281
Eusebius of Laodicea 237

Eusebius of Pelusium 169
Eustathians 252-253, 271
Eustathius of Sebaste
  252, 261-263
Eutaxias, I. 184
evangelists 6
Eve 246
exorcists 7, 279

Fabian, pope 195, 281
faith as criterion for
  ordination 283-288
fasting 151
fathers, apostolic 31-43, 307
Felix, an Alexandrian 197-198
First Ecumenical Council *see*
  Nicaea, Council of (325)
forbearance *see* gentleness
fornication 83, 190-191

Galerius, emperor 250
gambling 85
Gangra, Council of (ca.
  350) 253, 261-263, 271
Geminius Victor,
  African layman 242
gentleness 115-116
Gibbon, Edward 174
gnosis 44, 45
Gregory of Cappadocia 178
Gregory the Great 174
Gregory of Nazianzus 105,
  118-128, 131, 173, 175,
  176, 202, 220, 247, 260-
  261, 276-277, 279, 280,
  291, 299-300, 304, 308
Gregory of Neocaesarea 50-51
Gregory of Nyssa 8, 162-163,
  173, 248, 276, 279, 303
Gregory Thaumaturgus 231